en
di

Benvane

Stob
Binnein

Ben
More

Ben

Ben
Cleuch

Forth

Dumyat

Rail Bridge

D1180862

Firth of Forth

Cramond Island

Fettes
College

N

Caleb's List

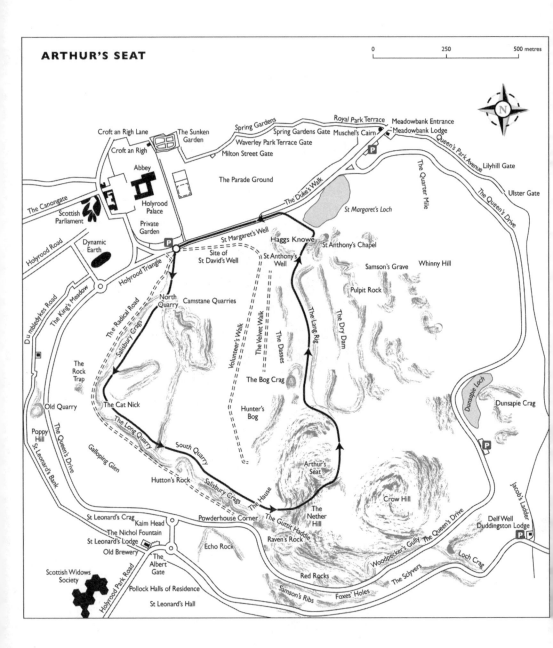

Caleb's List

Climbing the Scottish mountains
visible from Arthur's Seat

KELLAN MacINNES

Luath Press Limited

EDINBURGH

www.luath.co.uk

First published 2013

ISBN: 978-1-908373-53-3

The paper used in this book is sourced from renewable forestry

Mixed Sources
Product group from well-managed
forests and other controlled sources
www.fsc.org Cert no. SA-COC-1565
© 1996 Forest Stewardship Council

and is FSC credited material.

Printed and bound by
MPG Books Ltd., Cornwall

Typeset in 11 point Sabon
by 3btype.com

Drawings by Kaye Weston

The moral right of Kellan MacInnes to be identified as the author of this
work has been asserted by him in accordance with the Copyright, Designs
and Patents Act 1988.

A percentage of net sales of this book will be donated to Waverley Care,
Scotland's leading charity supporting people living with HIV and Hepatitis C.

Contents

Weathering the Storm...

SOMETIMES A MOUNTAINEERING BOOK is born out of human drama, suffering and struggle against the odds. In the chaos and bloodshed of World War Two while serving with the Highland Light Infantry in Egypt in 1942 the legendary Scottish climber WH Murray was captured by Rommel's 15th Panzer Division. He spent the rest of the war in German Prisoner Of War camps where he wrote the classic *Mountaineering in Scotland* on sheets of toilet paper kept hidden from his prison guards. When Joe Simpson broke his leg at 19,000 feet on the north ridge of Siula Grande in the Peruvian Andes in 1985 with no hope of rescue he began to crawl down the mountain. The result was *Touching the Void*. Sometimes a climbing book has its origins in more mundane circumstances. *Hamish's Mountain Walk* was conceived on a hot, stuffy day in the office and Muriel Gray wrote *The First Fifty* as an antidote to all those climbing books with pictures of men with beards on the cover. *Caleb's List* falls somewhere between these two extremes, a book about mountaineering with its roots in the AIDS crisis of the late 1980s and early '90s.

Acknowledgements

I WOULD LIKE TO THANK above all the following people for their help with this book; Kaye Sutherland for the drawings, Sue Collin for her critique of the draft manuscript, Alan Fyfe archivist at the Edinburgh Academy for the photographs and sketch of Caleb... and my partner Scott for understanding my long nights on the computer.

I'd also like to thank Chris Fleet for showing me Timothy Pont's maps and June Ellner at the University of Aberdeen for giving me access to the copy of Blaeau's Atlas once owned by Caleb. I am very grateful to the following people for various reasons; Marcia Pointon, Monica Jackson, Martin Moran, Alison Higham, Karin Froebel, the Royal Scottish Geographical Society, the Ladies Scottish Climbing Club, The Greek Consulate, John Paul Photography, Roy Dennis, Peter Stubbs, Colin Liddell, Bruce McCartney, Jonathan de Ferranti and Mercy Eden. Thanks to Tom Prentice for use of Munros Tables® which is a registered trademark of the Scottish Mountaineering Club.

Peter Drummond's definitive work *Scottish Hill Names*, Ian Mitchell's *Scotland's Mountains Before the Mountaineers* and Andy Wightman's pioneering website www.whoownsscotland.org.uk were of great help while I was researching *Caleb's List*. Finally thanks to Gavin, Kirsten and Louise at Luath for the expertise, care and patience shown during the publishing of this book and for their commitment to a first time author.

CHAPTER ONE

Caleb's List

*The views from Arthur's Seat are preferable to dozing inside on
a fine day or using wine to stimulate wit.*

ROBERT BURNS, 1786

EDINBURGH. 1898. On the cusp of the modern age. Caleb George Cash –
mountaineer, geographer, antiquarian and teacher – stands at the rocky
summit of Arthur's Seat. Sounds drift up from the city below; the chime of
church bells striking the hour; a horse and cart rattling down the cobbled
streets past the tenements of Dumbiedykes. From the hillside nearby comes
the bleating of sheep grazing on The Lang Rig. Caleb breathes in a yeasty
smell of beer from the brewery beside the Palace of Holyroodhouse. A
hundred years later a reconvened Scottish Parliament will meet where
the brewery stands, but for now Edinburgh is quietly comfortable, part
of Britain and its empire, sending its young men to fight in foreign wars
like the one that will soon break out in South Africa.

The sound of a steam whistle. Clouds of white smoke pour from a
blackened locomotive hauling a long line of coal wagons up the steep
gradient of the Innocent railway to the sidings and engine shed in the
Pleasance. At the base of Arthur's Seat in wooded grounds stands a
mansion, St Leonards, its four storey tower topped with pepper pot turrets.
Nearby serried rows of glass roofs, Thomas Nelson's Parkside printing
works and on Queen's drive figures in linen suits and straw boaters
stroll by St Margaret's Loch.

Caleb looks across to Calton Hill, its lower slopes encircled by the
Georgian sweep of Regent Terrace. On its summit Caleb sees the telescope
shaped Nelson Monument next to a half completed Greek temple.

Opposite the Royal High School stands the Calton Jail, and where
the St James centre squats today are the slate roofs and chimney pots of
Georgian tenements in St James Square.

The spires of the Scott monument rise above Princes Street but the
clock tower of the North British Hotel, a landmark on the city skyline
in the century to come, will not be completed until 1902. Cable hauled
trams slide across North Bridge. When a cable jams, as frequently happens,

it brings the entire tram network to a grinding halt until the fault can be repaired. The problems with the trams generate much heated discussion among the citizens of Edinburgh.

A crow on a nearby rock eyes Caleb sceptically. The crows were here when Iron Age farmers hewed the cultivation terraces on the slopes of Arthur's Seat, and will hang on the breeze still after Caleb has gone to his long rest.

To the west at the edge of the Meadows, the domed roof of the recently built McEwan Hall. Nearby, George Square where the tower blocks of The University of Edinburgh stand today.

To the east Holyrood Park merges into the open countryside of East Lothian. At Lilyhill the new houses will soon stretch almost to the boundary wall of the Queen's Park. Past the barracks at Piershill a ribbon of sandstone villas straggles along Willowbrae Road petering out around Northfield Farm, and Duddingston Mill a mile or so from the seaside resort of Portobello with its beach and pier. To the north beyond the tenements of Leith Walk and Easter Road and the chimneys and clock tower of Chancelot Mill lie the docks. White water foams against the Martello tower, and close by steam ships and sailing ships lie at anchor in the Forth waiting to enter the Port of Leith. Cranes and sheds dominate the shoreline near the new extension to the docks, but 60 years will pass before the tower blocks of Restalrig and Lochend are built.

Puffs of smoke rise from the funnels of steam trawlers moored beside the east breakwater at Granton harbour. Fettes College stands on the very periphery of the city among fields and trees. Beyond are islands: Inchkeith, Inchmickery and Inchcolm. Closest to Edinburgh is Cramond Island linked to the land by the Drum sands at low tide. Caleb can see the Fife fishing villages nestled into the north shore of the Firth of Forth. The Forth rail bridge completed nine years earlier spans the estuary where it narrows at South Queensferry.

Without the buildings of the 1960s and the big housing estates of the '30s, Caleb's Edinburgh is smaller and leafier. But it's a smokier more industrial city too. Where the trees and grass of the Queen's Park end, the chimneys of London Road iron foundry and the St Margaret's locomotive works begin. Brewing, printing and banking are the main industries of this city. Among Edinburgh's financial institutions are the National Bank of Scotland, the Commercial Bank of Scotland and the Royal Bank of Scotland.

Approaching the summit of Arthur's Seat.
© Alastair White

As yet there are few motor cars, and children and dogs still wander freely on the streets. In winter late Victorian Edinburgh is a cold city of draughty windows, high ceilings and coal fires, each tenement belching smoke from two dozen or more chimney pots.

This is the city where a decade earlier Robert Louis Stevenson imagined Dr Jekyll and Mr Hyde; its medieval old town crammed with slum tenements. Caleb lives and works in the city teaching the sons of the wealthy middle class at the Edinburgh Academy. The spire of the Tron Kirk and the dome of St George's are prominent on the skyline of Caleb's Edinburgh, and the general assembly of the Free Church of Scotland meets every summer at the Mound. Morningside ladies take tea at Jenners department store on Princes Street, but it's only a ten minute tram or train ride to Great Junction Street in Leith where children play barefoot round the corner from the Sailors' Mission at the Shore and the prostitutes.

To the south, a mile or so from Arthur's Seat, Craigmillar Castle stands among fields of cows and copses of trees. The suburb of Morningside is spreading around Blackford Hill and the Braids as the city tide line creeps towards the Pentlands. South-east lie the Lammermuirs, the Moorfoots and the hills of Peebles-shire. But Caleb stands with his back to the hills of the Scottish Borders beyond which lie the Cheviots and England, his country of birth. It is to the north Caleb looks, beyond the shoreline where the city ends and across the Firth of Forth with its islands to the Lomond Hills of Fife, to the Ochils and Dumyat, to Ben Ledi, Ben Venue and Ben Lomond straddling the Highland boundary fault.

In places at the summit of Arthur's Seat the rock beneath Caleb's feet has been worn smooth by the passage of many feet, by generations of people over the years climbing the hill to see this view. Since he came to Edinburgh a dozen years earlier and climbed Arthur's Seat for the first time Caleb has been fascinated by the view from the summit and by the topography of the city, the River Forth and the panorama of mountains to the north.

Alice sits beside Caleb, a notebook and pencil in her hands. Spread out around them are several Ordnance Survey one-inch to the mile maps weighted down with stones. Nearby is a brass theodolite on a simple wooden stand, carefully levelled and pointing north-west. Caleb puts his eye to the telescopic lens of the theodolite. After a moment he speaks; 'Ben Lomond degrees west of north 73.' Alice writes down the name of the hill and the bearing under the heading *Mountains Visible From Arthur's Seat*. Caleb adjusts the theodolite glances down at one of the maps speaks again; 'Ben Venue degrees west of north 68...'

A few hours later the notebook Alice holds contains a list of 20 Scottish hills and mountains... Ben Lomond... Ben Venue... Ben Ledi... Benvane... Dumyat... Stob Binnein... Ben More... Ben Vorlich... Ben Cleuch... Ben Lawers... Meall Garbh... Ben Chonzie... Schiehallion... Meall Dearg... Beinn Dearg... Ben Vrackie... Beinn a'Ghlo... West Lomond... East Lomond and Lochnagar.

And so a new hill list was born.

In July 1899 Caleb published his list in the form of a simple table printed on page 21 of *The Cairngorm Club Journal*. Hugh Munro had published his list of Scottish mountains over 3,000 feet in *The Scottish Mountaineering Club Journal* eight years earlier in 1891. During the 20th century Munro's list became famous while Caleb and his list were all but forgotten. This is the story of Caleb, me and the Scottish mountains visible from Arthur's Seat. Somehow the Cashs or the Calebs didn't sound right so I have called the hills on Caleb's list *The Arthurs*.

The Heart of Darkness

The Congo flows through the provincial city of Leopoldville. The wide muddy river has been a trading route since biblical times. In the central market, among the baskets of yams and cassava, people and flies crowd around the bush meat stall... Sometime around 1912, while Caleb, thousands of miles away in Scotland sketched cup and ring marked stones in the Perthshire countryside a trader or perhaps a sailor left a ship in the port and went ashore into the hot African city night... a spherical particle of virus floating in his bloodstream spikes itself to a white blood cell, strands of DNA mutate... a new sickness incubates far-away, very distant for now, for decades to come, moving undetectably slowly as the years pass but transmitting from one to another, to two, to three, to four... across central Africa... a shadow spreading out from the heart of darkness.

CHAPTER TWO

Kellan

And when he thus had spoken, he cried with a loud voice,
Lazarus, come forth.

JOHN 11:43

IN THE YEARS AFTER World War One Edinburgh gradually expanded. During the early 1930s blocks of flats designed in the fashionable new art deco style were built in Comely Bank Road just along from the tenement where Caleb had lived 30 years before. Into one of the new flats moved Thomas, a printer by trade, and his young wife Margaret.

Tommy worked in a small printer's workshop round the back of Broughton Street. On Saturday afternoons he would be sent to the Star Bar in Northumberland Place to carry back jugs of whisky for the men at the printers. Margaret worked as a buyer at the clothing chain Jaeger's fashionable North Berwick branch. One weekend Tommy, showing off to Margaret in the outdoor swimming pool by the sea accidentally belly flops from the top diving board and winds himself. He has to be carried from the water.

After a miscarriage Margaret had one son Douglas. When he was 12, Douglas went to George Heriot's, one of Edinburgh's oldest private schools. Tommy and Margaret struggled and sacrificed to pay the school fees out of a printer's wage.

Their flat in Comely Bank Road is furnished with the latest in art deco sideboards, armchairs, cut moquette sofas and glass light fittings. Margaret reads Proust while waiting for the potatoes to come to the boil in the tiny cluttered kitchenette. As women did then, Margaret had given up work when she married and suffered badly from post natal depression. Douglas would come in from school and find the hoover lying abandoned in the hall and know Margaret was not feeling well that day. 'The evening paper rattle-snaked its way through the letter box and there was suddenly a six-o'clock feeling in the house', wrote Muriel Spark of the Edinburgh of the 1930s.

His parents' sacrifices had not been in vain and Douglas left Heriot's to study English at The University of Edinburgh where he met Susan from Yorkshire. Susan's father comes to visit her at university for the first time... it is the late 1950s and they walk along the path skirting the foot of Salisbury Crags and Arthur's Seat. Douglas and Susan married in 1962 and their eldest child a boy, Kellan, was born at the Western General Hospital in December 1963, the year, according to Philip Larkin, sexual intercourse began.

Douglas and Susan buy a house in Craighouse Avenue with £1,000 given to the young couple by Susan's grandfather, James Edward Collin. In the 1960s Kellan walks to school along the quiet back streets of Morningside.

Towards the end of primary school in the mid-'70s Kellan's class are taken on the bus (dusty fabric seats) to the Lothian Outdoor Centre on Macdonald Road. In a former classroom Chris Bonington, the famous mountaineer, is delivering a lecture. Kellan remembers the bearded man sitting behind the school-type table, but what formed a lasting impression on a 12 year old mind were the brown blotches on the skin of his hands, the scars of frostbite sustained climbing the south-west face of Everest.

Douglas and Susan's marriage folded under the pressures of the sexual revolution of the 1960s (or the '70s by the time it reached Edinburgh) and Susan moves with the children to a flat in Marchmont. Kellan and his younger sister go to secondary school at James Gillespie's High founded by a rich Edinburgh snuff merchant and rumoured to have been the school that inspired Muriel Spark to write *The Prime of Miss Jean Brodie*. To Kellan the school with its modern brick classroom blocks surrounding the medieval Bruntsfield House bore little resemblance to the school described in the pages of Muriel Spark's novel.

The 1970s was the golden age of outdoor education in Scotland and Kellan was introduced to mountaineering by pioneering outdoor education teacher, Pete Main. He joined his innovative Tuesday Group, a moun-taineering club for pupils at Edinburgh secondary schools, and spent two weeks climbing in the Austrian Alps. Back in Scotland with a school friend Kellan climbed the Five Sisters of Kintail, Ben Nevis and the Devil's Ridge in the Mamores.

University in Aberdeen passes in a haze of sweet smelling hashish smoke and Friday night amphetamine. Summers are spent in Greece where it is too hot to walk further than the beach or climb anything higher than a bar stool. One morning awoken by the blinding Greek sun shining through a gap in the shutters Kellan climbs down a wooden ladder from the only inhabitable upstairs bedroom in the house. Bare rock forms the back wall on the ground floor of the 300-year-old villa. Kellan's bare feet on cool stone as he climbs down through the trapdoor to the kitchen. Sees on the simple wooden table a plastic carrier bag with pots of Greek yoghurt, a jar of honey, Nescafé in a tin, bread. Someone's bought an English newspaper too. Reads in *The Guardian*'s mid-'80s font *Rock Hudson Victim of* AIDS *Dies at 59*.

Kellan left university with a degree in psychology and a boyfriend, and during the summer he graduated spends three weeks in Assynt in the far north-west of Scotland. One sunny day he climbs Suilven with Bridget, Morag, Graham and Aunty. Bridget was the 'camp' name of Kellan's first boy-

Monica Jackson and Sherpas Mingma and Ang Temba on the first ascent of Gyalgan Peak, Nepal in 1955 and at home in Edinburgh in 2012 with the 'eye-remover'.

friend. Morag was David, and he and Graham had been a couple since meeting in a Gents public lavatory in Dundee in the early-'70s. Aunty, his boyfriend's rotund, very camp ex-landlord climbs Suilven in knee length motorbike boots. And David and Graham's collie Meg. There always has to be a dog... It's a hot July day and on the way back Kellan and his boyfriend go skinny dipping in the sandy loch that lies at the foot of Suilven.

In the early-'90s Kellan was a once a month and summer holiday kind of hill walker. Being continually skint, equipment for winter mountaineering was a problem. Monica Jackson who led the first women's climbing expedition to the Himalayas in 1955, lent Kellan her husband Bob's ice axe. An old style two and a half foot long alpenstock it stuck out from the back of his rucksack and quickly acquired the nickname 'the eye-remover'. In the days before Munro bagging really took off we climbed Schiehallion, the Tarmachan ridge, Bynack Mhor in the Cairngorms, Ben Chonzie, An Caisteal, Aonach Beag, Bidean nam Bian, Buchaille Etive Mor, the South Glen Shiel ridge, Liathach and Ben Vrackie.

The Heart of Darkness

One summer I noticed a spot on my left thigh. It stayed there for a couple of months, then after a Greek holiday and two weeks of sunshine the spot disappeared. But by the following January a similar kind of spot had appeared on my face. My left eye had begun to water uncontrollably at times and I felt more tired than a 33-year-old ever should. A young GP asked me if I had been squeezing the spot, I hadn't. He arranged for me to see a dermatologist, but before the hospital appointment letter arrived, suspecting what might be wrong, Scott (my new partner) and I both went to the Edinburgh genito-urinary medicine clinic one bleak Monday morning in March.

I asked the doctor if he thought the spot on my face was Kaposi's sarcoma, a rare form of AIDS related cancer. The doctor brought his face very close to mine as he examined the spot and said the best way to find out would be by taking blood and testing it for HIV. That was at 9.30am. After a traumatic six hours sitting on the sofa in our flat in Leith, we two boys together clinging, we were back at the hospital just after 3pm to be told I had AIDS... Scott's blood test had tested HIV negative. I left the clinic dazed, clutching a prescription for valium.

CD4 count is a measure of the relative health of your immune system, usually somewhere between 800–1,200 in a healthy adult. Mine was 174. At an appointment with another doctor a week or two later my CD4 count had fallen to 66. The consultant thought I'd been HIV positive since the 1980s. I watched as the doctor hid the form he was filling in with his elbow. I didn't read what he'd written. I didn't need to. I knew the significance of the form. It was for patients who had less than six months to live.

If there can ever be a good time to get sick with HIV/AIDS I picked a good time. Combination therapy had been introduced a year earlier and I started on the drugs saquinavir, AZT and epivir plus a prophylactic antibiotic to ward off pneumonia. Since 1997 I have taken between six and 25 tablets per day to stay alive. The drugs reduced the level of virus in my blood to undetectable levels and slowly my CD4 count began to rise.

At a dental appointment it was found Kaposi's sarcoma had spread to the inside of my mouth. Within weeks I couldn't breathe through my left nostril as the tumours spread. Six months of chemotherapy and radiotherapy were needed to treat the cancer. At the Western General Hospital a little man in a white coat and thick glasses takes a plaster cast of one side of my face and makes a lead mask for me to wear during radiotherapy. Every fortnight for three months I arrive at the oncology ward of the Western General Hospital, the most frightening place I have ever been. A nurse takes my blood to be tested and I wait for two or three hours to see if my immune system is strong enough to cope with a chemotherapy treatment. Then I would sit for an hour hooked up to a drip of liposomal donna rubicin.

I'm sure most of the other patients in the ward at the same time as me are long dead. As a boy I started to read Alexander Solzhenitsyn's *Cancer Ward*, never imagining (no one does) I would end up in an oncology ward one day. Side effects caused by HIV medication and cancer treatment included nausea, chronic diarrhoea and fatigue. I realised I was going to have to live the rest of my life with a chronic life threatening medical condition which fluctuates on a sometimes daily basis.

Some mornings I felt I could climb a mountain. Other days I could hardly get out of bed or go further than 10 feet from a toilet. Gradually though I began to recover. I was 33 years old. I didn't plan on dying of AIDS.

A Dog Called Cuilean

Scott had always wanted a dog. Since he was a kid. I'd read research showing people recover faster from serious illness and tend to stay better if they have a pet, but uncertain about the idea I stalled; 'maybe we'll find a nice dog when we go on holiday to Assynt'. Hoping that might be the end of it.

Assynt... like Muriel Gray I've always fancied Assynt; 'If Assynt was a boy I'd have knocked it to the ground with a rugby tackle and pulled its trousers down years ago.'

The first morning of the holiday, Scott drove the seven miles from Stoer to the nearest shop for supplies; rolls, bacon, Marlboro Lights. A brown envelope was sellotaped to the window of the newsagent's in Lochinver, (life changing) words scribbled in black biro;

Free to a good home
Two border collie puppies
One black and one tan
Alan MacRae, Torbreck

'Oh yes', said the wifey in the shop, Mr MacRae was very keen to find homes for the pups... they were driving him mad... The next day Scott drove to Torbreck but couldn't find Alan MacRae, only a herd of Highland cattle who surrounded the car thinking he'd come to feed them.

Kellan at the summit of Sgorr Dhearg near Ballachulish in 1982.

Scott (second from left with Ben) had always wanted a dog. Since he was a kid...

Ann who we were staying with was less impressed; 'you don't want one of Alan MacRae's dogs – they stand in the road and bark at cars'. I can't say we weren't warned.

Scott found the right house and Alan MacRae took him out to see the pups. A hole in the barn door was blocked with a plastic crate held in place by a tractor wheel. High pitched squealing could be heard coming from within, and as Alan MacRae rolled back the tractor wheel then pushed aside the plastic crate, a brown furry nose appeared.

We called her Cuilean (*koo-lan*), the Gaelic word for a pup, a cub, a whelp or a *sweetheart*. I took the name from a Gaelic dictionary in Primrose Cottage at Stoer while the rain swept in from the sea.

The Stoer collies are a breed apart, nothing like Shep from *Blue Peter*. The puppy grew up in to a long haired brown shaggy thing referred to variously as The Wookiee (*Star Wars*) or, 'is your dog a mop/sheep?'

When the Vikings sailed in long ships past the Old Man of Stoer and the pillar mountain Suilven, to land on the white sands of Achmelvich (I like to think) a long haired brown dog with a wild look in its eyes, a distant ancestor of Cuilean, splashed ashore with them and raced off after a sheep.

That was 12 years ago. Cuilean the whelp mellowed into Cuilean the sweetheart. She doesn't go on the high hills so often these days… asleep in the dog basket by the Rayburn as I write this.

We Have Won The Land.

Alan MacRae in 1993 celebrating the purchase of the North Lochinver estate for the people who lived there. The dog in the picture is Cuilean's mother. The mountain is Suilven.

© John Paul Photography

Leith

Three years before I was diagnosed with HIV I bought a flat in Leith on what was then one of the cheapest streets in Edinburgh. It was an elegant Victorian flat upstairs from a Scots Asian-owned food shop and off-licence. Every Friday night the kids from the nearby tower blocks congregated to swig bottles of cheap booze in a derelict side street across the road from the flat. Then around 9pm as eight per cent alcohol hit teenage brain cells there would be a loud bang as one of the plate glass windows of the shop downstairs was smashed.

Old sofas were set on fire in the street, the window above the entrance door to the tenement was smashed and lighter fluid poured onto the plastic door entry phone system and ignited. The benches in the park across the road from the flat were a popular venue for drinking large blue plastic bottles of cider. One day two policeman arrived at the front door to say a disabled man on crutches had gone berserk in the street and smashed up several cars including ours, front and back windscreen shattered.

In 2007 Leith police told Jabbar who owned the shop directly below my flat of a threat to firebomb it. I fitted smoke detectors in every room and made plans to move. With help from our families we sold the flat in Leith and relocated to one of the streets that skirts Arthur's Seat. On the shelves of the local library in Piershill I found *A Guide to Holyrood Park and Arthur's Seat* published in 1987. Turning the pages I came across a list, *Mountains Visible from Arthur's Seat by CG Cash*, FRSGS. The list intrigued me. Who was CG Cash and why had he made a list of hills?

I took a compass and climbed to the top of Arthur's Seat to identify the hills on the list. The day was cold, air clear, it was easy to make out the mountains – most were snow covered. Ben Lomond I could see to the west, next to it must be Ben Venue between two church spires... Ben Ledi – easy... Benvane over Dumyat yes, Stob Binnein and Ben More to the right of Fettes College, Ben Vorlich behind the Ochils, Schiehallion hmm? East Lomond, West Lomond, not sure about Lochnagar...

I sat there at the summit of Arthur's Seat where Caleb stood a hundred years before. Watching the crows floating on the breeze with the city spread out below me. Sometimes I sit at the top of a hill and think. How lucky to be here... A long term survivor of HIV. All the lives still stolen by AIDS. From somewhere came the idea of climbing the Scottish mountains visible from Arthur's Seat. Making a journey through a distant line of hills from 73 degrees to 1 degree west of north. I could survive HIV/AIDS... I could weather the storm... I could climb the mountains on Caleb's List.

CHAPTER THREE

The Arthurs

The question has been many times asked, What Grampian and
other summits can be seen from Arthur's Seat?

CG CASH WRITING IN NOVEMBER 1898

EDINBURGH 2008. Standing on the orange carpet in Piershill library between the rows of large print and audio books... Arthur's Seat is visible from the supermarket car park outside. While a librarian chases some kids from the Square across the road out the door, the first thing that strikes me about Caleb's list is the similarity of its layout to Sir Hugh Munro's famous tables of Scottish mountains over 3,000 feet. It strikes me that Caleb must have looked at Munro's Tables in *The Scottish Mountaineering Club Journal* and copied the layout for his list of Scottish mountains visible from Arthur's Seat. During the 20th century Munro and his list would become famous while Caleb's list was all but forgotten. It resurfaced, briefly rescued from obscurity in the 1980s, in Gordon Wright's (long out of print) *Guide to Holyrood Park and Arthur's Seat*, which is where I came across it one afternoon in Piershill library.

I'm curious. Who was CG Cash FRSGS? I wonder? What led him to compile a list of the Scottish mountains visible from Arthur's Seat? The FRSGS bit is easy – in tiny print along the foot of the table I read *Reproduced by kind permission of the Royal Scottish Geographical Society*. The list seems older than the 1980s guidebook it is reprinted in. I see a 1960s university lecturer with sports jacket and sighting compass taking bearings from the summit of Arthur's Seat.

In fact the list is older and the truth more interesting. As well as being a geographer the remarkable CG Cash will turn out among other things to be one of the early Scottish mountaineers, a pioneer who explored the Cairngorms a decade before the Scottish Mountaineering Club held their first meet there. A man described by fellow climbers as having 'a familiarity with, and a knowledge of the Cairngorm mountains almost unequalled' and by historian Ian R Mitchell writing in 2001 as 'a Scottish mountaineer of some note.'

Though I don't know it as I stand on the orange carpet in Piershill Library, searching for Caleb will take me from the summit of Arthur's Seat to the place known as the heart of the Cairngorm mountains. From concrete Strathclyde University to the forgotten volumes of *The Cairngorm Club Journal* in the National Library of Scotland. I will see an osprey for the first time and climb to the summit of Scotland's highest mountain. I'll sit under the ancient pines on the shore of Loch an Eilein and wander the narrow cobbled streets of Old Aberdeen. I'll stand on the bridge over the Falls of Dochart and explore stone circles in the Perthshire countryside and cycle to a sandstone house near Cramond.

But all that lies in the future... for now back to Piershill library and Caleb's list... rediscovered.

MOUNTAINS VISIBLE FROM ARTHUR'S SEAT C.G. Cash, F.R.S.G.S.

NAME	Height in feet	POSITION	Distance in Miles	Direction	Degrees W. of N.	GUIDE LINE
Ben Lomond	3192	E. side of Loch Lomond	59	W. by N.	73	Towers of Free Church College
Ben Venue	2393	S. side of Loch Katrine	53½	W.N.W.	68	Between St. George's and Tron Churches
Ben Ledi	2875	N.W. of Callander	48½	W.N.W.	63	Left of Fettes College, over north approach viaduct of Forth Bridge
Ben Vane	2685	W. of Loch Lubnaig	52	W.N.W.	62½	Over Dumyat
Dumyat	1375	S.W. extremity of Ochils	31	W.N.W.	62	Over Fettes College
Am Binnein or Stobinian	3827	Braes of Balquhidder	60	N.W. by W.	61	Just to right of Fettes College
Ben More	3843	Braes of Balquhidder	60¼	N.W. by W.	60	Just to right of Am Binnein
Ben Vorlich	3224	S. side of Loch Earn	48½	N.W. by W.	57	Left-hand end of Cramond Isle
Ben Cleuch	2363	Highest point of Ochils	28½	N.W. by W.	55	Right-hand end of Cramond Isle
Ben Lawers	3984	N. Side of Loch Tay	57¾	N.W.	44	Left-hand end of Inchcolm
Meall Garbh	3661	E. peak of Ben Lawers	58	N.W.	43½	Left-hand end of Inchmickery
Ben Chonzie or Ben y Hone	3048	N. of Comrie	47	N.W.	43	Right-hand part of Inchcolm
Schiehallion	3547	S. of River Tummel, between Lochs Rannoch and Tummel	60½	N.W. by N.	35	East Breakwater at Granton
Meall Dearg	2258	N. side of Strath Bran	48	N.W. by N.	31	Chancelot Flour Mill
Ben Dearg	3304	W. side of Glen Tilt	69	N.N.W.	22	
Ben Vrackie	2757	E. of Pitlochry	58	N.N.W.	21	To left of steep scarp of Benarty
Ben y Ghlo	3671	E. side of Glen Tilt	63½	N.N.W.	20	
W. Lomond Hill	1713	Between Falkland and Loch	21	N. by W.	15	Over entrance to Leith Harbour
E. Lomond Hill	1471	Leven	20¼	N. by W.	7	To right of Leith Martello Tower
Lochnagar	3786	S. of River Dee, E. of Braemar	68	N.	5	East end of Imperial dock at Leith

Caleb's List of Arthurs as it appeared in *The Cairngorm Club Journal* in 1899.

Caleb's list is printed as a table with seven columns. I run my eyes down the first column. It lists the names of 20 Scottish mountains visible from Arthur's Seat, sometimes giving an old spelling of a hill name, *Am Binnein* for Stob Binnein and *Schichallion* for Schiehallion.

The second column gives the height of the mountain in feet as marked on the Ordnance Survey maps of the 1890s – Ben Lomond is 3,192 feet while on today's maps it is 974 metres or 3,195 feet. The Scottish mountains visible from Arthur's Seat range in height from Dumyat, the lowest at 418m/1,371ft to Ben Lawers the highest at 1,214m/3,983ft. All the Arthurs are over 300m/1,000ft in height.

TABLE I.—THE 3,000 FEET TOPS ARRANGED ACCORDING TO DISTRICTS.

SECTION 1.

Number of Mountain in order of Altitude.	Number of Separate Top in order of Altitude.	Height. The smaller figures within parentheses are the Contour height from the 1-inch O.S. Map.	Name.	Position.	County.	Best Ascended from	See Page
179	315	3192	Ben Lomond	3 m. N. by E. from Rowardennan, Loch Lomond	Stirling	Rowardennan Inn	319
254	462	3086 (3000)	Beinn Narnain¹ ..	1½ m. S.E. from Beinn Ime	Argyll	Arrochar (3½ m.) ..	63 et seq.
117	198	3318 (3250)	Beinn Ime	3½ m. N.W. from Arrochar ..	Do.	Arrochar	Do.
278	506	3004	Ben Vane	3½ m. N.N.W. do. ..	Dumbarton	Do.	
262	480	3021	Beinn an Lochain¹ ..	Glencroe	Argyll	Cairndow Inn (3 m. E.S.E.), Arrochar or St Catherine's, Loch Fyne (5½ m.)	
		(>995ft.1-in.O.S.)					
232	405	3092	Ben Vorlich, South Top ..	2½ m. S.W. from Ardlui, L. Lomond	Dumbarton	Ardlui	65 et seq., 334
	440	3055	Do. North Top ..	2½ m. do. do. ..	Do.	Do.	Do.
211	385	3106	Beinn Buidhe	4 m. N. from head of Loch Fyne ..	Argyll	Dalmally or Cairndow Inn ..	237
273	498	3008	Beinn a' Chlèibh ..	1 m. S.W. Beinn Laoigh ..	Argyll & Perth	Dalmally (5 m.) ..	247
26	46	3708	Beinn Laoigh² (Ben Lui) ..	6 m. E. from Dalmally ..	Do.	Tyndrum or Dalmally ..	120, 207, & 247
102	172	3374	Beinn Oss	1½ m. E.S.E. from Beinn Laoigh ..	Perth	Tyndrum (4 m.) ..	247
176	300	3204	Beinn Dubh Chraige ..	3½ m. S.S.W. Tyndrum ..	Do.	Do.	247
242	442	3053	Beinn Chabhair ..	3½ m. E.N.E. Ardlui, Loch Lomond	Do.	Ardlui or Crianlarich..	120 and 247
145	241	3265 (3250)	An Caisteal²	1 m. N.E. from B. Chabhair ; 3¾ m. S. from Crianlarich	Do.	Crianlarich	119 and 248
	419	3078 (3000)	Beinn a' Chroin, West Top ..	4½ m. S. by E. from Crianlarich ..	Do.	Do.	119
216	394	3101	Do. East Top ..	4½ m. S. by E. do. ..	Do.	Do.	119 and 326
219	401	3099	Beinn Tulachan ..	4½ m. S.S.E. do. ..	Do.	Do. or Balquhidder ..	119 and 326
72	124	3477 (3250)	Cruach Ardran, N.E. Top³ ..	3 m. S.S.E. do. ..	Do.	Do.	84, 119, & 326
	148	3429 (3250)	Do. S.W. Top ..	¼ m. from N.E. Top ..	Do.	Do.	
	465	3034 (3000)	Top between Cruach Ardran and Stob Garbh..		Do.	Do.	
	319	3148	Stob Garbh	2¼ m. S.E. from Crianlarich.. ..	Do.	Do.	84 and 119

Munro's List of Scottish mountains over 3,000 feet.
Caleb set out his list in a similar layout. [SMC]

Next the position of the mountain is given; Ben More and Stob Binnein are located in the *Braes of Balquhidder* and Ben Cleuch is *Highest point of Ochils*. Thus confusion is avoided between the two Ben Vorlichs in the southern Highlands and the Meall Dearg north of Strathbraan which is but one of Scotland's numerous 'red hills'.

Many of the hills on Caleb's list lie along the Highland boundary fault which stretches from Loch Lomond in a north-easterly direction through Aberfoyle, Callander and Comrie then along Strathbraan to Dunkeld and Blairgowrie before reaching the east coast at Stonehaven. Formed when ancient continents collided the fault separates the sandstones of the central valley of Scotland from the older, harder rocks of the Highlands. The hills of the Scottish Highlands were once part of a much larger mountain range that stretched from Norway to the Appalachians. Many of the mountains on Caleb's list are frontier hills... hills straddling an ancient geological boundary that remains a cultural dividing line today.

The fourth column gives the distance of the mountain visible from Arthur's Seat in miles, again as measured on the Ordnance Survey maps available to Caleb in 1899. East Lomond is nearest at 20¼ miles away and Ben Dearg furthest 69 miles to the north.

Another column gives the general direction of the mountain from Arthur's Seat – Ben Venue is WNW (west-north-west) and Ben Vrackie is NNW The most southerly Arthur is Dumyat, the furthest west Ben Lomond, the most eastern and northerly Lochnagar.

Column six gives the mountain's position in the form *Degrees West of North*. Meall Garbh is 43½ degrees west of north and East Lomond 7 degrees west of north. The bearings are given in the form of degrees west of north because Caleb used a theodolite to compile his list. It is relatively difficult to pick out individual mountains from Arthur's Seat using a compass because of the long distances involved. The way the light slants on the hills at different times of the day affects the view from Arthur's Seat and a dusting of snow makes it easier to see the Arthurs.

The Lost Horizon

The final column of the table, headed *Guide Line*, gives the name of a landmark building on Edinburgh's skyline, one of the islands in the Firth of Forth or a nearby hill which is in line with one of the 20 mountains visible from Arthur's Seat. Unlike many British cities Edinburgh suffered little from the bombs of the Luftwaffe or the Brutalist architects of the 1960s, and the city's horizon has changed comparatively little in the hundred years since Caleb stood at the summit of Arthur's Seat compiling his list and noting landmark buildings on Edinburgh's skyline.

Today Free Church College is better known as the meeting place of the general assembly of the Church of Scotland on the Mound and St George's Church in Charlotte Square, easy to spot with its green dome, became West Register House in 1964. In the 21st century there are two, soon to be three, Forth bridges. Leith is more built up than a century ago and the east end of the 'new' dock extension on Caleb's list can be identified today by a tall concrete grain elevator on the quayside of the Imperial Dock. Only two of Caleb's 1899 'guide lines' – Chancelot Flour Mill and the Leith Martello tower – are no longer visible from Arthur's Seat.

Lists of Hills

As the recent 'demotion' of Sgurr nan Ceannaichean (913m/2,997ft) from Munro to Corbett status demonstrates, unlike mountains, hill lists are not set in stone. And like all hill lists, Caleb's table of Scottish mountains visible from Arthur's Seat contains it fair share of inaccuracies and inconsistencies. Most glaringly Caleb, a geography teacher who was always quick to draw attention to errors on Ordnance Survey maps, has himself erred in the guide lines column of his table confusing Bishop Hill and Benarty in Fife. Beinn Dearg, Ben Vrackie and Beinn a'Ghlo are in fact to be seen from Arthur's Seat to the left of the steep scarp of Bishop Hill not Benarty.

Caleb's list of 'mountains' includes Dumyat and East and West Lomond, usually described as hills but included because they are such notable landmarks from Arthur's Seat. They are the hills most often visible when the higher Arthurs are obscured by low cloud. Caleb had seen the Lomond Hills of Fife from the summit of Cairn Toul in the Cairngorms in August 1894.

Caleb's list is of 20 mountains visible to the north of

The First Chancelot Mill

The Cooperative Wholesale Society's Chancelot roller flour mill in Dalmeny Road, Bonnington. Caleb used the mill as a guideline for Meall Dearg. The building in the photo was demolished around 1970 when the present day Chancelot Mill opened at a site on the edge of Leith Docks.

© Allan Dodds

Arthur's Seat in an arc stretching from Ben Lomond in the west to Lochnagar in the east. The Pentland Hills and the hills of the Scottish Borders to the south are omitted. On a sunny day looking at the view from the top of Arthur's Seat it becomes clear that Caleb's list does not include *all* the mountains visible to the north of Arthur's Seat. Caleb it seems settled on a round figure of 20 hills from west to east. Ben Ime and Ben Vane in the Arrochar Alps can be seen from Arthur's Seat, between Ben Lomond and Ben Venue, but do not appear on Caleb's list and to the north-east in good visibility Driesh and Ben Tirran in Angus can be seen as well as Lochnagar.

Why Caleb omitted some of the mountains visible from Arthur's Seat is an unknown. Another book could be written about the hills visible to

Leith Martello Tower. In 1899
the tower stood on offshore
rocks, as seen in this RAF
aerial photo taken during the
Second World War. On Caleb's
List the tower is given as the
guideline for East Lomond Hill.
Today the Martello Tower is
half buried on reclaimed land
near the East Breakwater of
Leith Docks.
[© *Courtesy of RCAHMS (RAF
WWII Air Photographs Collection).
Licensor www.rcahms.gov.uk*]

the south of Arthur's Seat. Caleb knew his list was incomplete; in a letter
to *The Scotsman* newspaper he referred to his table as including;
'... *most* of the 'tops' that can be seen from Arthur's Seat.' Caleb's list
of mountains is an arbitrary one, but omissions, inconsistencies and mistakes on hill lists seem to add interest and form part of their intrinsic fascination for some. As with old maps the errors on Victorian hill lists
need to be seen in the context of their making, and are less important
than what Caleb's list of Scottish mountains visible from Arthur's Seat
symbolises; that to the early mountaineers the view of the distant hills
was something new and exciting.

In May 1907 Caleb published 'in response to numerous inquiries' an
'amended and extended' version of his table which resolved many of the
errors and inconsistencies of his original 1899 list.

Caleb climbed in the Scottish hills at the same time as the best known
list compiler of them all, Sir Hugh Munro of Lindertis. Both Caleb and
Munro died within months of each other at the end of the First World
War, but Caleb remains a shadowy figure in the background of the
world of Edwardian mountaineering, outshone by his more famous con-
temporaries, middle class men like Munro and AE Robertson.

Munro's list of Scottish mountains over 3,000 feet contained many
inconsistencies too. Over the past hundred years Munro's Tables have
been subject to several revisions. Most notoriously, in Munro's original

list the Inaccessible Pinnacle in the Cuillin Mountains on Skye was listed as a mere 'Top' despite being 26 feet (8 metres) higher than nearby Sgurr Dearg which was listed as a Munro.

Errors in early hill lists can be partly explained by the maps and navigational tools available to mountaineers at the time. Caleb's list was compiled using a theodolite and Ordnance Survey maps a century before the creation of digital elevation models and computer drawn mountain panoramas.

Like other mountaineers of his generation Caleb encountered problems with the maps available to him in the 1890s. At the time Caleb compiled his list the Ordnance Survey produced two sets of maps for mountaineers; one-inch to the mile and six-inch to the mile maps. The problem was the two sets of maps contained separate, independent and different information! The one-inch maps (early versions of today's familiar Landranger 2cm to 1km/1:50000 maps) had 250 foot contours, but few spot heights or names, while the six-inch maps (large scale maps roughly equivalent to 1:10000 today) contained numerous spot heights and names, but no contour lines. This must have made for traumatically complicated navigation, and certainly made life difficult for Hugh Munro when he was compiling his tables of Scottish mountains over 3,000 feet in height. About the absence of contours Caleb wrote in *The Scotsman* newspaper in September 1901; 'Mountaineers are loud and frequent in their complaints...'

Geography Class-Room
EDINBURGH ACADEMY, 14 November 1898

GENTLEMAN. The question has been many times asked, What Grampian and other summits can be seen from Arthur's Seat? I have made many pilgrimages to that pleasant spot, and have drawn up a table of all the summits I have been able to identify in the quadrant from West to North. It will perhaps prove of interest to some of your readers. I must admit that the identification of Lochnagar is not certain. I am, yours faithfully,

C.G. CASH

From Letters to the Editors, *Edinburgh Academy Chronicle*.

The Mountain Panorama

Panorama from Greek πᾶνν 'all' + ὅραμα 'sight'
Wikipedia

What led Caleb to compile a table of the mountains visible from Arthur's Seat? Partly it was his interest in the landscape of Scotland, but Caleb's list also has its roots in the artist painted mountain panoramas of the Alps that became popular as tourism and mountaineering developed in Europe during the 19th century. Mountain panoramas handpainted in oil on canvas were quickly replaced by neatly folded paper panoramas which were included in guidebooks or sold to tourists. The mountain panorama never caught on to the same extent in Scotland as on the continent, but essentially Caleb's list of mountains visible from Arthur's Seat is a mountain panorama in tabular form.

Back home from the library a search on Google reveals Caleb was closely involved in the conservation of Timothy Pont's 16th century maps of Scotland which include panorama-like drawings of Scottish mountains and these too may well have influenced him. The Cairngorm Club Journals of the 1900s contain several hand drawn mountain panoramas. Caleb's fascination with the hills visible from Scottish mountains was a common characteristic of Victorian mountaineers. The view from the summit of a hill was still a new and novel phenomenon and a number of early Scottish climbers recorded the view from the mountains they ascended in great detail.

In Scotland, the most popular and successful mountain panorama was James Shearer's 360-degree drawing of the view from the summit of Ben Nevis published in 1895 and reprinted in 1935 and 1980. Caleb describes using Shearer's drawing to identify hills when he climbed Ben Nevis in August 1907 and this panorama may have inspired him to compile a list of the Scottish mountains visible from Arthur's Seat.

Another form of the mountain panorama is the mountain indicator, a polished circular slab of stone or steel cemented to a cairn with the names of the distant peaks visible from that hill engraved on it. Mountain indicators stand on the summits of several Scottish hills including Arthur's Seat, Ben Cleuch, Ben Vrackie and Lochnagar. Today the mountain panoramas of the 21st century are computer generated, based on digital contour data and available at the click of a mouse.

Later I will discover the Scottish mountains visible from Arthur's Seat was not Caleb's first list of hills, two years earlier in 1897 he had published a table of mountains in the Cairngorms over 2,000 feet. And while on holiday in the summer of 1898 Caleb was asked, 'could the summit cairn of Braeriach be seen from Aviemore?' Caleb did not know, but he set to work to find out by drawing a panorama of the Cairngorm mountains visible from Aviemore railway station. It may be that a similar question back home in Edinburgh prompted him to compile a list of the Scottish mountains visible from Arthur's Seat.

The First Arthurist?

Many people today enjoy ticking off hills from the lists of Munros, Corbetts and Grahams. In terms of their classification according to other (more famous) hill lists the Arthurs include eleven Munros, three Corbetts and three Grahams. There are only 20 Arthurs compared with 283 Munros, but they are a good 'mix' of hills; some classic southern Highland Munros, a couple of popular Corbetts and two of the best Grahams. The Arthurs have something to offer people of every age and level of hillwalking experience; from the family with young children climbing East Lomond, to the experienced hill walker making the long approach to Beinn Dearg in winter or climbing all the Arthurs in one expedition. Ticking off the mountains on Caleb's list could form a good introduction to the Scottish hills or a coda to a lifetime of mountaineering.

MUNRO, CORBETT OR GRAHAM?

An early president of the Scottish Mountaineering Club, Sir Hugh Munro was a landowner with a country house at Lindertis near Kirriemuir and an enthusiastic supporter of the Conservative and Unionist tendency in Scottish politics. Munro published his list of Scottish mountains over 3,000 feet in 1891 and there are currently 283 Munros.

John Rooke Corbett made a list of 219 Scottish hills between 2,500 feet (762 metres) and 3,000 feet (914.4 metres) with a drop of a least 500 feet (152.4 metres) between each listed hill and any adjacent higher one. Corbett was a Cambridge mathematician who became a district valuer in Bristol and joined the Scottish Mountaineering Club in 1923. His list was published posthumously in 1952.

A list of the Scottish hills between 2,000 and 2,500 feet in height with a re-ascent of at least 150 metres was compiled by Fiona Graham while she was convalescing from a skiing accident. The list of Grahams was published in 1992 and stands as a memorial to Fiona Graham who was murdered during a hillwalking holiday in Scotland in the 1990s.

Caleb's list presents possibilities; from climbing Arthur's Seat and – if the weather conditions are right – trying to see the Scottish mountains visible from its summit, to the challenge of climbing and ticking off the 20 hills on the list, the Arthurs. A list is a starting point. Finding Caleb's list that afternoon will lead me to try and spot the mountains visible from Arthur's Seat and then to climb all 20 of them (the first Arthurist? … hmmm) and, in time, to write these pages.

I leave the library, Caleb's list in my pocket, cut through the supermarket car park heading for the blaze of yellow whin on the lower slopes of Arthur's Seat.

CHAPTER FOUR

Ben Lomond

73 Degrees West of North

BEYOND THE TOWERS of Free Church College, 73 degrees west of north, Ben Lomond (974m/3,195ft) appeared a distant blue triangle on the skyline far to the west that day in 1898 when Caleb stood on the rocky summit of Arthur's Seat compiling his list of Scottish mountains visible from Arthur's Seat.

Anderson's Guide to the Highlands and Islands published 50 years earlier in 1834 was one of the first guidebooks to Scotland. Written by two brothers based in Inverness it included information about the Scottish mountains and on page 340 I read;

> Ben Lomond has perhaps been ascended by a greater number of tourists than any other of our highland mountains... the birds'-eye view of Loch Lomond itself, as seen from the shoulder of the hill, amply repays the labour of the ascent...

The mountain is a landmark on the edge of the Scottish Highlands visible from many places in Scotland's central belt; from Glasgow, right across to Stirling and, on a clear day, from Arthur's Seat in Edinburgh. Long ago an ancient language, Cumbric, was spoken in southern Scotland. The Cumbric word *llumon* means a beacon, blaze or light. Like the Lomond Hills of Fife, the name Ben Lomond may be derived from *llumon* and perhaps these hills were once used to send messages. The Scottish diaspora has led to hills across the planet being named Ben Lomond. There are Ben Lomonds in Canada, Australia and New Zealand. The Ben Lomond in the American state of Utah is thought to have inspired the opening credit of Paramount Pictures.

Scottish winter mountaineering could be said to have begun on the summit ridge of Ben Lomond in November 1812 when Colonel Peter Hawker and his companions were forced to cut steps in the frozen snow with their knives. In the early 19th century the idea of doing this for fun hadn't occurred to anyone yet;

To get to the most elevated point of the shoulder we found impossible, as the last 50 yards was a solid sheet of ice, and indeed for the last half-mile we travelled in perfect misery and imminent danger. We were literally obliged to take knives and cut footsteps in the frozen snow, and of course obliged to crawl all the way on our hands, knees and toes, all of which were benumbed with cold.

Climbing Ben Lomond

Sron Aonaich means *the nose of the ridge* and this is the easiest route up Ben Lomond sometimes referred to as the tourist path. *Anderson's Guide to the Highlands and Islands of Scotland* includes directions for climbing Ben Lomond;

> From opposite Tarbet the ascent (here rather steep) generally occupies two hours. At Rowardennan, opposite Inveruglas, five miles down the loch it is more tedious, but considerably more easy, and this is the route most commonly followed.

Begin from the car park at the end of the public road from Balmaha to Rowardennan just past the Rowardennan Hotel. Behind the visitor centre built in 2001 with creative use of local materials – oak frame, slate saddle-back roof and mud walls, a path leads off into the woods through rowans and silver birches. In October when I climb Ben Lomond devil's bit scabious is still flowering by the path and fungi sprout from the moss covered trunk of a fallen tree.

The footpath crosses a forest track and continues across ground where trees have been felled. Over the next 50 years the National Trust and the Forestry Commission plan to cut down the remaining conifers on Ben Lomond and replace them with native trees and shrubs. Clear felling looks ugly for a while but new trees and plants soon begin to cover the ground. The plan is to restore the mountain landscape recreating a natural transition from loch shore to mountain summit.

In *On Foot in the Highlands* Ernest A Baker has words of reassurance for those feeling a little daunted by the prospect of climbing Ben Lomond. He quotes John Stuart Blackie, the famously eccentric Victorian academic who described the mountain as;

> A Ben which possesses the double advantage of commanding a splendid prospect and presenting no difficulty of climbing, even to the most feeble and dainty-footed tourist.

The path climbs up through silver birches. All the time Ben Lomond and the Ptarmigan ridge draw the eye. In October the bracken has turned orangey-red and the heather faded from purple to brown. The hillside is turning to autumnal colours. The trees turning too. I pause and look down at Loch Lomond. Speedboats and jet skis create ripples and wave patterns on the surface of the loch as a sea plane flies past low over the water.

Chaffinches flutter around a solitary rowan, drawn to the tree's red berries. On the west shore of the loch, Glen Douglas and the white painted Inn at Inverbeg. The path is well constructed breaking out into a flight of stone steps at one place. The tree lined Ardess Burn curves down to Loch Lomond where stone built Rowardennan youth hostel with its red painted gables stands in woodland by the shore.

Birches and rowan grow beside the Ardess Burn. Birch leaves lie on the grass and float in the water. A little further on the path reaches the grassy lower slopes of Ben Lomond's south ridge, crossing the hillside through clumps of soft rush. Much work has been done on the Ben Lomond path by contractors and volunteers to repair erosion caused by the estimated 50,000 people who climb the mountain each year. At one time the old path was 25 metres wide in places. Today the path is paved with stones and impressive gullies draw rainwater away. Erosion by thousands of pairs of boots over the years has exposed the underlying rock. Bare rock now incorporated into the surface of the path.

If you climb Ben Lomond during the summer months and find you are not alone on the mountain, it was ever thus as Charles Ross's *Travellers' Guide To Loch Lomond* published in 1792 states;

> In the months of July, August and September, the summit of Ben Lomond is frequently visited by strangers from every quarter of the island, as well as by foreigners.

Some kids camping near the path have left crisp packets and a disposable barbecue among the yellow deer grass and mossy lichen covered rocks. My mind clicks back to one January early morning driving west in Morag's old Rover to climb Ben Lomond. Scott off work suffering from depression. The aftermath of my diagnosis with HIV... for him it was to be mountains as therapy. From Edinburgh through Stirling and the little villages on the road to Drymen, Scotland was asleep that Sunday morning.

WHO OWNS BEN LOMOND?

Ben Lomond was originally bought for the nation in 1950 with support from the National Land Fund, set up by Labour chancellor Hugh Dalton after the Second World War. In his speech to parliament announcing the creation of the £50 million fund Dalton waxed lyrical about the beauty of the British countryside; '... the sunshine on the hills, the mist adrift across the moors... the deep peace of the woodlands, the wash of the waves against the white, unconquerable cliffs which Hitler never scaled.' The post war Labour government saw conserving beauty and wildlife, coupled with peaceful outdoor recreation for the living as a way to commemorate those who had been killed in the Second World War or as Dalton put it in his speech; 'those who for our sake went down to the dark river...' In 1984, Ben Lomond, under threat from the Craigroyston hydro-electric scheme, was bought by the National Trust from the Forestry Commission, so the mountain has the dubious distinction of having been purchased *twice* for the nation.

Up through the woods. David missing his old dog Meg running ahead to get to the snowline. The summit ridge was icy and we put our crampons on, at least two of us did. Scott had only a pair of Blundstone boots with steel toe caps which conducted body heat away and slowly froze his toes. With no crampons he had to proceed rather in the manner of Colonel Hawker 'in perfect misery and imminent danger' though I see from my diary we did lend him an ice axe. And afterwards back to the warm beery fug of the Barony Bar in Broughton Street.

A red grouse flies up. I've already seen many small birds on the hillside and noticed grouse droppings on the track. As the path climbs Sron Aonaich the tree covered islands of Loch Lomond are seen; the view you remember from climbing Ben Lomond. To the west the hunched shape of the Cobbler, easy to recognise. The A82 snakes along the western shore of Loch Lomond and I can see down to Dumbarton Rock, the Clyde and the tower blocks of Glasgow. A yellow haze seems to hang over the city, the result of traffic and industrial pollution.

As you climb Ben Lomond, pause a moment and think about the early explorers and climbers who passed this way before. William Burrell who made the first recorded ascent of the mountain in 1758... Thomas Russell in 1771... the botanist John Lightfoot in June 1772 in search of rare flowering plants for his *Flora Scotica* published five years later... Thomas Wilkinson from Westmoreland who climbed Ben Lomond in 1 hour and 38 minutes in 1787... Jacques Louis de Bougrenet, Chevalier de Latocnaye, an exile from revolutionary France and early foreign visitor to Ben Lomond in 1797... Sir John Stoddart who in 1799 described reaching the summit of the mountain as a 'surprise, arising almost to terror... one side forcibly torn off, leaving a stupendous precipice' and Colonel Hawker in November 1812 who wrote that groups of ladies would often climb the hill, taking a piper with them for dancing on the summit.

Before the Second World War the legendary Scottish climber Jock Nimlin worked as a crane-driver in the Clyde shipyards and from the cabin of his 150 foot high crane could see Ben Lomond. He climbed the mountain many times as he described in *A Hundred Times up Ben Lomond* broadcast by the BBC Home Service in 1940. Surveying the view from the summit of Ben Lomond not long after climbing the Matterhorn Nimlin is said to have asked; 'Why go to the Alps when we have all this on our doorstep in Scotland?'

From around the 550 metre contour line a level section of the Sron Aonaich ridge gives easy walking with the summit of Ben Lomond peppered with white quartz boulders visible to the north. The Arran hills are seen to the west and the little top of Conic Hill to the south-east marks the line of the Highland boundary fault.

At about 800 metres where the path steepens to zig zag its way to the summit ridge, I stop to munch an apple. Nearby a plastic bottle lies discarded among the rocks and alpine ladies mantle. Scottish Natural Heritage designates Ben Lomond a site of special scientific interest because;

The mountain ringlet: a rare butterfly is found on Ben Lomond.

> It is distinct from other southern Highland hills as it retains remnants
> of the full range of upland plant communities from low to high altitude,
> a feature that has been lost from neighbouring hills.

Everything from the ancient oak trees that shade the road along Loch Lomondside to the miniature mosses on the mountain's summit. Among the flowering plants still found on Ben Lomond's higher slopes and rocky ledges: alpine mouse-ear, downy willow, hoary whitlow grass, alpine saxifrage, alpine cinquefoil, sibbaldia, alpine willowherb, spiked woodrush, black alpine sedge and alpine meadowgrass.

I remember a cold day in autumn. I stood on the sandy beach at Luss looking across the loch at Ben Lomond. Bracken on the lower slopes turning gold, further uphill the fading purple of ling heather giving way to dark green blaeberry, followed in turn by yellowing deer grass merging into thin soil and stony, frost shattered rock at the summit of the mountain.

As the path climbs onto the summit ridge you become aware of the hillside beginning to fall steeply away to the north, Ben More and Stob

---

THE FIRST RECORDED ASCENT OF BEN LOMOND

William Burrell (1732–96) was a young English lawyer from a wealthy family. In 1758 he visited Scotland and described his ascent of Ben Lomond;

'On the opposite side [of Loch Lomond] stands a mountain of the same name of a prodigious height overshadowing all the neighbouring rocks. The way to it is very irksome and in some places so steep that we were obliged to crawl on hands and knees... In several parts we sunk up to our knees in mire. We were fortunate enough to have a fine day and from the top on one side we could see Edinburgh and Sterling [sic] castles at 40 miles distance. On the other that of Dumbarton, Port Glasgow, the Clyde and all the country beyond, many miles. About two miles from our landing place we experienced the hospitality of the laird of Blairvochy... [who] furnished me with a little horse that carried me up to the steep, part of the hill (where I was obliged to dismount)... when I got within 100 yards of the top, I had the misfortune to be seized with a dizziness which prevented my quixotism being carried to so great a height as that of my friends, who feasted very heartily on the summit, whilst I was descending with the utmost caution or, rather, creeping down on all fours.'

Binnein on the skyline. I look down to the winding river in Gleann Dubh and the house at Comer, once home to Mary MacGregor, wife of Rob Roy. The River Forth has its source in the burns to the east of the Ben Lomond watershed. They flow into the river at Comer and then the Duchray water which in turn becomes the River Forth.

At about 930 metres the summit ridge is gained and the path continues north-west just below the crest. The knobbly Ptarmigan ridge comes into sight climbing up towards the top of Ben Lomond. The cliffs that fall away into Ben Lomond's northern corrie come as a shock after the gentle Sron Aonaich ridge. A white boulder above the path perches right on the crest of the ridge. At the start of the 20th century the Scottish Mountaineering Club explored these crags but found them too mossy to provide much rock climbing. The rock of Ben Lomond is schist. Schists are the most common rocks across much of the central and western Highlands. They usually appear grey but often sparkle in the sun because of the presence of flakes of mica.

The path squeezes between boulders and then up a last rise where erosion has exposed the underlying rock, to reach the trig point at the summit of Ben Lomond (974m). From here Loch Sloy dam and the power

---

THE DAM THAT NEVER WAS

The Cailness burn has its source in a shallow grassy corrie on the north-west side of Ben Lomond. In the 1970s the Craigroyston hydro-electric scheme was proposed; the corrie would become a reservoir with a power station almost 1,000 feet below on the eastern shore of Loch Lomond, opposite Inveruglas. A pumped storage hydro-electric scheme of the type built on Ben Cruachan was planned to supply the then industrial heartland of Glasgow. The North of Scotland Hydro Electric Board, concerned about how people might react to a huge construction project on an iconic mountain like Ben Lomond, carried out environmental and economic studies in an attempt to win the support of politicians and public for the plan. The dam would face north and not be visible from the west side of Loch Lomond, announced the Board, all the rest of the scheme would be underground. Construction was expected to take 8 years, including two years building access roads and a workforce of 1,000 men was to be employed. However by 1980 increase in demand for electricity in Scotland had slowed markedly and the Craigroyston scheme was never put forward for planning permission.

station at Inveruglas on the west side of Loch Lomond can be seen. A hydro-electric scheme was once planned up here on Ben Lomond too. On the severely eroded summit people today will look in vain for the covering of moss heath with its cushions of pink flowered moss campion described by early visitors to the mountain top. Some species early botanists collected from Ben Lomond such as the arctic bramble are now extinct in Scotland and today exist only in herbarium collections.

While William Burrell's ascent of Ben Lomond in 1758 is the first for which a written record exists hunters and shepherds climbed the mountain before him. In 1724 Alexander Graham of Duchray who lived near Loch Lomond wrote;

> In this paroch is the mountain of Ben Lomond, reckon'd the highest in Scotland, off the top of this mountain in a clear day a person will discover not only the Cape of Kintyre... but also some of the mountains of the County of Donegal in Ireland.

Ben Lomond was a popular stop on the 19th century tourist trail as a painting from 1834 by John Knox, a Glasgow landscape painter shows. In the second half of the 19th century railway engineers from Snowdonia investigated the possibility of building a mountain railway up Ben Lomond.

The first Munroist Archibald Eneas Robertson bagged Ben Lomond on a leisurely day trip by train from Glasgow leaving at 8am for Balloch, and the steamer to Rowardennan, and returning exactly 12 hours later. In beautifully clear weather from the summit cairn he was able to make out the newly built Forth Rail Bridge.

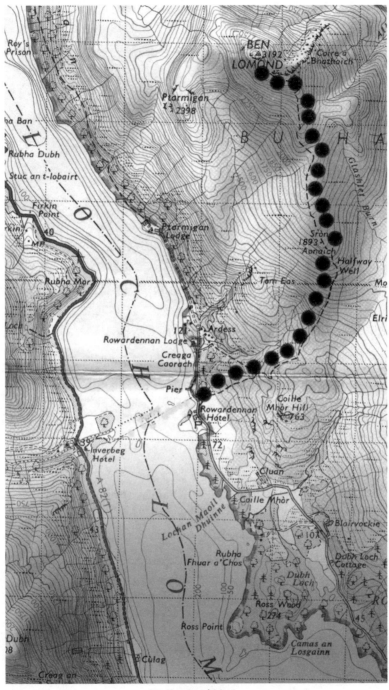

Ben Lomond Map

BEN LOMOND (974m)

Grade: **
Map: OS Sheet 56
Distance/Ascent: 11km/954m
Starting Height: 20m
Time to Top: 3h + breaks
Start/Finish: Rowardennan

In summer this is probably the easiest ascent of a Munro in the southern Highlands with a good path to follow all the way.

ROUTE

1   Start from car park NS35968 98631 (signposted) at end of public road from Balmaha to Rowardennan, just beyond Rowardennan Hotel.

2   Path starts behind toilets (signposted *Ben Lomond Hill Path*).

3   Footpath to Ben Lomond crosses forest road (90m) NS36448 98702 and continues through area where trees have been felled.

4   Go through gate with sign *Welcome to Ben Lomond*.

5   NS37655 9987 (400m) go through another gate.

6   NN37630 00415 (550m) follow path along flattish section of Sron Aonaich ridge with summit visible to N.

7   NN37253 02321 (800m) follow path as climbs steeply in zig zags to summit ridge.

8   At about 930m reach summit ridge NN37114 02563. Follow path NW along summit ridge.

9   Reach summit Ben Lomond (974m) NN36714 02851 (trig point).

10 Return by same route.

DOGS: there are cattle and sheep on Ben Lomond after first gate with sign warning of livestock grazing on hillside.

WINTER CONDITIONS: ice axe and crampons needed for summit ridge.

Swimming with the Osprey

Strathspey. 1894. A man stands on the sandy shore of Loch an Eilein in the forest of Rothiemurchus. Ancient Scots pines surround the loch. On an island stands the ruined castle. The man wades into the loch, still a memory of last winter's snow melt in the cold of the water even in August. He swims now, a few strokes. The osprey circles on the blue air above the loch. Seeing the man in the water the osprey flies over him, uttering its screaming cry. The first time this happened the man was afraid. Now when the bird of prey does not come he feels its absence. He misses swimming with the osprey. As the man turns back towards the shore, the osprey draws away, rising so high the man loses sight of it in the vertical distance.

CHAPTER FIVE

Ben Venue

The Fragments of an Earlier World

Imagine how bleak our hills would be if no golden eagles swept over the ridges, no arctic-alpine flowers shone like jewels on the dark rocks...

ADAM WATSON, 1979

IN THE FOLKLORE of the Gaels only those gifted with the second sight, the ability to foresee the future, could see ùruisgs. Gaelic for goblins or leprechauns, ùruisgs are associated with water and according to William Gillies writing in 1938 haunted deep gorges and high moorland lochs. Some ùruisgs had names – the Allt Coire Phadairlidh, one of the streams flowing down from Meall Greigh, a mountain to the west of Fearnan on Loch Tay is named after (and was home to) the famous ùruisg Paderlan. An ùruisg was half man, half spirit, a lover of solitude who became sociable towards the end of harvest time. Tending to be mischievous rather than malign ùruisgs though lazy sometimes carried out work in the house or on the farm at lightning speed – kind deeds done without bribe, fee or reward for any payment offered would banish the ùruisg forever.

Below the Bealach nam Bo on the precipitous north eastern slopes of Ben Venue lies Coire nan Uruisgean, the corrie of the ùruisgs. Uruisgs loved cream, milk and cheese, and this love of dairy produce has led some to speculate that Ben Venue may mean milk mountain, from the Gaelic *beinn a' bhainne* (pronounced vanny*a*) because of the way Highland burns foam white like milk when in spate. Not far away on the west side of Loch Lomond are Ben Ime the butter mountain and the Cobbler with its Buttermilk burn.

In *The Old Statistical Account*, an historical source which gives a good snapshot of Scotland in the last decade of the 18th century, the mountain's name is spelt *Benivenow*. James Robertson who lived in Callander in the 1790s wrote; '*Ben-venu*, is called the *small mountain*, because it is less than *Ben-ledi*, or *Ben Lomond*, from which it is almost equally distant, forming nearly a straight line with both.' Caleb saw this

The bed of Loch Katrine had suddenly collapsed...

In 1859 Jules Verne visited Scotland and toured the Trossachs, the experience inspired him to write *The Underground City.*

line of hills too. On his list of mountains visible from Arthur's Seat Ben Lomond is first from the west, Ben Venue second and Ben Ledi third. Seen on a clear day from Arthur's Seat between West Register House and the Tron church, 68 degrees west of north, Ben Venue is the smallest of the three hills. The Gaelic for small mountain, *beinn mheanbh*, is pronounced like the anglicised 'Ben Venue'. Though Walter Scott wrote of 'huge Benvenue', at 729m/2,391ft the hill seems large seen towering over Loch Katrine, it is a small mountain compared to nearby hills and dwarfed by Ben More (big mountain) a few miles to the north.

Ben Venue is a much loved hill in the way Arthur's Seat, Ben Lomond and Dumyat are. The north-east face above the Achray water is very steep; crags and trees on the lower part of the hillside make the mountain look a difficult climb. To Ralph Storer Ben Venue rises above Loch Katrine giving the 'impression of a miniature Highland scene'.

At the beginning of the 19th century Sir Walter Scott sat and wrote by Ledard Pool at the foot of Ben Venue. His writing inspired people to visit Scotland and put the forests, lochs, mountains and rivers between Callander and Aberfoyle – the Trossachs – at the heart of the 19th century tourist trail. One visitor was Jules Verne. He heard the tales about the goblin's corrie and went on to imagine an underground city and vast coal mine beneath Ben Venue and Loch Katrine haunted by an ùruisg like creature.

Climbing Ben Venue

The most scenic route up Ben Venue starts from the pass of Aberfoyle. Long ago this was Clan MacGregor country and the scenery around here features in Sir Walter Scott's novels *Rob Roy* and *Waverley*. Begin from a parking place beside the B829, half a kilometre east of Kinlochard where swallows fly low over fields bordered with hedgerows. In summer the verges of the road are yellow with buttercups and next to the parking place brown, black and white sheep and geese share the same field on the shore of Loch Ard. The south side of the loch is heavily wooded and from the parking place there is a fine view of Ben Lomond.

Cross the road, go through a gate signposted *Ben Venue* and walk a short distance along the private road to Ledard. Before reaching the farm buildings a signpost by a high stone wall points the way. Go through a gate in a deer fence and across a wooden footbridge over the Ledard Burn. The stream flows down among moss covered stones and ferns. Through trees and bracken I glimpse white washed Georgian farm buildings with black painted window sills – Ledard Farm. Nearby is Ledard waterfall and pool where Sir Walter Scott used to sit on a rock by the burn to think and write. It features in his novel *Rob Roy*.

Continue uphill on the west side of the stream through a stand of oak skirting the edge of a conifer plantation with the Ledard burn in a deep gorge below. Foxgloves and bracken grow high by the sides of the path and as it climbs up above the gorge the view opens out over the tree tops. The path winds between the silver birches. A fallen tree lies on the hillside its branches moss covered and bare of leaves, its roots exposed. Marsh orchids grow by the eroded and muddy track. Bear left uphill at arrows on a wooden post to keep to the driest path. As open hillside is reached the birch trees become more scattered, tormentil grows among the grass and there are glimpses of deep pools down in the gorge.

The rocky hillside of Creag a' Bhealaich rises ahead. The burn clear of the trees now, heather overhangs its banks and ferns grow beside little waterfalls and pools. A golden ringed dragonfly hovers over the water. Looking south the endless trees of Loch Ard forest seem to stretch to the foot of the distant Campsie Fells.

THE GOBLINS' CORRIE

Legend has it that all the ùruisgs in Scotland would come to Ben Venue and gather in Coire nan Uruisgean to plan and plot amid the deep heather, crags and boulders. In *The Guide to Mysterious Perthshire* Geoff Holder puts forward an explanation of the origin of the legend of the ùruisg. About 2,500 years ago the Celts were the predominant tribe in Scotland. Their religious leaders were Druids – warrior priests who led from the front. The Roman invasion of southern Scotland and the introduction of Christianity put the Druids under great pressure in a changing world. The Romans feared and persecuted the Druids and their last stronghold was in Coire nan Uruisgean. Here they survived and continued to be consulted by those who had need of their powers. Sometimes the Druids hid from their enemies among the flocks of goats that graze on Ben Venue and they began to cultivate a half animal, half human appearance. To protect themselves in an increasingly hostile world, so no one would know if the Druids really existed or not, they began to spread strange rumours about sprites or ùruisgs. In a faint echo centuries later Andersons' 1834 *Guide to the Highlands and Islands of Scotland* translated Coir Nan Uriskin [*sic*] as 'the den of the ghost'.

At a height of 350 metres the path crosses to the east side of the Ledard Burn at a ford. Old iron tram rails have been laid across the stream as a makeshift bridge but in wet weather when the burns are high the crossing may be difficult. Once over a stile the path continues along the line of a deer fence through patches of heather dotted white with cotton grass.

Ospreys were once a common sight in the southern Highlands. In the 1790s Patrick Graham, the minister at Aberfoyle wrote; 'The osprey, or water eagle, builds in an island of Lochlomond, in this neighbourhood, and pays us frequent visits.' As the sunshine glints on the waters of Loch Ard a thousand feet below I scan the sky for a glimpse of the ospreys that returned to the lochs and forests of the Trossachs in the 1970s. And I think of Caleb at the dawn of the 20th century standing on the shore of another Highland loch waiting for the ospreys to return. Caleb realised why ospreys were so popular with 19th century visitors to Loch an Eilein and his words written in 1903 still have relevance today for the many people who visit osprey viewing sites like David Marshall Lodge on the A821 outside Aberfoyle;

> There is, perhaps, no other of our raptors at once so interesting and so easy to observe. The dark, stern golden eagle will not brook observation, but sails off indignant on majestic wing; the smaller falcons and hawks dart in arrowy flight from the presence of man. But the osprey allows of moderately near approach, and permits itself to be inspected as it stands or sits on its nest, or as it soars in wide curves above the loch.

Cross a side stream in an eroded little cleft lined with rowan trees. Common butterwort with its purple flowers grows here. Grass stalks hold gobs of cuckoo spit – the mass of frothy white liquid surrounds young nymphs of an insect called the common froghopper. The path climbs up towards the col between Beinn Bhreac and Creag a'Bhealaich. Bare rock, outcrops of little crags on the hillside and deer grass in bright green clumps. When the col is reached, a sudden eye catching view of the summit of Ben Venue and the southern Highland mountains across Loch Katrine, Stob Binnein stands out among them.

Cross a low stile and head north-east on a level traverse across grassy hillside through clumps of heather and blaeberry. At the lowest point of the ridge linking Creag a'Bhealaich and Ben Venue the path

---

CLIMBING IN THE 1930s

'Sunday 26 January: Slept in blacksmith's shelter above Aberfoyle. Very keen frost. Climbed Ben Venue from Kinlochard in perfect weather.' So reads Jock Nimlin's diary for 1930. The blacksmith's shelter he slept in was a howff or doss at the Aberfoyle slate quarries. Loch Lomond and the Trossachs were as far as people could travel before the Second World War without cars, and with only one day off a week, Ben Venue must have seemed a world away from the slums, pollution and poverty of Glasgow. Some unemployed Glasgow men in the 1930s first discovered the mountains around the Trossachs by walking out of the city following the track which ran alongside the pipes carrying Glasgow's water supply from Loch Katrine. It led them out of the city and into the hills and glens and for some into a new life of mountaineering.

joins the route up Gleann Riabhach from Loch Achray at a large cairn. The dog... nose to the ground. Concentrating on an intense new aroma in a world of scent. A herd of wild goats roams the slopes of Ben Venue. I've typed the word 'wild' but 'feral' is more accurate. Perhaps these goats are truly wild, descended from the flocks the Druids hid amongst in Coire Nan Uruisgean but more prosaically they are probably 'feral' goats, descendants of livestock abandoned in the late 18th and early 19th centuries as the people left the glens. The goats that wander the Scottish hills are still tied to the breeding cycle of their Mediterranean ancestors and their kids are born in February, a month which in Scotland sometimes brings the cruellest weather of the winter.

Goats with horns and bells... suddenly I'm back sitting on the warm stones of the Temple of Apollo on Thassos, the chatter of cicadas filling the Greek island night. The purple spot there on my leg. The virus has closed the circle eight decades after the journey of replication begun in the African night, though I don't know it yet. We climbed to the bronze age temple to exchange rings... it will be another decade before civil partnerships so we two boys sit up here on the hill looking down on the lights of the town... the white car ferries manoeuvring into the 2,000-year-old harbour and in the darker patches of night watch the fireflies.

A big cairn on flat boggy ground where pools of water form in wet weather marks the lowest point in the rugged ridge linking Creag a Bhealaich to Ben Venue. The day I climbed this way Ben Ledi and the higher peaks were cloud covered while the summit of Ben Venue drifted in and out of the mist.

As I sit by the cairn two ravens suddenly wheel into view, rolling and tumbling high in the air, flying upside down at great speed with the wind behind them; gliding, soaring, nose diving, putting on an aerobatic show. They are only there long enough for a couple of distant photos before they are swept away on the strong wind over towards Gleann Riabhach. In spring time this behaviour is thought to form part of a courtship display but at others times it seems to be simply *joie de vivre*, like when the dogs run round and round in mad circles.

The path climbs up through little crags towards the summit. Clumps of pink heather still flower on the hillside. The morning sunshine is long gone. The dogs look wet and bedraggled; Cuilean the older dog missing her basket beside the Rayburn in the kitchen at home. I have a glimpse

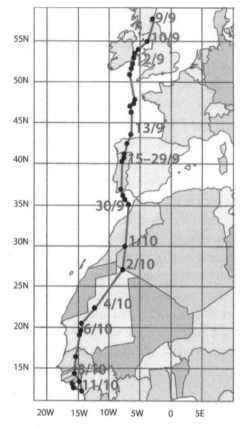

Osprey:

The incredible 5,000km autumn migratory flight south (beginning on 9 September and ending on 11 October) of a juvenile osprey from a nest near Carrbridge in Strathspey to Senegal in Africa as tracked by a miniature radio transmitter attached to the bird.

© Roy Dennis

of Glen Finglas reservoir and can just make out the flat plain around Stirling and Dumyat. The only hills I can see are Creag a' Bhealaich, Beinn Bhreac and Beinn an Fhogharaidh, the near neighbours of Ben Venue.

Walk about 500 metres north-east past the big cairn to a little dip in the ridge at about 680 metres where the path forks. Take the left hand fork and look out for some old iron fence posts which the path follows as it climbs steeply up and along the knobbly ridge, over some little crags to reach the north-west summit of Ben Venue (729m), marked by a little stone cairn.

WHO OWNS BEN VENUE?

Most of Ben Venue is owned by Forestry Commission Scotland, Silvan House, 231 Corstorphine Road, Edinburgh, EH12 7AT.

Ben Venue has twin summits and this can be confusing in misty weather. The north-west summit NN47440 06328 at 729 metres is 2 metres higher than the south-east top (727m) with the trig point on it. The Ordnance Survey (OS) 1:25000 map shows the height of both summits but the OS 1:50000 shows only the trig point and the height 727 metres. The first time I climbed Ben Venue in low cloud and strong winds navigating by GPS I missed the true summit. Puzzled by the line of red and yellow cagoules heading into the mist on the ridge above me I conferred with my most constant, enthusiastic and untiring hillwalking companion;

What are they doing up there Labradoodle? Woof... I expect they don't have GPS, pack leader dog and are a bit lost. Now let's get after those goats...

Alpine ladies mantle, wild thyme and fir clubmoss grow among the grass and rocks on the summit ridge. Caleb a pipe smoker enjoyed 'indulging in tobacco' and on Ben Venue I spot the first cigarette end I've seen on a hill for a while bringing back memories of forbidden pleasures... Embassy Regals puffed on top of mountains.

From the cairn at the north-west summit of Ben Venue follow the line of rusty iron fence posts along the ridge for about 400 metres skirting around little rocky outcrops to reach the remains of a trig point at the lower south-east top. I don't linger; it is September, very windy and the dogs look cold tethered to an old iron fence post while I take photos of Loch Katrine in the mist.

THE FIRST RECORDED ASCENT OF BEN VENUE?

John MacCulloch was employed as a geologist on the Trigonometrical Survey of Scotland and made an early ascent of Ben Venue sometime between 1811 and 1821.

The extensive view of the southern Highlands from either summit of Ben Venue on a clear day includes – Ben A'an, Loch Venachar, Loch Drunkie, Loch Achray, Loch Katrine, Loch Arklet, Ben Ledi, Benvane, Ben More, Stob Binnein, Ben Vorlich, Stuc a' Chroin, Ben Lawers, Dumyat, The Cobbler, the Arrochar Alps, Ben Lomond and the Island of Arran.

To the south Ben Venue slopes down to Gleann Riabhach and the Queen Elizabeth forest while to the north the mountain drops steeply away to Loch Katrine. By the mid-19th century, cholera and typhoid were endemic in Glasgow and the city's drinking water was described as the colour of coffee. At Loch Katrine at the foot of Ben Venue Victorian engineers built the pipes and aqueducts that deliver tens of millions of litres of water to Glasgow each day. In summer the steamship *ss Walter Scott* (launched in 1900) still plies the loch sailing past Eilean Molach, Ellen's Isle immortalised in *The Lady of the Lake*. Lines from Scott's epic of hunting, clan warfare and rivals in love reveal how the poet instinctively understood the nature of geology and plate tectonics; *High on the south, huge Benvenue Down to the lake in masses threw Crags, knolls, and mounds, confusedly hurled, the fragments of an earlier world.*

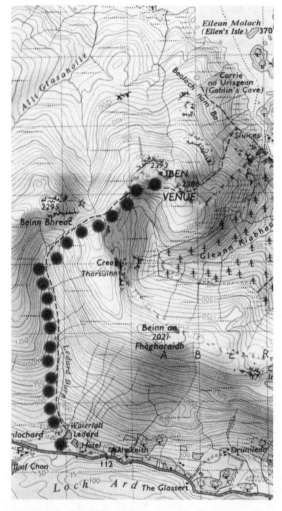

Ben Venue Map

BEN VENUE (729m)

Grade   **

Map: OS Sheet 57

Distance/Ascent: 10km/694m

Starting height: 35m

Time to top: 2h30min +breaks

Start/Finish: Kinlochard

Ben Venue is one of the most spectacular Grahams and forms the back-drop to Sir Walter Scott's epic poem The Lady of the Lake.

ROUTE

1   Begin from parking place NN45937 02259 on B829 500m east of Kinlochard.

2   Cross road and go through gate opposite parking place signposted *Ben Venue* and walk 200m up private road to Ledard. Before reaching farm buildings go through gate in deer fence signposted *Ben Venue* and across wooden footbridge over Ledard Burn. Follow the path up between two fences.

3   Follow path uphill on west side of Ledard Burn (on board walk at one point).

4   Path eroded and muddy in places. Bear left uphill where arrows on wooden post indicate better path.

5   Where path comes out of forest signpost reading *Footpath* indicates to keep following the stream.

6   Path crosses to east side of stream at a ford NN45755 04532 (350m). Might be difficult after heavy rain. Cross stile and follow path along line of deer fence.

7   Path comes close to another fence as it climbs up towards col between Beinn Bhreac and Creag a'Bhealaich.

8   Cross low stile NN46227 05639 and follow clear path NE across hillside below Creag a' Bhealaich for 1km on a level traverse to lowest point of the ridge between Creag a'Bhealaich and Ben Venue.

9   Path descends a few metres to large cairn NN46909 06084 where it meets the path that comes up Gleann Riabhach from Loch Achray.

10 From cairn follow path about 500m NE to a little dip in ridge (about
    680m) where path forks NN 47310 06251. Take left hand fork (*not*
    right fork in path which skirts below the crags and leads directly to
    the lower SE top, bypassing the higher NW summit).

11 Follow iron fence posts as path climbs steeply up and along craggy
    ridge to NW summit of Ben Venue (729m) NN47440 06328 (small cairn).

12 From NW summit continue to follow line of iron fence posts along
    ridge for about 400m. Path skirts rocky outcrops to reach remains of
    trig point on SE summit of Ben Venue (727m).

13 Return by the same route.

DOGS: Keep dogs on leads/under close control until clear of the trees as
    there are wild goats in the woods. Just past ford on Ledard Burn
    NN45755 04532 is a stile over a deer fence. At time of writing there
    was a gap in the fence which dogs can squeeze through but should
    fence be repaired it would be difficult to get a dog over the stile
    which is high with ladder type rungs – no steps.

Somewhere Else: the Byre Inn, Brig o' Turk.

CHAPTER SIX

Mountaineer

*Caleb the son of Jephunneh the Kenezite said unto him... now
therefore give me this mountain.*

JOSHUA 14

THE NORTH BRITISH RAILWAY'S LINE to Edinburgh from the south is a
dramatic run along the east coast passing cliffs and ruined cottages by the
shore, and on clear days gives passengers a glimpse of Holy Island across
the grey waters of the North Sea. In 1886 when he was almost 30 Caleb
travelled to Scotland to take up the post of assistant master at the
Edinburgh Academy, a fee paying school where Edinburgh's prosperous
middle classes sent their sons to be educated. How different was Caleb's
background to that of his pupils at the Edinburgh Academy.

As the train slowed to cross the Royal Border Bridge at Berwick high
above the River Tweed Caleb surely felt he was leaving his old life in
England behind and beginning a new life in Scotland. When the train
emerged from the darkness of the Calton tunnel and pulled into
Waverley station Caleb and Alice peered through the grimy windows of
the railway carriage straining for a first sight of Edinburgh Castle or the
Scott Monument. Edwin Muir wrote in *Scottish Journey* 'the first sight
of Edinburgh... is invariably exciting. Its bold and stony look recalls
ravines and quarried mountains.' How tall and black the buildings rose
so different from the low terraces of brick back to backs they'd left
behind in Sheffield. Truly this was another country.

All mountaineers remember the first hill they climbed. In the 1970s
mine was 308 metre high Beinn Lora that rises over the Argyllshire
village of Benderloch. A century earlier Caleb spent his childhood in
Birmingham, a city more famous for its rolling mills than its rolling hills.
In the early 1880s he moved to Sheffield where he had lodgings in the
Ecclesall area of the city. During the Victorian era Sheffield had grown
to be an industrial giant. The population rose from 9,000 in 1736 to
110,000 in 1841 and 400,000 by 1901. The iron and steel industry
employed thousands of men, women and children in huge factories.

For Caleb, by now a young teacher in his early 20s it would have been relatively easy to escape from the smoke and grime of the city. William Street where Caleb lived was within reasonable walking distance of Burbage and Hallam moors so it may have been here, on the moors above Sheffield, that Caleb first developed his love of hillwalking and the outdoors.

Walking in the countryside around Sheffield has a long history, a guidebook to walks in the area was published as early as 1831 and the city's first Sunday rambling club, the Sheffield Clarion Ramblers was formed in 1900. Or perhaps it was one of the new Ordnance Survey maps which first led him from Sheffield up onto the moors or to Stanage Edge in nearby Derbyshire. The Peak district has rounded hills, wide views and rocky tors; topographical features Caleb would later find on a grand scale in the Cairngorms. Perhaps that's why he felt a special affinity to places like the Argyll Stone, the rocky tor that stands on the Sgoran Dubh ridge high above Gleann Einich.

When they first arrived in Edinburgh Caleb and Alice lived at 5 Barclay Place, Tollcross. The census of 1891 records that a general servant Josephine Borthwick lived there too. The girl aged 16 would have slept in the boxroom of the flat and provided Alice with much needed help in an age where clothes had to be washed by hand and to heat a tenement flat, like the one in Tollcross, involved carrying heavy buckets of coal, laying, tending and raking out two or three open fires and a kitchen range.

Behind Barclay Place, from nearby Bruntsfield Links there are good views to Arthur's Seat and the hill's 'striking topography' seems to have attracted Caleb almost from the moment he arrived in Edinburgh. Though busy with the demands of a teaching job and settling into life in a new city Caleb would still have found time at weekends to explore his new home town.

It is reasonable to infer Caleb climbed Arthur's Seat soon after arriving in Edinburgh in 1886. Indeed Arthur's Seat may well have been the first Scottish hill Caleb climbed. Perhaps he walked from Tollcross, over the Meadows, along Melville Drive, through the streets of Newington, crossing the bridge over the Innocent railway line before passing St Leonard's Lodge at the Albert Gate to the Queen's Park and climbing Arthur's Seat by the dramatic Guttit Haddie path. In 1894 he wrote about Arthur's Seat for the journal of the recently formed Cairngorm Club making Arthur's Seat his first ascent for which a record exists.

In 1891 Caleb was promoted to special master for geography and music at the Edinburgh Academy. That summer Caleb and Alice took their first holiday near Aviemore and around this time Caleb began hillwalking in the Cairngorms. By 1894 Caleb was clearly a keen mountaineer, writing in *The Cairngorm Club Journal* that Arthur's Seat gives; '... good scrambling to keep one in training for work on the bigger hills away north.'

Caleb as sketched by one of his pupils.

Caleb also explored the easily accessible Pentland Hills just to the south of Edinburgh and knew them well enough to be able to point out errors like the omission of the footpath from Dreghorn via Howden Burn that passes over the col between Capelaw and Allermuir on Ordnance Survey maps of the time. In the 1890s hillwalkers reached the Pentlands from Edinburgh by taking a train from Princes Street station to Colinton and then walking to Bonaly. Caleb may also have taken school pupils from the Edinburgh Academy hillwalking. An unaccredited article in *The Cairngorm Club Journal* of 1896 describes two teachers taking a group of schoolboys hillwalking on the Pentlands, an early example of outdoor education.

Between 1891 and 1907 Caleb spent 25 holidays in Strathspey. He spent the summer of 1891 at Inverdruie near Aviemore and probably began hillwalking in the Cairngorms that first summer though no record exists of Caleb doing any climbing until 1894 when he began to write about mountaineering for the new *Cairngorm Club Journal*, first published in 1893.

They say if you can climb in the Scottish mountains you can climb anywhere. Though only a handful of Scottish hills exceed 4,000 feet in height, their northerly latitude and at times Arctic climate make them as challenging as any mountain range in the world. Caleb was one of that first generation of mountaineers who began exploring the hills following the publication of the first Ordnance Survey maps in the 1870s. Caleb's first recorded Cairngorm ascent was of Cairn Toul from Loch an Eilein in August 1894, almost a decade before the Scottish Mountaineering Club visited the Cairngorms for the first time in 1902. Caleb walked to the Shelter Stone at Loch Avon probably for the first time on 2 September 1895 accompanied by three other climbers, later reporting in the 'Excursions and Notes' section of *The Cairngorm Club Journal* that he had seen a flock of eight goats. Caleb was a mountaineer who, in his own words, knew the central and western Cairngorms best. Alexander Inkson McConnochie, first editor of *The Cairngorm Club Journal* and a pioneer of Scottish winter mountaineering wrote that Caleb had 'a familiarity with, and a knowledge of the Cairngorm Mountains almost unequalled.'

A picture of Caleb as mountaineer emerges in a series of articles he wrote about hillwalking in the Cairngorms with evocative titles like 'Mist on the Sgoran Dubh' and 'Nights and Days on the Cairngorms'. Caleb's prose is at its most interesting and readable in his writing about mountaineering. Likewise his articles on Pont's maps are more accessible than his writing on topography and archaeology. And Caleb wrote more on mountaineering than on any other subject.

The Brindled Upland

Caleb loved the wild land of the Cairngorms. He enjoyed solitary hillwalking;

> ... the sheer impressiveness of the wilderness is most felt when one strays alone, scarce conscious of one's own physical presence, and entirely open to the appeal of great nature... it is for these joys that I turn more and more often to that great plateau of Braeriach and Cairn Toul, and to the huge Garbh Coire...

An Garbh Choire, the great hollow forming the innermost recess of Braeriach has been described as perhaps the most intriguing corrie in the Cairngorms on account of its size, remoteness, wildness, climate and beauty. In *The Cairngorm Club Journal* Caleb described seeing in August 1894 the semi-permanent snow beds that are found in An Garbh Choire;

> Skirting the corrie on our way to Sgor an Lochan Uaine we looked down some of the gullies, and saw the soiled and shrunken remnants of the winter's snow…

These lingering snow patches are obvious indicators of climate change and would generate volumes of research later in the 20th century.

The Cairngorm plateau and An Garbh Choire of Braeriach were wild places Caleb visited many times; '…[I] returned to the edge of the Garbh Coire crags, a place that has great fascination for me', he wrote in 1902. Caleb was one of the first mountaineers to fall under the spell of the Cairngorms experiencing something similar to the poet Nan Shepherd who in *The Living Mountain* describes;

> The young Dee, as it flows out of the Garbh Choire and joins the water from the Lairig Pools, has… astounding transparency. Water so clear cannot be imagined, but must be seen. One must go back, and back again, to look at it, for in the interval memory refuses to recreate its brightness. This is one of the reasons why the high plateau where these streams begin, the streams themselves, their cataracts and rocky beds, the corries, the whole wild enchantment, like a work of art is perpetually new when one returns to it.

On Easter Monday 1897 Caleb climbed Braeriach in winter conditions alone and without an ice axe. Just after crossing the snowline on the mountain's northern ridge he briefly experienced a strange light effect he later wrote about in a letter to the journal *Nature*;

> I witnessed a phenomenon of great beauty, the explanation of which I cannot give. The edge of my plaid, of my gloved hands, of my knicker-bockers… was bordered by a two-inch band of brilliant violet light, at the moment of beginning any movement…

It must have been a pleasant September day when Caleb climbed Carn na Criche, an outlier of Braeriach, in the autumn of 1898, for he lingered at the top and made a sketch of the summit rocks which was later printed in *The Cairngorm Club Journal*. By contrast in August 1903 Caleb climbed Cairn Toul, the Angel's Peak and Braeriach from Inverdruie in gale force wind, rain and snow. As the weather deteriorated Caleb debated whether to turn back but decided; 'that the experience of walking the Braeriach ridge in such a storm would be worth having.' It was a tough day's mountaineering and the storm was at its height as Caleb reached the summit ridge of Braeriach;

> The thing was a nightmare of wild turmoil, and I have no recollection of anything along there but the dogged strenuous effort to keep my line and not be blown over or buffeted out of it by the fierce blasts that leaped roaring from the many gullies.

In August 1904 Caleb ascended Braeriach from the Lairig Ghru, climbing up by the Falls of Dee whilst collecting rare alpines. Though he may not have known it he was repeating the first recorded scramble in the Cairngorms which took place in 1810 when the Rev Dr George Keith Skene climbed Braeriach while following the Dee to its source. Though Caleb was in his own words a mountaineer not a rock climber; '... I am not a "climber", for I have never been "roped"...' he was a competent and confident scrambler with a good head for heights who thought nothing of scaling 30–40 feet high crags to get a good view of an eagles nest or as he describes while on the ridge summit of Braeriach; '... scrambling warily out on some of the pinnacled buttresses, the better to gaze into the depths below...'

In the pages of *The Cairngorm Club Journal* Caleb describes climbing Braeriach in a wide spectrum of weather conditions. From days when it was hot enough to swim (naked) in the pools of the infant Dee to days when; 'the hard blown snow smote the face with the sting of small shot.' Caleb climbed Braeriach in his own words 'many times'. Braeriach was his favourite mountain and exerted a fascination over him. Today mountaineering is all about ticking off peaks on lists and it seems strange to us that Caleb climbed the same hill again and again. But other early mountaineers did this too among them Jock Nimlin who climbed Ben Lomond more than 100 times in the 1930s.

In many ways Caleb was more like the climbers who came along a decade or two later among them Ronnie Burn and Jock Nimlim than the well-heeled members of the Scottish Mountaineering Club like Sir Hugh

Munro and the Reverend AE Robertson. Like Burn and Nimlin, Caleb's mountaineering was restricted to weekends and holidays by the need to earn a living.

Caleb was in the prime of life those years of the long Cairngorm walks, a tough mountaineer who wrote that climbing Braeriach from Loch an Eilein, a round trip of about 26 kilometres with 1,036 metres of ascent was 'an enjoyable stroll'. He was in his forties and described by his friend and fellow mountaineer Alexander Inkson McConnochie as having a 'never-wearying step'.

Caleb sometimes approached the Cairngorms from Braemar in the east and spent holiday time at Inverey staying on at least one occasion at Thistle Cottage, home of the legendary Maggie Gruer who befriended so many climbers. An article in *The Cairngorm Club Journal* describes a 50 mile (80km) two day stravaige across the hills from Inverey to Spittal of Glenshee then over Glas Tulaichean and back to Braemar via Glas Maol and Carn an Tuirc. Caleb is not mentioned by name in the piece but can only be the 'mulishy obstinate' hill walker referred to as the 'geographer royal' by the writer. I wonder if a shy rather prickly man like Caleb saw the funny side of this description of him when it appeared in print in *The Cairngorm Club Journal*.

An engaging picture of Caleb on the hill emerges; the summit of Glas Maol strewn with his 'paraphernalia' of barometer, prismatic compass, spirit level, notebook and Ordnance Survey maps. When they reached Spittal of Glenshee at 6.45pm after a 26mile/42km walk;

> … a warm bath and a good supper revived the Geographer's weary frame… But as the evening wore on he called for water and a kettle, for sugar and a lemon, for whisky of the glen, and soon he had forgotten graphs and bearings, altitudes and angles. He made hot toddy, and strong toddy, and toddy both strong and hot. And he drank it and we drank it, til at length all that was earthly of him slipped to the floor, and the "Geographer Royal" was asleep.

The next day the party stopped for lunch at 3,500 feet on the flat summit of Glas Maol. Picture the scene. Bitterly cold, a howling gale, the mist racing by on all sides and Caleb sat on a fencepost; '… singing, – singing nothing in particular, but singing like the last swan of summer.'

Nights and Days on the Cairngorms

John Allen, for many years leader of the Cairngorm mountain rescue team, describes flying over the Cairngorm plateau in a Sea King helicopter on a beautifully clear night; 'cloudless and starlit, with visibility of many miles. For those who are experienced and prepared the plateau is a joy to visit in such conditions.' A century before in 'Nights and Days on the Cairngorms' Caleb recounted how at 10 o'clock one evening in July 1901, after dinner and a short sleep, he picked up his rucksack and left the house where he and Alice were staying in Coylum Bridge. He walked for 17½ hours, climbing Cairn Toul and Braeriach by moonlight covering an impressive distance of about 45 kilometres.

Caleb waited for two hours on the summit of Cairn Toul in the early hours of the morning hoping the mist would clear and give a view. Years before he had arranged some granite boulders to form a seat at the Wells of Dee and on reaching them in the small hours he wrapped himself in his cape and had an hour's sleep. At 3.15am on Sgor an Lochan Uaine;

> The silence was broken by only two sounds, the continual roar of the Dee falls, a mile away across the corrie, and the occasional croak of a ptarmigan somewhere below…

The following month, August, he climbed Cairngorm and Ben Macdui from Coylumbridge again by moonlight, visiting the Shelter Stone en route and spending 18½ hours on the hill. From the summit of Cairngorm in the darkness Caleb could see the flashes of the light house at Tarbet Ness on the Moray Firth.

Caleb also knew the Sgoran Dubh ridge above Loch Einich well, most visited by hillwalkers today for the Munro Sgor Gaoith that is its highest point. On 4 September 1899 along with members of the Cairngorm Club, Caleb climbed the ridge from Loch an Eilein in wild conditions; '… we went on over Sgoran Dubh and to Sgor Ghaoith [sic], in a roaring wind that made conversation impossible…' In August 1905 Caleb crossed the Cairngorm plateau in poor weather. Walking from Inverdruie he entered Coire an t-Sneachda where 'I crossed the corrie to its south-west section, where several gullies can be ascended to the plateau…' Then Caleb passed the top of Hell's Lum Crag, visiting the Garbh Uisge Mor lochans before re-crossing the plateau south of Cairn Lochan. A round trip of about 30 kilometres much of it in rain, mist and a 'heavy buffeting… chill wind'.

ALICE

Caleb's wife Alice features only occasionally in our story but she is there in the background through all his adult life. In August 1894 Caleb wrote an account of climbing Cairn Toul from Loch an Eilein via Glean Einich and Coire Dhondail. Following this route on the map the total distance is an arduous 35 kilometres (22 miles). Alice accompanied Caleb on this hill walk. This seems to have been a rare occurrence but one Caleb clearly enjoyed describing it as '... a day unequalled in my mountaineering experience for excellent weather, good performance of programme, and marvellous scenery.' There is no mention of Alice climbing after 1894 so perhaps she didn't enjoy the 'performance of programme' as much as Caleb did. Maybe she found it a bit on the gruelling side.

One senses in Alice a reluctant hill walker. In 'Nights and Days on the Cairngorms' Caleb refers to the 'occasional disaster of over late return', a scenario every mountaineer who has gone on the hill leaving an anxious wife or partner at home will be familiar with. How did Alice spend the long summer days like the one at the end of August 1904 when Caleb left their cottage at Inverdruie at 5am, climbed Braeriach reaching the summit at 2pm and eventually returned home at 7pm.Or for that matter, the long summer nights when Caleb was away climbing Ben Macdui by moonlight for 18½ hours? While Caleb wrote a lengthy account of his night on the hill no record survives of Alice's presumably equally sleepless night at Inverdruie spent worrying her husband had sprained his ankle in the dark on top of Braeriach. Caleb's walking by moonlight 'experiment' seems to have been undertaken with Alice in mind, perhaps to avoid being late back or because she was tired of him being away all day. While Sir Hugh Munro sometimes climbed at night to avoid disturbing landowners' sport, Caleb climbed at night to avoid upsetting his wife.

We meet Alice again on a walk in 1903 accompanying Caleb to view an eagles' nest though they nearly give up and go home due to a heavy shower of rain. In 1907 Alice cycled up Glen Nevis with Caleb and later visited many chambered cairns and standing stones around Killin and Aberfeldy with him. But when it came to mountaineering, like the hillwalking widows Muriel Gray describes in her climbing book *The First Fifty* Alice's role was; 'being expected to have the white-bearded, old sod's tea ready for him on the table when he comes home from a fabulous day on the hills.'

By 1907 perhaps Alice had decided it was time for a change from Strathspey for she and Caleb travelled to Fort William on the West Highland railway which had opened 13 years before in 1894. Caleb missed the Cairngorms and the weather didn't help. In the course of a month's holiday Caleb had hoped; 'to get in at least a dozen visits to the Ben...' But on his return to Edinburgh he wrote; 'the August of 1907 will, I expect, long remain in the memory of holiday-makers as the worst for many years...'

Caleb spent the few dry days that summer exploring Ben Nevis; 'it was a relief to get out of the cramped narrowness of the little town...' He walked up Coire Leis to the foot of the cliffs of the north face of Ben Nevis, delighting to find a tin rain gauge that had fallen from the observatory on the mountain's summit. A few days later Caleb climbed the Ben by the pony track enjoying a cup of tea in the hotel that then stood on the top of the mountain. While at the summit he used James Shearer's panorama of the view to identify the mountains visible from Scotland's highest peak and; 'just as I turned from the Observatory, a Snow-Bunting flew past me, uttering its pretty tinkling cry.' Caleb's ascent of Scotland's highest mountain in August 1907 was his last climb for which a written record exists. And the snow buntings are still there on the ruins of the Observatory when Kellan climbs Ben Nevis more than a century later.

It seems likely Caleb's mountaineering was not confined to the climbs he wrote about in the pages of *The Cairngorm Club Journal*. He explored an archaeological site to the west of Meall Dearg during August 1910 and knew the hill track that runs from Aberfeldy to Glen Quaich, so perhaps Caleb did some hillwalking as well as archaeology that summer of 1910. Staying in Aberfeldy it seems likely as a keen mountaineer he might have climbed Schiehallion (it was his kind of hill after all) but if he did no record exists for by this time Caleb no longer wrote about mountaineering for *The Cairngorm Club Journal*. Nor is it known how many of the Arthurs Caleb climbed.

In 1911 near Morenish on Loch Tay Caleb and a companion had trouble finding a cup marked rock; 'Even with the assistance of a local farmer we had much difficulty in finding it, and had searched many hundreds of yards of ledges before Mr Haggart rediscovered it.' So at the age of 54 we can infer Caleb was still fit enough to traverse rough hillside and climb mountains. Our last glimpse of Caleb on the hills is in 1912 when he visited the Megget stone which stands at 450 metres at a high point in the road across the Tweedsmuir Hills in the Scottish borders and from which it is an easy climb to the top of Broad Law.

CG Cash and Alexander Inkson McConnochie explored the Cairngorms at the same time as famous early climbers like William Naismith and Harold Raeburn were discovering the mountains of the West Highlands. Caleb was a skilled navigator (not the case with all the early Scottish mountaineers by any means). Caleb was expert at finding his way across the Cairngorm plateau – a navigational test piece today used to test the skills of candidates for mountain leader certificates. Caleb navigated with map and compass and seems to have experimented with the use of timings in navigation around the period Naismith was formulating his famous rule; mountaineers walk at 3mph + ½ hour for every 1,000 feet climbed.

Caleb's mountaineering writing appeared in *The Cairngorm Club Journal* alongside articles by Hugh Munro and Seton Gordon and take us back to a Scotland where the mountains are subtly different. Corries are unexplored and mysterious, summits seldom visited. Official Ordnance Survey heights are queried and maps corrected. In 1891 when Caleb first visited Strathspey the Highlands were little known from a mountaineering point of view. Nobody even knew how many mountains there were.

But the mountaineer is recognisable; the thermos flask dropped and smashed at the summit of Cairngorm; Caleb's pause at the top of the headwall of Coire an t-Sneachda 'to do all his buttons up' before stepping onto the Cairngorm plateau in a gale; building cairns or making scrapes in the gravel as navigational markers; Caleb using a stick like today's mountaineers with their walking poles; using Ordnance Survey maps on the hill; Caleb cycling through Glen Einich and Glen Nevis; swimming in streams; the rucksack packed the night before.

While Caleb's mountaineering achievements appear modest by today's standards his climbing has to be seen in the context of a very different world. Caleb was a mountaineer of his time. When hillwalking in the two decades before 1914 he had to be completely self-reliant in a world without mobile phones or rescue helicopters. Equipment too was very limited... no GPS, survival bags or Gore-Tex. The village of Inverdruie, from where Caleb set off many times to wander the high tops of the Cairngorms is today where the Cairngorm Mountain rescue team has its base. Had her husband failed to return from a hill walk Alice would have raised the alarm but Caleb perhaps injured and hypothermic would have faced a very long wait while a makeshift rescue party of stalkers, ghillies, shepherds and their dogs searched for him. At the dawn of the 20th century the Cairngorms were a remoter range of mountains than today and little explored by mountaineers before 1886 so Caleb was something of a pioneer – hence all those articles about Braeriach and An Garbh Coire. No ski road existed to transport hillwalkers effortlessly half-way up Cairngorm. From Coylumbridge it was literally 'a long walk in' to the foot of Cairngorm. There is an echo of this era in WA Poucher's exhortation to hillwalkers climbing Cairngorm to start from Loch Morlich;

> Park your car, put on your climbing boots, shoulder your rucksack and proceed on your way joyfully, ignoring completely all pressing offers of a lift up to Coire Cas!

In some ways Caleb's accounts of scrambling up by the Falls of Dee in search of rare Alpines and sleeping on Braeriach wrapped in a coat are reminiscent of the early 19th century explorers, cartographers and naturalists who climbed Scotland's mountains before the mountaineers. But essentially Caleb was a modern hill walker who climbed for recreation, a 'holiday mountain wanderer', as he once described himself.

A number of times over the years, Caleb walked to the Shelter Stone at Loch Avon, a place often described as 'the heart of the Cairngorms'. Most memorable was the occasion in 1901 when alone at the Sticil, as the cliffs above the Shelter Stone were then called, he observed a spectacular effect of light and mist;

> The top edge of the crag was outlined in a vivid silver band, and flying outwards over it were multitudes of brilliantly shining silver sparks that fell through the air and disappeared as they entered the shadow.

CHAPTER SEVEN

Ben Ledi

The Hill of God

FIRST OF THE HILLS beyond the Highland line, Ben Ledi is in the vanguard of the Scottish mountains. A familiar landmark that is one of the most distinctive outposts of the Highlands. 'Ben Ledi is a frontier mountain,' wrote Jim Crumley,

> ... Each new sighting advances the mountain, redefining its lynch-pin role in Scotland's Southern Highland skyline. Stirling, they like to say... is the buckle at Scotland's waist which clasps Highland and Lowland together, in which case Ben Ledi is a dark jewel in Scotland's navel.

But Jim Crumley goes on to describe how he fell out of love with Ben Ledi because of its eroded paths, the presence of too many walkers, too many cars and car parks, too much litter left on the hill. Crumley felt the sanctity of the mountain had been lost though he later relented when walking on a quieter part of the hill, discovering his 'beautiful friendship' with Ben Ledi was not over after all.

Caleb's table of Scottish mountains visible from Arthur's Seat lists Ben Ledi as lying 63 degrees west of north. On a clear day from the top of Arthur's Seat Ben Ledi is to be seen to the left of Fettes College, over the north approach viaduct of the Forth Rail Bridge.

Long ago Ben Ledi was the site of ancient ritual. In the 1790s James Robertson wrote;

> By reason of the altitude of Benledi, and by reason of its beautiful conical figure, the people of the adjacent country, to a great distance, assembled annually on its top, about the time of the summer solstice, during the Druidical priesthood... to get as near to heaven as they could...

Andersons' Guide to the Highlands and Islands of Scotland describes; 'The lofty mountain... Benledi', The Hill of God;

> upwards of 3,000 feet in height. In early ages, tradition reports that it was customary for the people to assemble, for three successive days, on its summit, for the worship of their deity; most probably of Baal, or the sun.

The first ascent of the mountain may have been by people climbing Ben Ledi for Druidical rites and ceremonies. Rennie McOwan has written about how on the first day of May, the old Celtic New Year, people walked up Ben Ledi to celebrate an old Druidic rite, the lighting of the Beltane fires. Bel was a Celtic sun god. In the houses in the glens below Ben Ledi all hearth fires were extinguished before midnight to symbolise the dying of the old year. A fire was lit on the top of Ben Ledi and the fires in the villages were then relit from the purifying hilltop flames.

In November 1837 the Reverend P Robertson wrote Ben Ledi was a contraction of *Beinn-le-Dia* meaning the hill of god, a seemingly appropriate name given the mountain's history.

And although 'the hill of god' explanation is still around, today it is generally accepted the name Ben Ledi comes from the Gaelic *leiter* or *leathad* meaning a slope and probably referring to the long southern flank of the hill that runs down to Loch Venachar. Back in 1898 George Williams writing in *The Cairngorm Club Journal* complained Ben Ledi;

> is persistently and poetically explained as 'the hill of God', but… is more correctly and characteristically interpreted as 'the hill of slopes' Ben Leathadich.

Climbing Ben Ledi

Ben Ledi can be climbed from Edinburgh or Glasgow using public transport; trains run every hour to Stirling and buses continue to Callander from the bus station (three minutes' walk from Stirling railway station). When the bus reaches Callander get off at the Dreadnought Hotel near a large car park where most buses seem to terminate anyway. Opposite the bus stop a cycle/walkway starts at a sign reading *Strathyre 9½ miles*. From here it's about half an hour's walk to the foot of Ben Ledi.

Keep following the signs as you walk along the cycleway out the back of the car park which stands on the site of the old railway station and along Tulipan Crescent to cross Leny Road (the A84) at traffic lights. Continue along the cycleway through the trees past a red semaphore signal, a relic from the days of the Callander and Oban railway.

Follow the walkway across a footbridge spanning the Garbh Uisge and on into open countryside where the trees overhang the slow moving water. At the side of the old railway line grow herb-Robert and cow parsley. In the fields to the south of the track a high stone wall surrounds the old clan Buchanan burial ground among the trees. Forty-five-year-old silver birches line the edge of the walkway, grown tall in the decades since the railway closed. On either side of the track rusting iron gates erected by the railway company in 1870 mark an old crossing point. In a field next to the walkway two roe deer stand watchfully in the long grass. In the distance radio masts top Ben Gullipen. Bluebells and forget me nots next to the yellow of broom. A glimpse of wooden eaves, stone cottage through the trees and white hawthorn blossom.

OS Nock described the view from the footplate of a locomotive heading west out of Callander. The train he wrote;

> ... strikes out across green meadows for a frontal attack... upon a solid wall of mountains towering up to the summit of Ben Ledi. The rocky heights crowd so closely round the Pass of Leny, and are so thickly wooded that it is only when close at hand that the gap in the mountain wall can be descried, and the railway begins to wriggle its way uphill on a track that looks more like a sylvan lane among the birch woods. The gradient here is 1 in 50...

The walkway passes through fields where hoodie crows strut among grazing sheep and lambs. Near NN61458 07792 the outline of low grass covered walls can be made out. Ben Ledi dominates the passes to the north, south and west. When the Romans reached Callander they built a marching camp or temporary fort here at Bochastle. Almost two millennia later Victorian navvies built the railway on top of the grassy Roman ramparts. Archaeologists first carried out excavations here in 1949. Over time river erosion by the Garbh Uisge (the rough water) has destroyed the north-east corner of the fort.

Bochastle Roman fort like others along the Highland line (there's one near Comrie) was strategically placed at the mouth of a narrow glen to control access to and from the Highlands. There is a theory these forts were built as the springboard for a planned Roman invasion of the Highlands that failed to materialise, but I reckon the Roman empire never extended north of the Highland line because the Roman legions, kitted out in a uniform featuring short tunics and bare legs two thousand years before the invention of insect repellent met an unconquerable foe in the dreaded Highland midge.

Some of the soldiers based at Bochastle came from Italy but most were Britons recruited into the ranks as the Roman Empire expanded northwards. The Romans sent out patrols from the forts they built, some never returned. In thick mist on Ben Ledi or walking past Bochastle at dusk listen for the ghostly cohort of Roman soldiers sometimes heard marching through the night near here, orders still being shouted in Latin.

Beyond the fields and the river to the north the pine tree covered slopes of Callander Craig rise gently. Just a kilometre to the west of the Roman camp stands the hill fort on Dunmore. Around 700BC a sudden change in the climate to the colder wetter weather of the Highlands today made much of the land too boggy for agriculture. Good farmland was harder to find and people prepared to fight for it. Dunmore (a big fort) with its commanding view over the river valley was constructed around this time. Thick walls encircled it providing a refuge for local farmers. Armed camps. The Roman legionaries on the flat plain by the river, the native tribes in the hill fort on Dunmore.

On a low hill blue with wild hyacinths beside Dunmore a large boulder stands on the skyline. Left by a glacier it is called an erratic by geologists. At some time in the past it was named Samson's Putting Stone giving a Christian twist to the legend that it was thrown from the top of Ben Ledi during a trial of strength between two Celtic giants.

The walk way crosses an unsurfaced road at a pair of gates where wild roses grow. Keep straight on towards Ben Ledi which rises ahead to the north-west. Just past an arched stone bridge over the walkway (Victorian engineers built to last) cross the A821. On the far side leave the cycleway and turn left along a path which follows the verge for about 100 metres. This short stretch of path leads to Bochastle car park and a forest road that climbs the southern slopes of Ben Ledi.

Follow the forest road through serried ranks of Sitka spruce past a small quarry. Look closely at the rock in the quarry, embedded in it are big rounded pebbles, this lumpy brown rock is (appropriately) known as 'puddingstone' and shows, geologically, you are still in the Scottish Lowlands. The forest road crosses the Highland Line (Ben Ledi stands just north of it) a boundary defined by geology where the rock changes from the lumpy 'puddingstone' of the quarry to the Dalradian schist of Ben Ledi. The grey slaty schist on the north side of the Highland Boundary Fault is a much older rock than 'puddingstone'. Ben Ledi is grey schist making it a mountain of the Highlands, these different rocks of the Highlands and Lowlands a result of the collision and drifting

Callander railway station in 1965 with Ben Ledi in the background and Black 5 no 45423 about to leave with the 1.30pm to Glasgow, Buchanan Street. The early Scottish mountaineers travelled by train using the stations at Balquhidder and Callander as starting points for hill walks in the days before car ownership was widespread. Opened in 1880 the Callander and Oban line ran from Dunblane to Crianlarich through glorious southern Highland scenery. The Beeching axe already hung over the route when a landslide in Glen Ogle blocked the line in September 1965. It never reopened and Edinburgh lost its direct rail link to the West Highlands. Trains were rerouted via Glasgow resulting in longer journey times. Subsequent improvements to the A84 and A85 have made train travel to the West Highlands much slower compared to driving.

Substantial sections of the line have been preserved for transport use as a cycle way. With the advent of climate change there is a strong case for reopening the line for commuters from Callander to Stirling, a rail link would reduce traffic on the busy A84. The line along Loch Lubnaig and over the viaducts high on the hillside above Glen Ogle must have been a spectacular run and the line has great potential as a tourist attraction. Witness the success of the steam train service from Fort William to Mallaig. Reopening the line would restore a vital link in the West Highland railway network and if powered by renewable energy from the nearby Breadalbane hydro-electric scheme could give Scotland one of the greenest transport systems on an overheated planet.

© Robin Barbour

apart of ancient continents during Scotland's journey across the surface of the planet.

Near NN 59953 BNG07755 at a break in the trees it is possible to walk to Dunmore Fort; follow the fence/dry stone wall along until you come to a stile. Further along the road is an area where trees have been felled and replanted. It's good to be clear of the conifers, to see the hills around Loch Lubnaig. The forest road along the hillside gives an aerial view of the Pass of Leny below. I see many white moths and butterflies here and high above a bird of prey scans the hillside. *Where to Watch Birds in Scotland* lists the Pass as a good place for bird watching and pine martens have been seen hereabouts. The Garbh Uisge rushes through the oak trees. The A84 snakes along beside the river. Through the Pass of Leny Roman legionaries marched north and black cattle came south. Red coated soldiers built a military road and later Irish navvies constructed the Callander and Oban railway line.

Pine marten tracks

Near the road old dry stone walls still stand among dense rows of conifers, moss covered memorials to the people who farmed here before the Second World War and the planting of the Queen Elizabeth Forest. Speaking at the Edinburgh Book Festival Andy Wightman (tongue in cheek) compared the Forestry Commission's effect on rural Scotland to Stalin's collectivisation of Soviet agriculture in the 1930s. The natural woodland by the Garbh Uisge, the round shapes of the oak trees, stand in marked contrast to the ubiquitous conifer. At over 7,000km² commercial forestry plantations cover much more of Scotland's uplands than native woodland. Mostly these plantations are dominated by Sitka spruce, a conifer introduced from North America which thrives on poor wet soils. Sometimes to break the monotony there are larch or lodge pole pines too.

Kellan tramped through forests like these on childhood walks in the 1960s. The rows of tree seedlings uniformly spaced in endless lines separated by drainage ditches. Plantations like these the visible remains of an outdated forestry policy – today there is more emphasis on native trees, better designed woodland and 'getting the look right' – no more perfect squares of forest. But these benefits won't be seen on a significant scale until existing plantations are felled and restructured in a 50 year cycle.

WHO OWNS BEN LEDI?

Much of Ben Ledi is owned by Forestry Commission Scotland, Silvan House, and 231 Corstorphine Road, Edinburgh, EH12 7AT.

The craggy eastern slopes of Ben Ledi begin to come into view but soon the forest closes in again. This is where you join the footpath coming up from Coireachrombie Bridge.

Continue to the summit of Ben Ledi by the south-east ridge. In Spring I have seen dotterel on this ridge pausing on their migratory journey north. One time Cuilean and the Labradoodle were tied to an old fencepost here while I was taking photos. Then from the hillside below – the steep eastern flank of Ben Ledi – I heard shouting and barking. A shepherd, youngish, about 30, came striding up the grassy hillside. He had at least seven dogs with him. Brown and white collie crosses, grey and white collie crosses, predominantly black collies and a beardy. The dogs relishing being out on the hill doing their job. The shepherd controlled this wild bunch of farm collies with fierce shouts. Unlike the Gore-Tex clad hillwalkers the shepherd carried no rucksack, or waterproofs, just a hoodie and on his belt, a two way radio.

An early ascent of Ben Ledi for which a written record exists was made around 1815 by Thomas Grierson a minister and keen walker from Galloway in the south-west of Scotland. His book *Autumnal Rambles Among the Scottish Mountains* published in 1850 became a bestseller.

As I climb towards the summit crags two ravens fly above the ridge. An iron cross near the top of Ben Ledi commemorates Harry Lawrie a policeman killed in a helicopter crash on Ben More during a mountain rescue in 1987. The day I climbed Ben Ledi a bunch of yellow roses was tied to Sergeant Lawrie's cross.

In 1827 the Reverend P. Robertson reported of Ben Ledi;

> The view from the summit is very fine. To the east is seen the Firth of Forth as far as the eye can reach; towards the south, the Firth of Clyde and the hills of Arran; and to the north and west is a splendid view of the Grampians, one rising higher than another.

A century later WH Murray wrote that from the top of Ben Ledi you can see 120 miles from Arran to the Cairngorms and from Ben Nevis to Tinto hill.

Tormentil: in *Hostile Habitats* the leaves of tormentil are described as 'narrow and deeply-toothed, appearing as radiating whorls of five which faintly resemble the foliage of a cannabis plant... The plant is also alleged to cure nervous diarrhoea and is conveniently – available on numerous belay ledges.'

On the way back down when you reach the forest road, cross it and continue on a footpath steeply downhill to Coireachrombie car park then follow the south bank of the Garbh Uisge for three kilometres through oak trees and blaeberry to re-join the outward route at the A821 near Bochastle car park. The walkway passes the Falls of Leny and the remains of railway bridges where the Callander and Oban line once switched from one side of the river to the other and back again.

The Journal of the Scottish Mountaineering Club for 1891 includes an account of climbing Ben Ledi on Christmas Day. John Macharg and two unnamed friends accompanied by HB Watt, set off from Callander at 11.20am walking via Kilmahog and Coilantogle. No car park handily situated at the foot of the hill in those days and sounds like it wasn't the best of weather;

> Dripping thaw, roads bad, with snow, ice and water; a slow rain falling, and a close mist all around. Could not see fifty yards ahead.

Things improved when they got to 1,700 feet and the rain turned to snow and the mist cleared giving them a view of the tops of nearby peaks, some even with a bit of sun on them. Leaving the summit cairn at 2.10pm, they ruefully note they didn't use their alpenstocks (old fashioned long handled ice axes) all day, they tried a glissade but there wasn't enough snow. Macharg and Co must have set a cracking pace all day as they were back in Callander just in time to catch the 3.55pm train south. Not a transport option available to the 21st century hill walker who has a bus journey or the M9 to contend with before reaching home, the fireside and a dram.

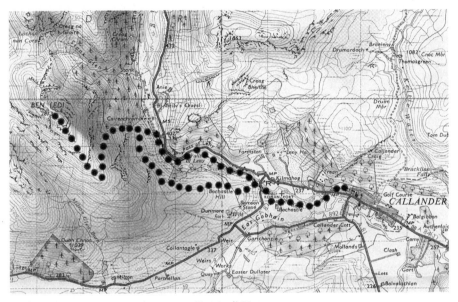

Ben Ledi Map

BEN LEDI (879m)

Grade	**
Map	OS Sheet 57
Distance/Ascent:	21km/810m
Starting height:	90m
Time to top:	3h30min +breaks
Start/Finish:	Callander

A scenic route up Ben Ledi which starts by following a disused railway line and passes the site of a Roman marching camp and a hill fort.

ROUTE:

1   Get off bus at Dreadnought Hotel in Callander or park in adjacent large car park NN62623 08572. Opposite bus stop is start of walk/ cycleway signposted *Strathyre* 9½. Follow the track behind the car park toilets by some iron railings.

2   Keep following cycleway signs out back of car park then along Tulipan Crescent to reach main road (A84) at pedestrian crossing. Cross road and follow cycleway (signposted *Strathyre*) through trees past old railway signal.

3   Follow cycle track N for about 2km to where it crosses A821 NN60779 08200. On far side of road turn left (don't go through gate, leave the cycle way) and walk along path beside wooden fence which follows verge of A821 for about 100m to Bochastle car park NN60800 08100. Walk to back of car park where another few metres of footpath lead to a forest road.

4   Follow forest road (not marked on older editions of OS 1:50000 map) for 4km to where it crosses the footpath marked with blue waymarkers NN58000 09300 that comes up from Coireachrombie Bridge. Turn left here onto footpath.

5   Follow paved path above little gorge. Follow path down to ford burn. Cross stile.

6   Follow eroded path up towards Ben Ledi's SE ridge. Path swings round to right/N to reach ridge NN57097 08578.

7   Follow wide path up broad SE ridge passing several cairns on upper section of ridge (not summit).

8   Pass some small crags before reaching trig point and cairn that mark summit of Ben Ledi (879m) NN56241 09768

9   Return by the route of ascent as far as blue waymarkers on forest road NN58027 09263. Cross road and continue steeply downhill on footpath to reach Coireachrombie Bridge NN 58600 09200.

10 Do not cross bridge. Instead turn right and follow sign posted cycleway S through car parking area. Go through metal gate then follow cycleway for 3km on S bank of Garbh Uisge to re-join outward route at A821 near Bochastle car park.

DOGS: allowed on bus to Callander. Sheep on hillside where forest ends at stile and fence.

PUBLIC TRANSPORT: train to Stirling leaves Edinburgh/Glasgow 7.33am/ 8.06am (not Sundays). Then bus to Callander (buses hourly) arriving 9.42am. Last bus back from Callander 8.47pm. Most buses seem to terminate at bus stop at Dreadnought Hotel near large car park. Full public transport details at www.travelinescotland.com or phone 0871 200 22 33.

Something Else: Mhor Fish in Callander (used to be the Ben Ledi Café) for chips.

Wheatear

CHAPTER EIGHT

Benvane

Bracken Cigarettes

TOPOGRAPHICALLY OVER SHADOWED by its more famous neighbour Ben Ledi, mountain number four on Caleb's list, Benvane, stands 821m/ 2,693ft high to the west of Loch Lubnaig at a distance of 52 miles from Arthur's Seat and can be seen 62½ degrees west of north in line with Dumyat. In *Climbing the Corbetts* Hamish Brown found;

> ... Benvane the more friendly [hill] with its green and open northern aspects rising above cheery Glen Buckie while Ben Ledi has been strangled with dank forestry plantings... and dotted with grim names like 'loch of the corpse', and Stank Glen.

Benvane is an anglicised version of the common Gaelic hill name *beinn mheadhoin* meaning middle hill. In this case Benvane is the middle hill between Ben Ledi and Beinn a t-Sithein. In Gaelic as well as meaning 'in the middle '*beinn mheadhoin* also has connotations of being at the centre or 'heart'. On Timothy Pont's map of Scotland the Ben Vane near Loch Lomond appears as *Ben Vian* a good phonetic version of *beinn mheadhoin* based on how local people pronounced the name in the 16th century.

The Benvane in the Trossachs, the hill on Caleb's list lies between Glen Finglas in the south and Glen Buckie in the north. The route through these glens was once an important trade route. Benvane lies halfway between Balquhidder and Brig o' Turk and to the soldiers, tinkers, Highlanders, horseman, Kings and cattle drovers who once travelled this route Benvane would indeed have been the middle hill.

To complicate things the Ordnance Survey 1:25000 map shows Benvane with the name Beinn Bhan in brackets underneath. Several 20th century hillwalking guidebooks also give this name which means 'white hill' for Benvane. Perhaps both names are right as in past centuries mountains were sometimes given different names according to where people lived and the direction from which they saw the hill.

Climbing Benvane

It was going to be a very hot day. I realised that when I stopped at the old station car park in Callander and had to find a parking space in the shade (for the dogs) at 8.45am.

To climb Benvane leave the A84, following signposts for *Balquhidder*, at the historic Kingshouse hotel. Just past Balquhidder old kirk and Rob Roy's grave turn left along a road that crosses the River Balvag following signposts to Ballimore. At a crossroads keep straight on; don't take the right turn that leads to Stronvar.

A roe deer hind with two calves running at her tail crosses the road here and leaps the fence back into the woods as I creep along the very narrow single track road that leads through Glen Buckie down to Ballimore farm between dry stone walls enclosing old meadows and mature broad-leafed trees. Later looking at the map I see Benvane is bounded to the west by Gleann nam Meann which translates from Gaelic as the glen of the young roes.

At a gate and cattle grid with a sign reading *Ballimore* continue straight on till you come to Ballimore Farm. There is limited space to park on the verge where the narrow and pot holed public road through Glen Buckie ends at a sign *Immeroin Private Road*.

Go through a small gate beside a cattle grid and cross the single round-arch bridge over the Calair Burn. Before you set off to climb Benvane pause for a moment on the bridge. Look over the parapet at water tumbling over smooth stones under birch trees. Look down at the drainage holes at road level. Solid and well designed, this bridge has much to tell about the past of historic Glen Buckie. It was constructed during the Improvement period which began in the late 18th century and was a time of modernisation in agriculture when innovations such as adding lime to the soil to increase yields of some crops were introduced. Renovated in 1991, the bridge has retained its traditional long, narrow character and may be one of the five bridges mentioned in *The Old Statistical Account* as; 'built this year upon rapid burns in different parts of the parish by subscriptions.'

THE LAST JACOBITE

The Stewarts of Glen Buckie were supporters of Bonnie Prince Charlie during the 1745 Jacobite uprising. It was in Glen Buckie that the undercover agent Dr Archibald Cameron, the last Jacobite to be executed in Britain (in 1753) was captured by a Redcoat patrol; a story retold by the writer DK Broster in the romantic historical novel *The Gleam in the North*. A very private person, when she died in 1950 critics were astonished to learn that Dorothy Kathleen Broster was neither male nor Scottish. *The Flight of the Heron, The Dark Mile* and *The Gleam in the North* were written in the 1920s and some have detected a homoerotic undercurrent running through the Jacobite trilogy with its storyline of intense male friendships spanning class and race.

Glen Buckie was well populated in centuries past and historical records describe many trees and meadows and fields of crops. The broad upper glen is open and sunny and there are shielings here, more evidence of past population. Ballimore and nearby Immeroin were once relatively large settlements (Ballimore means big township) and during the 18th and 19th centuries very large numbers of cattle were driven through Glen Buckie to the Falkirk trysts which explains why there is a substantial bridge here.

Ballimore farm stands on the site of an old *ferm toun*. *Ferm touns* were small settlements of half a dozen families who lived in single storey cottages with stone foundations, turf walls and roofs of heather, without windows or chimneys, surrounded by small fields of oats, barley and potatoes separated by bigger stretches of bog and moorland where black cattle grazed. In past centuries in rural Scotland the *ferm toun* was the basic unit of the community in countryside without the hedges, fences, roads and ditches of the modern landscape.

On the far side of the bridge is a signpost *Footpath to Brig o' Turk via Glen Finglas.* Leave the track here and strike up a steep bank. Follow a faint path across a field where in spring heath speedwell and cuckooflower grow among the clumps of soft rush, to reach a dry stone wall with a large gate and a small pedestrian wrought iron gate a few metres away. Go through the iron gate and walk across the upper field dotted with birch trees, it rises gently up onto the long north ridge of Benvane. Head due south through thistles and patches of bracken aiming for a small plantation of fir trees.

BRACKEN CIGARETTES

I read in the pages of *Hostile Habitats* that bracken is; 'characteristic of economically marginal hill farms, as the plant requires periodic relief from grazing in order to spread.' This factual botanical description of Scotland's most abundant upland fern (*raineach* in Gaelic) belies the reality of bracken on the hill as I found out a couple of years ago in July on the Island of Mull. Be warned Corbett baggers, the recommended route up Dun da Ghaoithe starts from the rundown farm at Scallastle and involves negotiating THE BRACKEN. It had to be eight feet tall, was visible from the ferry in the Sound of Mull and covered the entire eastern lower slopes of the hill. I had to trample a way through it, slithering over its slippery flattened stalks, gasping up steep hillside for about two hundred feet until at last I escaped from it. Luckily for hillwalkers the fern's root system is susceptible to damage by frost so bracken is only found at low altitudes.

Bracken adds a rich russet colour to autumn in the Scottish glens but it also chokes out other plants and provides an ideal habitat for sheep ticks that lie in wait on the end of its leaves before attaching to a passing bare (human) leg or the Labradoodle's nose (twice).

As children on holiday in Knapdale in the 1970s we made 'cigarettes' out of dried bracken wrapped in toilet paper and happily oblivious to the cocktail of carcinogenic toxins present in the plant wreathed the family tent in garden bonfire smelling smoke.

Sudden panic. I remember I've forgotten to take the daily medication people with HIV have to take at exactly the same time each day to keep the virus in the bloodstream at an undetectable level. Missed doses risk giving HIV the chance to become drug resistant entailing a change to new drugs and new side effects. So I leave my rucksack on the hillside and plod back down to the car at Ballimore to take six tablets washed down with coffee and biscuits (food to reduce nausea) before starting up the hill again.

Near the plantation of fir trees climb over a fence onto the open hillside. There is no gate, I lift Cuilean and the Labradoodle over. Now make a rising traverse onto the north ridge of Benvane with the view starting to open out back down to Balquhidder and Ballimore Farm with the track winding along to Immeroin and the old shielings by the burn at the edge of the forest.

Heath bedstraw grows here. Sun bleached sheep's bones lie in the long grass. The dogs find deep pools in the little burns and marshy ground to cool off in.

The crest of the broad ridge is soon gained – matts of sheep's wool among tussocks of deer grass. Past peat hags at a height of 600 metres a fence is reached. Keep the fence on your left, it's a useful navigational aid. A faint footpath has formed and heads south along the grassy ridge towards the summit of Benvane with Stob Binnein and Ben More prominent on the skyline. Where the grassy hillside ends dense pine forest, dark green older trees and light shades of younger plantations scored with lines of firebreaks, sweeps down to Loch Lubnaig.

WHO OWNS BENVANE?

Most of Benvane is owned by The Woodland Trust Scotland, South Inch Business Centre, Shore Road, Perth, PH2 8BW and Forestry Commission Scotland.

High on the north ridge of Benvane a little marshy pool is home for a few brief weeks of summer to the four spotted chaser dragonfly. Tadpoles wriggle in the peaty water and common butterwort grows among the cotton grass on the boggy ground nearby.

The Labradoodle sniffing at something in the grass. A fox scat. White. The fox had eaten bones. It must be the fox from Creag a'Mhadaidh, I think. I check GPS and map – sure enough I am standing at a point on the north ridge of Benvane just below the M in Creag a'Mhadaidh – the Gaelic name for crag of the fox. The foxes are here on Benvane still, though the people who named the crag of the fox, and their language, are long gone, spoken today only by hillwalkers to name the mountains they climb.

At about 740 metres a rusty fence stretches across the hillside. The wires trail in the grass. A little higher up an iron fence post indicates the way to the summit though in bad weather navigation will be needed. As I climb the ridge three swifts catching insects in the warm summer air, whirl like black scimitars across the azure blue sky. I stand and watch them for a little while.

As I climb on towards the summit of Benvane a big cloud of black flies buzzes around my head; they are bothering the dogs too. I can't shake them off and there being not a breath of wind I can't stop to eat. I wish the swifts would catch them all.

It isn't just me they swarm around, the Labradoodle is pawing its face and another hill walker I meet at the top of Benvane is accompanied by his own cloud of flies. Not just flies – midges and clegs too and the whine of a mosquito in my ear. All despite it being broilingly hot, 28 degrees on the car thermometer when I get back to Ballimore at 3.30pm. Big anvil shaped clouds form in the east with little ragged grey outliers like puffs of smoke from cannon... one of the thunderstorms forecast on the radio for eastern areas in the afternoon.

The views from the small summit cairn of Benvane (821m) are far more striking than from many higher hills. Clouds cast huge shadows on nearby Ben Ledi and I recognise Ben Lomond, The Cobbler and the Arrochar Alps, the Arran hills, Stob Binnein and Ben More, Dumyat and the Ochils, the Campsies and the Wallace monument. Below lie Strathyre and Balquhidder, Loch Lubnaig with its marshy wetlands shone in the heat and Glen Finglas reservoir lay blue and sparkling to the south-west.

I explore the summit of Benvane with the dogs in an attempt to escape the flies and find a big white lichen covered split rock and a second cairn a little to the west of the summit cairn which the altimeter measures as 805 metres. Midges lurk in the shade below every big boulder, it's where they go to hide from the sun. So different from the snowy February day I climbed Benvane one winter. It is slightly hazy (and it doesn't show up in photos I take) but beyond Dumyat I think I can make out the familiar shape of Arthur's Seat.

Return by the same route; on the way down its worth looking out for the point where you came onto the ridge as you need to bear north eastwards from about the 550 metre contour in order to get back to the little plantation of pine trees. If you go too far north along the ridge on descent you end up coming down over some little crags. The dogs swam in the Calair Burn on the way down their coats wet and cool for getting back into the blisteringly hot car. For us three Benvane will always be the hill of the flies. No record exists of the person who first climbed Benvane; a shepherd from Ballimore or a fox hunter perhaps. Or just someone who wandered up the hill from the old shielings one evening in summer long ago.

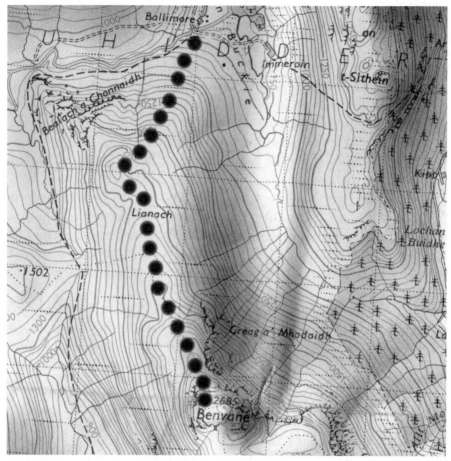

Benvane Map

BENVANE (821m)

Grade:	***
Map:	OS Sheet 57
Distance/Ascent:	8km/620m
Starting height:	210m
Time to top:	2h +breaks
Start/Finish:	Glen Buckie near Balquhidder

A straightforward ascent of a fairly remote southern Highland Corbett.

ROUTE:

1 North of Callander leave A84 following signposts to *Balquhidder*. Just past ruined church at Balquhidder/Rob Roy's Grave, turn left following signposts to Ballimore.

2 At crossroads keep straight on. At gate with sign *Ballimore* continue straight on to Ballimore Farm. Limited space to park NN52933 BNG17476 beside gate with sign *Immeroin Private Road* and cattle grid (be careful not to block gates).

3 Go through small gate beside cattle grid. Cross bridge over Calair Burn.

4 On far side of bridge is a signpost *Footpath to Brig o' Turk via Glen Finglas*. Leave the track here where a footpath strikes up a steep bank and follow a faint path across a field.

5 Reach dry stone wall. Go through small wrought iron gate (*not* large gate with sign on it). Walk due south (no path) through upper field heading for small plantation of pine trees.

6 Near plantation of fir trees climb over fence onto open hillside.

7 Now make a rising traverse onto the long north ridge of Benvane.

8 Past peat hags at 600m a fence is reached NN52696 BNG15141. Keep fence on left and head south along ridge.

9 At 740m cross dilapidated fence NN53233 BNG13999.

10 Head to iron fence post at 790m NN53270 BNG13848 (in bad weather navigation will be required).

11 Reach small summit cairn of Benvane (821m) NN53500 13700.

12 Return by same route. On way down its worth remembering where you came onto ridge as you need to bear north-eastwards from about 550m in order to get back to plantation of pine trees. If you go too far north along ridge on descent you end up coming down over some little crags.

DOGS: lots of sheep and lambs around on this walk. One fence to lift dogs over – no barbed wire.

WINTER CONDITIONS: ice axe and crampons needed.

Somewhere Else: The Kingshouse, Balquhidder

CHAPTER NINE

CGC

Caleb gently closes the heavy wooden double doors of the bright south facing twin windowed classroom with its view across the schoolyard to Raeburn Place. CGC straightens his black gown and turns to the boys crowded into the geography room on a January afternoon at three o' clock just as the light is fading. Comets are not stars... he begins.

AT THE START OF THE 19th century Ladywood Lane near Birmingham ran from the toll gates at Five Ways through rolling green countryside and elm trees to Spring Hill. The construction of the first canals changed Ladywood forever. By the 1840s factories lined the banks of the canal that ran from Ladywood into Birmingham. This rapid industrialisation soon led to the uncontrolled building of working class housing in the nearby countryside.

Caleb George Cash was born in Birmingham in June 1857 the eldest son of Caleb and Sarah Cash. The census of 1861 records Caleb's family as living at 69 Ladywood Lane. By now Ladywood Lane was a busy city street soon to be renamed Ladywood Road. In Victorian times the lane consisted of two or three storey brick built houses with shops on the street corners. People in Ladywood were poor. Most of the terraced back to back houses had no bathroom, no hot water and an outside toilet in the backyard.

Number 69 where Caleb spent his childhood was above a grocer's shop. Caleb's father was 41 years old in 1861 and the census gives his occupation as a brass finisher and grocer. The enumerator's handwriting is smudged and almost illegible but I can just make out that Caleb's mother's occupation is recorded as shop assistant. Brass finishing was often a part-time job so it may be that Caleb's family lived above the grocer's shop they ran and Caleb senior brought some extra income into the household by brass finishing for one of the many foundries that existed in Birmingham in the 19th century.

The author and academic JRR Tolkien lived in Duchess Road on the fringes of Ladywood at the start of the 20th century. The industrialisation

The Masters on the steps of the Edinburgh Academy in 1900. Caleb unmistakeable,
standing, second from right.

[*Edinburgh Academy Archive*]

of the countryside around Birmingham is known to have influenced
Tolkien's writing and perhaps Caleb's love of wild places developed out
of a childhood spent in an industrial area. By 1945 Ladywood had
become a slum and was extensively redeveloped in the 1960s. The mass
demolitions that occurred were a direct result of the cheap, quickly built
housing put up during the 19th century. In the 21st century Ladywood
Lane lies buried beneath Ladywood Middleway.

Educated at St John's school in Ladywood, even as a boy Caleb was
a hard worker and in 1871 at the age of 13 he was employed as a pupil
teacher. In Victorian schools intelligent pupils were sometimes kept on
after the school leaving age of 12. They would teach classes and receive on
the job training and a small salary. Caleb went on to St Mark's teacher
training college in Chelsea run by the National Society for Promoting the
Education of the Poor which sought to develop schooling in the growing
industrial towns of England. He matriculated from London University
and apprenticed to the National Society until the age of 21, and returned
to St John's as an assistant school master for two years. CGC's humble
origins perhaps explain why later in his career he unfailingly put the
initials FRSGS after his name whenever it appeared in print.

The census of April 1881 recorded that Caleb was now 23 years old and working as a schoolmaster in Sheffield at one of the School Board schools which the city opened after the 1870 education act. He was a lodger in the home of school board officer James Hanson in William Street. While living in Sheffield Caleb met 26-year-old Alice Octavia Randell. Alice did not have a job and lived with her father, a clerk, in the Eccleshall Bierlow area of Sheffield. Caleb and Alice were married at a Register Office in the town on Thursday 21 July 1881 and moved into 178 Ecclesall Road not far from Caleb's old lodgings in William Street. Caleb taught in Sheffield from 1882 until October 1886 when the couple moved to Scotland.

Behind high railings in Hamilton Place in the Stockbridge area of Edinburgh stand the Georgian buildings of the Edinburgh Academy with Greek Doric frontage above which is carved Η ΠΑΙΔΕΙΑ ΚΑΙ ΤΗΣ ΣΟΦΙΑΖ ΚΑΙ ΤΗΣ ΑΡΕΤΗΣ ΜΗΤΗΡ *Education is the Mother of both Wisdom and Virtue*. This was an altogether grander educational establishment than the schools in Birmingham and Sheffield where Caleb had previously taught.

Caleb taught at the Edinburgh Academy for 30 years and was closely involved in school life. As music and geography teacher he took part in performances of school plays such as the Greek tragedy *Antigone* when he sang bass in the choir. According to colleagues Caleb was always glad either to learn or teach and did not let personal likes or dislikes get in the way. Colleagues described Caleb as 'a zealot for knowledge' who enjoyed the process of learning.

Caleb joined the recently formed Royal Scottish Geographical Society in 1892 and over the years contributed articles and book reviews to the *Scottish Geographical Magazine* mainly on subjects connected with the topography and cartography of Scotland. As well as writing articles for the journal *The Geographical Teacher* Caleb also found time to edit several books for young people with titles like *Cook's Voyages, The Story of the North-West Passage* and *Anson's Voyage Around the World 1740–1744*. On a globe in his classroom he had his pupils plot the route followed by the Norwegian explorer Fridtjof Nansen's expedition to try to reach the North Pole during the 1890s. For this was geography and history in the making: the equivalent of the Apollo moon landings in Caleb's world.

I order *The Story of the North-West Passage* from Abebooks (*Find over 140 million new, rare and collectable books at AbeBooks.com proclaims the website*). A few days later it comes through the letterbox in a brown jiffy bag. Inside a slim blue bound paperback, Volume No.11 in the *Nelson's Supplementary Readers* series, with illustrations of polar bears and Eskimo kayaks. Thomas Nelson and Sons – London, Edinburgh, and New York – their printing works in the shadow of Arthur's Seat published it in 1906 at a cover price of four-pence/4d.

By 1901 Caleb and Alice had moved to a large seven roomed flat at 49 Comely Bank Road just a five minute walk from the Edinburgh Academy. At the beginning of the 20th century Comely Bank was a suburb of Edinburgh. Tall tenements stood along one side of Comely Bank Road and terraced houses lined the other side. Across the street was the Edinburgh Academy rugby field, Inverleith Park was nearby and beyond the extensive grounds of Fettes College lay open fields.

The introduction of Dunlop's pneumatic tyre in 1888 gave a boost to the new sport of cycling. From Caleb's home in Comely Bank Road it was an easy bike ride through Inverleith Park to Ferry road and on to the old village of Cramond. By 1900 he knew the area around Cramond well enough to be able to point out inaccuracies on the Ordnance Survey map of Edinburgh; a letterbox near the ferryman's cottage is on the wrong side of the river and a farm mistakenly marked as being the Cramond Brig inn.

Nearby Davidson's Mains was then a village in the countryside outside Edinburgh, connected to the city by a branch line railway with a station at Barnton. Here sandstone villas were springing up on the streets near the old village of Cramond which Caleb had first come to know on cycle rides from Comely Bank and where sometime around 1913 Caleb moved to a house at 15 Barnton Gardens.

What did Caleb look like physically? The picture opposite the title page of his last book shows a lightly built man about 40-years-old, photographed with a stern (in the manner of the times) expression. His face framed by a thick wiry black beard beneath a broad nose and black bushy eyebrows. Caleb's hair is immaculately combed (perhaps cut by a barber on the way to the photographers in Leith Walk?) Crisp white shirt, bow-tie, jacket and waistcoat with watch chain. Handkerchief in his top pocket. Caleb looks away from the camera.

Alexander Inkson McConnochie described Caleb as being slightly shy but 'the most genial of men' and his pupils remembered him as 'benevolent, just and exact…' Several accounts mention CGCs 'unfailing

C.G.C. conducting the Edinburgh Academy choir circa 1904 as sketched by one of his pupils Robert J. Wallace.

[*Edinburgh Academy Archive*]

punctuality'. A drawing of Edinburgh Castle was prominently displayed in his classroom and every day at lunchtime he would go out into the schoolyard to set his watch by the one o'clock gun fired from the Castle battlements.

Possessing a 'great capacity for happiness and affection' Caleb had many acquaintances but just a few close friends. Caleb was described as a good neighbour who led a 'temperate and healthy' life. In an age before TV and computers he was 'a vivid talker' who kept his Birmingham accent all his life. Caleb's friend Henry Johnstone quoted a phrase by the ancient Roman playwright Terence to describe him; 'Homo sum: humani nihil a me alienum puto' which translates as 'I am human, nothing that is human is alien to me' saying this line could have been written for Caleb to speak. Johnstone also wrote rather obliquely referring to Caleb's love of wild animals that Caleb had serenity of spirit and 'a sense of the mystery that surrounds human life.'

Some of Caleb's colleagues felt his work should have been more generally recognised and that he deserved to be better known than he was, though Caleb himself did not consider his work to be undervalued. Later in his career CGC in addition to teaching at the Edinburgh Academy began lecturing in commercial geography at the Heriot Watt College. By 1914 he was on the council of the Royal Scottish Geographical Society, a member of the Society of Antiquaries of Scotland and had published several books as well as dozens of articles for various popular and widely read journals. As CGC stood up to lecture to the college students, did Caleb sometimes pause and think how far he had come from the boy who was a pupil teacher in Ladywood?

CHAPTER TEN

Dumyat

The Teacher's Hill

FROM A TRAIN APPROACHING Stirling across the flat plain of the Forth valley, a view familiar to the Edwardian mountaineers of Caleb's generation, the Ochil Hills appear as a wall of mountains some have likened to a wave. Dumyat (pronounced *dum-eye-at*) is described in Caleb's list as lying at the south-western extremity of the Ochils. A low hill in comparison to its neighbours Dumyat is easily identified from Arthur's Seat on a clear day over the towers of Fettes College. Close to Stirling and readily accessible from Scotland's central belt climbing Dumyat is relatively easy and straightforward. At 1,374 feet or 419 metres Dumyat is the lowest of the Arthurs and the most southerly hill on Caleb's list.

The name Ochils comes from the Cumbric word *uchel* meaning the high ground. Cumbric was an ancient language of pre-Gaelic times. Names in the Ochils reflect the fact that this area was once a meeting place of different cultures and are derived from several languages including Gaelic, Scots and English.

The name Dumyat is derived from *dùn miathi* meaning fort of the Miathi tribe. The Miathi were enemies of the Romans and feature in the writings of historian Cassius Dio in 197AD. The name *dùn* is common across Scotland and means a fortress or castle. When used as a name for a hill it indicates the site of a prehistoric hill fort. *Dùn* is found in the name Dunedin from *dùn èideann* which has become Edinburgh's Castle Rock. Another example is Dundee. A hill is a good place for defence and observation. From the summit of Arthur's Seat the strategically commanding position of the hill forts on Edinburgh Castle Rock, Dumyat and East Lomond overlooking the River Forth is clear. It's easy to imagine the ancient tribes watching invading Roman galleys sail up the Forth to land at Cramond.

The Old Statistical Account of Scotland compiled in the 1790s records; 'There is a high conical hill in this parish, called *Dunmyatt,* from the top of which, is to be seen part of 12 counties.' Almost 50 years later in 1841 William Robertson wrote; 'The most remarkable peak in this parish is

Demyet...' This demonstrates how over time in Southern Scotland the word *dùn* frequently changed to *dum* before the letter *b*, *m* or *p*... because it is easier to say. Another example is Dumbarton Rock which means fort of the Britons.

Rennie McOwan calls Dumyat the hill of ghosts and tells the story of Robert Bontine Cunninghame Graham (1852–1936) once the most famous Scot of his time. A writer, traveller and radical politician he was a co-founder of the Scottish Labour Party in the 1880s and first president of the Scottish National Party in 1934. Graham was nicknamed Don Roberto because of the time he spent in South America. Once he was on a hill in Paraguay when he met another horseman on the summit. The man was a stranger to Graham but he could tell by the man's accent he was Scottish and commented admiringly on the view. The stranger replied 'Aye, man, but it disnae beat the view from Dumyat.'

Climbing Dumyat

Despite being just a few miles from the City of Stirling there is a real feeling of remoteness about Menstrie Glen. This approach to Dumyat starts from the Hillfoots village of Menstrie which has a regular bus service from Stirling. Get off the bus near the Holly Tree pub (refaced in the 1950s in '30s style) on the main street at the west end of Menstrie and turn up Park Road. At the top of Park Road at a pink sandstone Victorian house with a palm tree in its front garden turn right along Ochil Road. At the far end of a row of cottages go through a metal gate and take the track that leads uphill through a field.

The November day the Labradoodle, Cuilean and I climbed Dumyat there were four black cows in the field. They seemed placid enough, accustomed to people and ignored the dogs as we slunk past. Nearby are the turrets of Broomhall Castle built in 1874 by James Johnstone owner of Elmbank Mill in Menstrie (the mill can be seen from further up the track). Industrial development began in Menstrie and the other hill foot towns during the industrial revolution with the building of woollen mills powered by the streams that flow down from the Ochils. Broomhall Castle was later used as a boarding school and burnt down in 1941. It has since been restored.

Follow the track as it zig zags up the hill side through gorse, bracken, scrub, brambles and low trees. Little crags protrude from the gorse. As height is gained the rooftops of Menstrie appear nestling below Dumyat with the flat plain of Stirling beyond. The large rectangular buildings near Menstrie are a bonded warehouse and the factory with all the pipes and tanks makes yeast.

I see watercress growing in a ditch beside the track and it reminds me of childhood holidays in the 1970s, spent in an old caravan on a croft in Argyll. We children used to pick the watercress that grew wild in a drainage ditch along the edge of a field.

As the track climbs higher up the hillside the twin summits of Dumyat come into view on the far side of Menstrie Glen. In the distance the flat plain of Stirling stretches out to Longannet power station. To the south the River Forth flows in winding ox bows to the two bridges at Kincardine. The smoky chimneys in the distance mark the Grangemouth petro-chemical complex. The flat industrial plain of the Forth estuary with its power station and oil refinery stands in stark contrast to Menstrie Glen's tree lined gorge and grassy hillsides dotted with yellow whin. In Menstrie Glen it's hard to believe you are so close to Stirling and the motorway. As if to emphasise the feeling of rural remoteness so close to the council houses of Menstrie a shepherd comes up the track behind us with sacks of sheep feed and two border collies riding on the back of his quad bike. One dog is called Mist.

Leave the track at a bend and follow a narrow but distinct grassy path through gorse and bracken parallel to and above the Menstrie burn for about half a kilometre to a wooden farm gate where an old rowan tree stands.

Rowan

At a wooden gate near the foot of Menstrie Glen stands an old rowan tree. Rowans were often planted to keep witches away. Believing the old superstition, on either side of my garden gate at home I planted two rowans. In Scotland's glens there is now declining evidence of this practice for a rowan only lives for about 150 years and in Menstrie Glen poignantly both the tree at the gate and the buildings at Jerah are falling together into ruin.

The author and journalist Rennie McOwan grew up in the then small village of Menstrie. From his bedroom window he could see the crags of Dumyat and as a child played in the pools of the Menstrie Burn and guddled for small brown trout. McOwan's writing evokes an idyllic childhood:

> My youthful memories were of the clean scent of water soaked moss, lichen and stones, of the heady smells of summer, of the burgeoning heather and of birch, willow and hazel in spring. The sounds were the cackling jackdaws which nested in rabbit holes, the croak of the occasional carrion crow or raven, and on the higher ground, the burbling call of the curlew, the cackle of the grouse and the musical piping of the golden plover, ... I was accustomed to the crying of sheep and lambs, the barking of dogs, the swish of the wind in the long grass, and at night, the eerie, shrieking cry of the vixen fox.

The young Robert Louis Stevenson spent holidays with his parents in Bridge of Allan. RLS climbed Dumyat and the hill is thought to have influenced his descriptions of the topography of his most famous book *Treasure Island*.

Today Menstrie Glen is deserted but in the 18th century there were farmsteads and houses along the Glen. As happened in the Highlands, Menstrie Glen was effectively cleared of people to make way for sheep.

In November the trees by the Menstrie Burn were bare. Autumn leaves covered the path and hazel trees shaded it. Ferns grow among moss covered rocks by the side of the First Inchna Burn. The streams were roaring down the day I climbed Dumyat the week after the Cumbria floods of 2009. In the distance I could see the shepherd on his quad bike and hear his dogs barking as they rounded up the sheep.

Fox tracks

The grassy path goes downhill to cross the Second Inchna Burn. Be careful this wooden footbridge and the next are slippery as ice in wet weather. Just here in the trees by a clump of thick gorse the swish of a brown tail tipped with white, a fox. The dogs on their leads drag me forward.

After crossing the Third Inchna Burn the path disappears. The names First, Second and Third Inchna Burn probably originate from 18th century farmers in the glen using the deep stream gullies as natural boundaries between properties. The symbol for a *homestead* marked on the Ordnance Survey map near the Sherrifmuir road gives only a faint suggestion the houses, farmsteads, animal enclosures, cultivation strips, turf walls and rig and furrow field systems recorded by archaeologists on the slopes of Dumyat, the only signs left of the people who once lived and farmed here. In winter when the hill is covered with a dusting of snow it's easier to see the outline of ancient walls and buildings.

Somewhere around here sudden twisting spasms of watery looseness in my guts send me heading for the nearest clump of gorse bushes. Sudden, unpredictable diarrhoea is familiar to many people who live with HIV/AIDS. The gut is one of the places the virus likes to hide. Yellow water on bad days, the consistency of cake mix on good days. Or maybe it's a side effect of anti-retro viral medication. The doctor says she really doesn't know.

Don't cross the Menstrie Burn, instead head right and uphill on an indistinct path through bracken into a grassy meadow with good views back down Menstrie Glen. Half a dozen pheasants suddenly fly up towards a line of trees at the end of the field. Keeping the Menstrie Burn, with its pools and little waterfall, to your left and walk along the edge of the fields towards the ruined farmhouse at Jerah. One of the pools on the burn is known as the Washing Linn, a reminder of the people who once lived here.

WHO OWNS DUMYAT?

In 2005 Friends of the Ochils commissioned Andy Wightman author of *Who Owns Scotland?* to try and find out who owns the Ochils. Andy Wightman mapped 78 land holdings in the Ochils ranging from the 6,750 acre Gleneagles Estate in the hands of the local Haldane family to the 15,000 acre Blackford Estate owned by a holding company from Liechtenstein on behalf of the Al Tajir family from Dubai. Smaller land holdings were owned by people with addresses ranging from Dunning in Perthshire to Berkshire and Hong Kong. Other landowners in the Ochils include Forestry Commission Scotland and The Woodland Trust. Friends of the Ochils found that with some of the smaller land holdings it was difficult to know where control actually lay. For example in 2005 one hill in the Ochils was listed as being owned by the Trustees of Roger MA Van Zwaneberg, c/o Kayser Ullman Investment Management Ltd of London.

The ruined house at Jerah may take its name from the Gaelic *dearg* (meaning red and pronounced *jerrack*) after red scree on the nearby hillside. In the 14th century the land at Jerah was owned by the Cistercians of Culross. Papers in the National Archives of Scotland record that when Thomas Henderson, tenant of Jerah, died in April 1687 he owned an old horse, five cows, three bullocks, 35 sheep and he had sown fields of barley and oats in the spring that was to be his last.

The farm at Jerah consisting of three roofed buildings is marked on the first Ordnance Survey map published in 1865. The farmhouse had two fireplaces downstairs and a kitchen range. Outside were kennels for the dogs. The farm was reached by a track from the Sheriffmuir road. Old stories were told of warlocks and faeries at Jerah in days gone by. The farm was occupied into the 1960s. They were the last people to live in Menstrie Glen.

Cross the Menstrie Burn near Jerah by an old stone bridge with a deck of railway sleepers. The shepherd and his two collies are at the bridge having a long chinwag across the gate with another man on a quad bike. Mist is ordered to lie down. The Labradoodle barks excitedly. The shepherd asks if Cuilean is a beardy.

On the far side of the bridge are the ruins of Loss, the home of James Wright. A wealthy and important figure who owned half of Menstrie Glen in the 1750s, Wright was a compulsive note taker and hoarder of documents concerning his farming and business interests. The Wright of Loss papers have survived into the 21st century and provide a valuable source for historians and archaeologists. The house at Loss was lavishly furnished. It had an ornate fireplace and wallpaper in the front parlour. This was a gentleman's house. James Wright was an early supporter of the agricultural Improvement movement; he laid out this part of Menstrie Glen as parkland, planting many of the trees still standing today and an avenue of lime trees leading to the house from the south.

I stop for a bite to eat and sit on the moss covered stone walls thinking what an isolated place this must have been to live. The head of Menstrie Glen feels remote in a cold cutting November wind. Toadstools and holly grow among the stones that were once a home. Nearby stands a tall tree with spectacular bracket fungi sprouting from its trunk. A flock of redwings flies up from the branches. Redwings are migrating thrushes which fly south to Scotland to escape the harsh winter weather in Scandinavia and Iceland. This old tree must have seen the people leave the glen and the houses turn to ruins.

A track leads from the ruins to cross the outflow of the Lossburn

Reservoir at a ford. You might get wet feet crossing here – take care if the stream is high after rain. Dumyat is a volcanic plug and volcanic soil is fertile soil. Lossburn reservoir supplies drinking water and its name comes from the Gaelic word *lios* meaning a fertile place, hence the ruined farms.

The track climbs uphill away from the reservoir. Pass two lonely old trees (they stand at the site of an 18th century farm that rejoiced in the name of Backside of Lipney) and where the track bends west leave it and continue south following a faint grassy path which though indistinct can be followed all the way to the summit of Dumyat.

From the northern slopes of Dumyat I can see a conifer plantation in the distance and the turbines of a wind factory. As I climb higher grass turning yellow at the onset of winter gives way to heather and little crags. The Forth Valley reappears with the hill foot towns tucked into the Ochils. Soon I reach the grassy summit of Dumyat (418m) with its trig point and beacon. Below lies Castle Law (374m). A hill fort once stood here, built by the Miathi after whom Dumyat is named, an ancient Pictish tribe who were old enemies of the Romans. The remains of a defensive ditch constructed to separate the fort from the rest of the hill can still be seen. What a location for a castle. The commanding views make it easy to imagine the Miathi up here watching columns of Roman soldiers on the plain below.

Some have complained the grassy top of Dumyat is cluttered. There is a trig point and a cairn with a beacon on top filled with stones. The beacon was commissioned for the Queen's Silver Jubilee in 1977. It was carried up and erected by the Menstrie Scout Group and was one of a chain of beacons lit across Britain as part of the Jubilee celebrations. Nearby is a concrete replica of the cap badge of the Argyll and Sutherland Highlanders, the local regiment at one time.

In 1841 William Robertson wrote;

> The most remarkable peak in this parish is Demyet... From its summit, the Forth, the chief of Scottish rivers, may be traced almost from its source in Loch Ard, as far as the German Ocean. Edinburgh is distinctly seen, and it even said the coast of Ireland is sometimes visible. The well-known windings of the Forth, and the more humble, but hardly less picturesque, meanderings of the Devon, 'Stirling's ancient tower and town', the ruins of Cambuskenneth Abbey, and the beautiful domain of Airthrey

Castle, form the most striking objects in the immediate foreground, while the view on the north and west, bounded by the lofty summits of the Grampians, extends on the south as far as the hills of Peebleshire.

South of the River Forth lies the site of the Battle of Bannockburn where Robert the Bruce defeated an English army in 1314. In the past all roads stopped at Stirling and the glens and straths to the north contained only footpaths and the tracks taken by cattle drovers. The area around Stirling was once politically, militarily and strategically the heart of Scotland. So much history can be seen from the summit of Dumyat it has been called the teacher's hill.

THE WALLACE MONUMENT

In the 1850s Charles Roger led a campaign to erect a monument in honour of Scotland's 13th century freedom fighter. He proposed constructing a giant statue of William Wallace on Abbey Craig, the high wooded crag that rises above the flat carseland around Stirling. Abbey Craig was chosen because it is near the site of Wallace's victory over an English army at the Battle of Stirling Bridge in 1297 after which he became Guardian of Scotland. In June 1856 20,000 people gathered in Stirling's King's Park to show their support for the project. In the end the design chosen for the monument was a rocket shaped tower which Nikolaus Pevsner's architectural guide *The Buildings of Scotland* describes as; 'the ultimate totemic expression of Scots Baronialism'.

The start of the path back to Menstrie is not immediately clear. It starts about ten metres north-east of the cairn (look out for eroded footsteps in the grassy hillside) and zig zags down in a north-easterly direction before flattening to an obvious grassy path. The path becomes clearer lower down as you descend through hummocky tufts of grass.

Near some iron railings reach a track. Cross over the track and climb a stile marked by a wooden post then follow a clear path down through the bracken and gorse towards the trees. At the foot of some concrete steps turn left and cross the Auld Brig (built in 1665) over the Menstrie Burn to return to the start of the walk.

The whin grows high up the steep slopes of Dumyat. Geologists call this steep southern escarpment of the Ochil Hills, the Ochils Fault. The sea once lapped against tree covered slopes here. In 1898 as Caleb drew up a list of Scottish mountains visible from Arthur's Seat, Harold Raeburn of the Scottish Mountaineering Club came to explore the rock faces of Dumyat but found the rock mainly too loose and crumbly for climbing.

The remoteness of Menstrie Glen is left behind as the rooftops draw closer with 15th century Menstrie Castle rising incongruously from the middle of a 1960s housing estate. As I walked down the path a blustery shower was being blown in and the sky was dark grey with a bright rainbow. Over the east side of Menstrie Glen a buzzard was hunting.

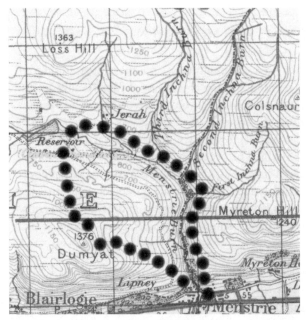

Dumyat Map

DUMYAT (418m)

Grade	**
Map:	OS Sheets 57 and 58
Distance/Ascent:	9km/401m
Starting height:	17m
Time to top:	2h30min (3h30min for whole circuit) +breaks
Start/Finish:	Menstrie

A quiet route to the summit of Dumyat through remote and historic Menstrie Glen.

ROUTE:

1 Get off bus at Holly Tree pub on A91 at west end of Menstrie and turn up Park Road. Car parking on street here NS84998 97015.

2 At top of Park Road turn right along Ochil Road. At end of row of cottages go through metal gate and follow track uphill through field to another (locked) gate with stile. Cross stile and continue along track as it zig zags uphill.

3 Leave track at bend NS84888 97526 and follow faint grassy path parallel to and above Menstrie Burn for 600m to wooden gate. Go through gate.

4 Cross bridge over first Inchna Burn NS84966 98238. Cross Second Inchna Burn and then cross bridge over Third Inchna Burn NS84439 98619.

5 Climb over locked metal gate (do not cross 'bridge' over Menstrie Burn that at time of writing consisted of two metal girders and foundations only). Head uphill on indistinct path through bracken into grassy field.

6 As path becomes fainter and then disappears head for little wooden gate in dry stone wall directly ahead.

7 Go through gate and follow fence along bottom of field as it gradually moves uphill into another field heading towards a ruined building.

8 Stay in lower third of field and continue to line of trees where there is a bridge and locked gate.

9 Cross bridge and follow track past ruin and ford outflow of Lossburn Reservoir at NS83430 98970.

10 Go through metal gate and follow track north towards Dumyat. As track turns west at NS83384 98714 leave it and follow faint grassy path to summit of Dumyat (418m) NS83567 97681.

11 Descend NE from summit Dumyat by path that starts at NS83599 97677 about 10m NE of cairn.

12 Cross a track just past area of hillside enclosed by railings and climb over stile marked by wooden post NS84666 97414.

13 Follow path down to trees in Menstrie Glen. Cross another stile and reach metal gate. Go down concrete steps to Ochil Rd. Turn left and walk past Menstrie Scout Hut to return to start of walk.

PUBLIC TRANSPORT: there is an hourly bus service from Stirling (bus station is three minutes walk from railway station) to Menstrie and the other Hillfoot towns. Last bus back from Menstrie 9.00pm. Full public transport details at www.travelinescotland.com or phone 0871 200 22 33.

DOGS: are allowed on the local buses from Stirling to Menstrie but not on Citylink coaches from Edinburgh/Glasgow to Stirling. There are a couple of locked gates on this walk that dogs have to be lifted over and a lot of sheep.

CHAPTER ELEVEN

Stob Binnein

Braes of Balquhidder

IN 1965 WA POUCHER WROTE 'Stobinian affords one of the easiest
ascents in Perthshire, providing always the atmosphere is clear and it is
not snowbound'. Stob Binnein and Ben More can often be seen from the
summit of Arthur's Seat, look beyond and to the east of Dumyat. When
Caleb compiled his list he noted that Stob Binnein was to be seen just to
the right of Fettes College. Stob Binnein (1,165m/3,822ft) is third highest
of the Arthurs and 18th highest Munro. Ben More and Stob Binnein
often appear as twin peaks separated by the Bealach-eadar-dha Beinn,
the pass between two hills, with Stob Binnein the more elegant peak, its
summit tip cut away to form a little plateau.

In *Highways and Byways in the Central Highlands* Seton Gordon
describes; 'the bare and wind-swept summit of Stob Inneoin, the Anvil
Hill, so named because of its resemblance to a huge anvil when viewed
from the south...' while *Scottish Hill Names* describes Stob Binnein as
having; 'a beautiful and distinctive summit, a long cone sliced off at an
angle just below its apex.'

Along with its twin Ben More, Stob Binnein reaches a significantly
higher altitude than other hills in the southern Highlands. Because Stob
Binnein is so high plants and flowers are found on the mountain that are
unusual so far south. On crags and cliffs, inaccessible to sheep and grazing
deer, alpine wild flowers grow, including several rare species of hawk-
weed. In 1987 Stob Binnein was designated a site of special scientific
interest and today the mountain lies within the Loch Lomond and
Trossachs National Park.

In the glen below Stob Binnein at the end of the road from Balquhidder,
lies Inverlochlarig Farm. On 28 December 1734 Rob Roy MacGregor
died at Inverlochlarig with the words 'It is all over. Put me to bed. Call
the piper. Let him play *Cha till mi tuille*' (I shall return no more). He is
buried at the old church in Balquhidder, his grave covered by an ancient
Celtic stone slab.

Climbing Stob Binnein

It is from near Inverlochlarig that the climb up Stob Binnein from the south begins. Drive west along the byroad from Balquhidder for about nine kilometres through the birch and oak woodland that lines the shores of Loch Voil. Past the Buddhist retreat centre Dhanakosa and the Monachyle Mor Hotel to where a sign reads *Inverlochlarig End of Public Road*. There is a car park here and a shelter that you can get changed in if it's raining. Birds nest in its roof. I can hear the cries of unseen fledglings from the rafters.

Leave the car park, cross the road and climb over the stile signposted *Am Binnein; Stob Coire An Lochan; Ben More*. Am Binnein is an alternative name for Stob Binnein used by Caleb in his list. From the stile a well-worn footpath leads up the steep southern slopes of Stob Invercarnaig across short cropped grass dotted with clumps of soft rush and yellow flowers of bog asphodel. Rocks capped with moss protrude from the bracken that covers much of the hillside. Follow the path up steep grass passing bushy clumps of bog myrtle. Marsh orchids grow on wet ground near the path and among the grass in summer grow the pink flowers of lousewort. On the lower slopes foxgloves rise above the dry stone walls that climb the hillside and the white heads of cotton grass wave in the breeze.

Sheep Tick

My most enthusiastic and untiring companion while researching the hill walks for this book was my five year old Labrador/Poodle cross. I often have to remove a tick (Gaelic name *mial-chaorach*) from her skin after a walk in sheep country. Ticks lie in wait on the end of blades of grass, fronds of bracken and heather. The tick waits until a mammal passes by and then attaches to a bare shin or a dog's nose or one unforgettable time in Knoydart, onto the left testicle of Truman, an enormous Rhodesian ridgeback, a breed of dog originally bred to hunt lions... Once on an animal, the tick crawls to a suitable feeding site, sinks its pointed mouthparts into the host's skin, injects an anti-clotting agent and feeds on blood. Ticks can be removed using tweezers or by smearing the tick with Vaseline causing the insect to suffocate and drop off. But the best method is to use a specially designed tick picker which can be hooked around the tick

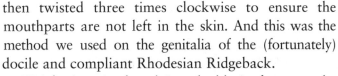

then twisted three times clockwise to ensure the mouthparts are not left in the skin. And this was the method we used on the genitalia of the (fortunately) docile and compliant Rhodesian Ridgeback.

Height is gained and Inverlochlarig farm can be seen below. This 10,000 acre hill farm has been in the same family since 1877 and has around 4,000 Scottish Blackface and Cheviot Ewes, a herd of 100 cattle and a sustainable number of wild red deer. One of the modern day farm buildings at Inverlochlarig stands on the site of the house where Rob Roy died. In 1914 archaeologists recorded that that some of the walls of Rob Roy's house could still be seen forming part of a shepherds' bothy near the farmhouse. By 1969 no signs of Rob Roy's house remained.

Pointed Stob Breac rises above the far side of the glen and the river Larig winds beneath birch trees down to Loch Doine. Fertile green fields border the river along the valley floor. The day I climbed Stob Binnein mist hid the tops of the hills across the glen.

Bog Asphodel

WHO OWNS STOB BINNEIN?

Stob Binnein is owned by The Braes Farming Company Ltd., Inverlochlarig, Balquhidder, Lochearnhead, FK19 8PH.

Keep climbing up the hillside following the hillwalkers' path worn by the passage of many boots. Although eroded in places it is a good path. Climbing Stob Binnein from the south, all the hard work comes at the start of the walk on the long climb up Stob Invercarnaig.

Higher up the hillside small crags are passed; on one a rowan sprouts from a crack. Among the rocks wild thyme with its pink flowers grows and in the grass melancholy thistle and common butterwort. I stop to catch my breath and admire the views of Ben Vorlich and Stuc a'Chroin. Seen from the steep grassy hillside here the buildings of Inverlochlarig look like a toy farm.

As a fence comes into view the path heads across the hillside to reach a stile at about 550m. Cross the fence and follow the path below crags through grassland dotted with wild flowers, among them heath bedstraw and the bluebells of Scotland.

Loch Doine and Loch Voil lie in the glen below, separated by a narrow bridge of land. Follow the path as it bears north-east for a short distance skirting the mossy crags, home to ravens.

Take note of where the path goes here in order to find it on the way back down. Apart from this point the narrow well defined nature of Stob Binnein's south ridge makes for straightforward navigation. A small stream with ferns growing on its banks is crossed and before long the broad deer grass covered ridge of Stob Invercarnaig is reached. The knobbly top of Cruach Ardrain can be seen across the deep trench of Inverlochlarig Glen. The path is fainter here but keep heading north, it becomes clearer as the ridge narrows. Yellow mountain saxifrage and alpine ladies mantle grow among the rocks and stones at the edge of the path.

The broad grassy section of the ridge ends at a cairn (890m) on an unnamed top. From here the climb becomes an enjoyable high level ridge walk above deep glens. The ridge well defined. The path easy to follow.

In May 1892 WW Naismith, the 'father' of the Scottish Mountaineering Club, climbed Stob Binnein. The last sentence of Naismith's report on the climb for the club's journal mentions;

> a simple formula, that may be found useful in estimating what time men in fair condition should allow for easy expeditions, namely, an hour for every three miles on the map, with an additional hour for every 2,000 feet of ascent.

This became known as Naismith's Rule, the classic formula for estimating time, used in mountain navigation today in the form 12 minutes per kilometre on the flat plus 10 minutes per 100 metres of ascent.

Continue along the grassy ridge passing little pools that have formed in folds and fissures in the hillside below the path. Pass the remains of an old wall.

The part of the ridge approaching Stob Coire an Lochain is known as Na Staidhrichean, *The Stairway*. At the top of Na Staidhrichean reach Stob Coire an Lochain (1,068m) a dramatic peak with a little lochan tucked in a fold in the ground next to the cairn.

From here follow the path to the summit of Stob Binnein. Although the last section of the ridge can look a bit daunting as it looms out of the mist there is no difficulty in summer. The last few metres before the summit are steep but the path winds its way round the crags to deposit you on the summit of Stob Binnein (1,165m/ 3,822ft) at its small cairn. WA Poucher wrote that from the top of Stob Binnein there is a 'stupendous panorama on a clear day'. In 1938 Seton Gordon climbed Stob Binnein and described approaching the summit and coming

> ... in sight of a vast country of hills, glens and lochs, all of them sunlit. Ben Lawers, Ben Dorain, Ben Nevis... each one was distinct.

Return by the route of ascent. As I climbed down the steep slopes of Stob Invercarnaig back towards Inverlochlarig I could see cattle grazing around the site of Rob Roy's house. Conifers blanket the hillside behind the farm but the high hills around Balquhidder are just as Rob Roy would have remembered them.

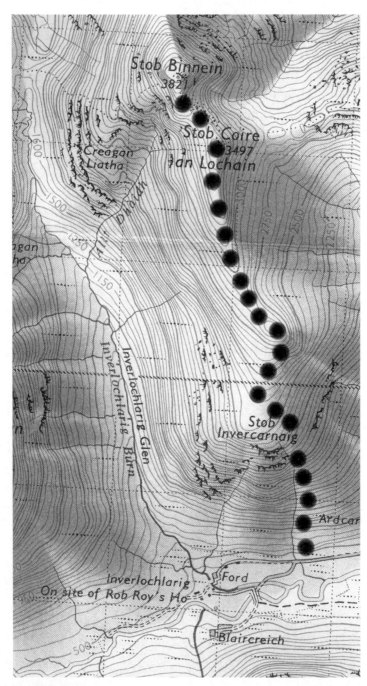

Stob Binnein Map

STOB BINNEIN (1,165m)

Grade	***
Map:	OS Sheets 51 & 57
Distance/Ascent:	8km/1,050m
Starting height:	135m
Time to top:	3h30min +breaks
Start/Finish:	Car park near Inverlochlarig farm

A dramatic high level ridge walk in Rob Roy country.

ROUTE:

1 Drive w from Balquhidder along N shore of Loch Voil for about 9km. Park at car park at road end NN44600 18450. Leave car park, cross road, climb over stile sign posted *Am Binnein; Stob Coire An Lochan; Ben More.*

2 From stile follow well-worn footpath steeply up s slopes of Stob Invercarnaig.

3 Reach stile at about 550m NN44321 19359. Cross stile and follow path NE/right, below crags. Take note of where path goes here in order to find it on way back down.

4 Walk up broad grassy section of ridge which ends at cairn (890m) at unnamed top NN44351 20559.

5 Follow path along narrower section of ridge (Na Staidhrichean) to reach Stob Coire an Lochain (1,068m) NN43845 22044.

6 Follow path up steep rocky ground to summit Stob Binnein (1,165m) NN43500 22700.

7 Return by route of ascent.

DOGS: the landowner asks that dogs be kept on a lead at all times and not taken on the hill during lambing time (20 April–29 May) and during periods of heavy rain when the burns are swollen. The Outdoor Access code only requires dog owners to keep dogs under close control.

STALKING: mid-September to 20 October estate asks that walkers keep to the route described above.

WINTER CONDITIONS: descent from summit of Stob Binnein can be difficult when icy even with crampons.

Somewhere Else: The King's House at Balquhidder.

CHAPTER TWELVE

Ben More

The Malhoulakins

'The top is exactly halfway... so keep concentrating.'
Legendary Scottish climber Mal Duff
on reaching the summit of a mountain.

IN THE SPRING OF 1891 the quiet of Glen Dochart was shattered by the sound of hundreds of navvies hammering, shovelling and blasting as they constructed the West Highland Railway. Members of the recently formed Scottish Mountaineering Club (SMC), in Crianlarich to climb Ben More and Stob Binnein, were not impressed. They had a good day on the hill but the atmosphere in the pub afterwards seems to have been less convivial, as they later wrote in the club's journal;

> Let us draw a veil over the West Highland Railway desecrations at Crianlarich. We advise members of the SMC to avoid the hotel there during the next twelve months or so, unless they are more than usually anxious for the society of drunk navvies.

Ben More is the anglicised form of the Gaelic *Beinn Mhòr* meaning big mountain. Ben More is spelt this way because early English speaking Ordnance Survey map makers recorded Gaelic mountain names as they sounded. The Ben Mores are the highest hills relative to nearby hills rather than being the highest hills in the whole of Scotland. So there is a Ben More on Mull and a Ben More Assynt in Sutherland. Of all the Ben Mores in Scotland, Crianlarich's Ben More is the highest.

According to Caleb's list Ben More is 60¼ miles distant in the Braes of Balquhidder and can be seen from Arthur's Seat just to the right of 'Am Binnein' on a bearing 60 degrees west of north. Ben More (1,174m/ 3,852ft) is the second highest of the Arthurs and 16th highest mountain in Scotland. WA Poucher said of Ben More; 'The 3,300 feet of steep, grassy slopes have a foreshortened aspect and as a result the climb seems endless.' In the southern Highlands only Ben Lawers is higher than Ben More. Ralph Storer declares; 'you can be assured that the word relentless was coined to describe the ascent.' Seen from Arthur's Seat Ben More seems bulkier than its neighbour Stob Binnein and is higher by a few metres. Cameron McNeish describes these two mountains as; 'the Castor and Pollux of the Scottish Highlands, heavenly twins joined together by a high bealach'.

Climbing Ben More

In the 21st century the West Highland Line is considered to be one of the great railway journeys of the world. According to the Scotrail timetable by catching the 8.21am from Glasgow it is possible to be in Crianlarich by 10.09am. A southbound train departs Crianlarich at 7.33pm arriving in Glasgow at 9.31pm thus leaving sufficient time to climb Ben More at a leisurely pace (no suitable trains on Sundays). Pick a long summer's day with a good weather forecast to enjoy the views of 'mountain, moor and loch' from the train window.

From Crianlarich railway station walk down into the village. Turn right along the main road signposted 'Stirling'. Walk east along the pavement until you reach the outskirts of Crianlarich. To avoid having to walk along the busy A85 go past the Ben More Restaurant and at the white painted Inverardran cottage, which belongs to the Ochils Mountaineering Club, turn left and walk through the cottage's parking area to a metal gate. Go through the gate and turn right along the sometimes muddy track bed of a disused railway (a sense of humour and an interest in industrial archaeology is recommended for this section of the walk). This line, the old Callander and Oban railway connected Stirling and Crianlarich and is a missing link in Scotland's rail network, the reinstatement of which would give Edinburgh back its direct rail link to the West Highlands and greatly reduce journey times.

Follow the footpath along the track bed for about two kilometres until you reach the east end of Loch Dochart. The ruined castle engulfed by vegetation on the tree covered island in the loch is said to be one of the seven towers built by Black Duncan of the Cowl. *The Black Book of Taymouth* records that it was burnt down in 1646. According to *The New Statistical Account of Scotland* one severe winter;

> This castle was... taken by the MacGregors, who approached it on the ice, and having surprised the inmates, put them all to the sword.

Leave the path here and walk a few hundred metres along the grass verge of the A85 past Portnellan holiday lodges then cross the road. A small wooden sign about 150 metres east of Benmore Farm reading *To Ben More* points the way. There is limited space to park cars here on the verge of the A85.

Go through the undergrowth at the side of the road and over a stile (dogs have to be lifted over). Once over the fence turn left along a track. The bulky mass of Ben More's grassy slopes can be seen ahead. Higher up are crags and a hanging corrie with an old wall along the edge of it. Near the track a large boulder, out of reach of grazing sheep and deer, has sprouted a bonnet of heather. Meadow pipits flit from boulder to dry stone wall and back. Follow the track as it climbs up through the fields in a series of hairpin bends.

Climb over a stile next to a gate at the 300 metre contour line (again difficult for dogs – the Labradoodle managed to leap it on the way back). In summer there is sometimes a herd of cattle on the hillside beyond the gate.

WHO OWNS BEN MORE?

Most of Ben More is owned by Ben More Farm and Judith Bowser, Suie Estate, Auchlyne, Killin, FK21 8RG.

Past the gate stay on the track and walk south through Benmore Glen for about one and a half kilometres with the Benmore Burn closes by on your right most of the way. The hills on the west side of Benmore Glen are thickly forested. Where the lower slopes of Ben More form the east side of the glen a few Scots pines and birch trees climb up the boulder strewn craggy hillside. Prominent on the skyline at the head of Benmore glen is the low col linking Stob Binnein and Cruach Ardrain. Grass grows on the floor of the glen providing good grazing. Clumps of soft rush sprout around an old sheep pen. In autumn dead thistles stand in clusters near the path, and on the wetter bits of hillside common butterwort can be found. Although I climbed Ben More on a sunny day in the middle of September there were still midges around at grass level.

Walk past a large lichen and moss covered boulder that stands by the path. The morning I walked up Benmore Glen the tops of the mountains were shrouded in mist. It was autumn again and on the grassy banks of the Benmore burn a rowan tree was red with berries.

The track ends at a fallen down wooden bridge by a few lonely birch trees. The deck of the bridge looks to have been constructed from the chassis of a wheeled vehicle possibly a railway carriage. To the left the col between Ben More and Stob Binnein, the Bealach-eadar-dha Beinn, can be seen. *The Ultimate Guide to the Munros* advises against taking 'a diagonal shortcut up the grassy hillside to reach the bealach'. This is good advice; it's best to keep on the rough footpath that continues south beside the Benmore Burn along the grassy floor of the glen for another kilometre past the bridge.

THE MALHOULAKINS

Edward Burt was a military surveyor in the Highlands. In 1754 he published a book called *Letters from a Gentleman in the North of Scotland*. His job as a surveyor necessarily entailed working out of doors where Burt encountered the dreaded highland midge, the Gaelic name of which is *meanbh-chuileag*;

I have been sometimes vexed with a little Plague (if I may use the Expression), but do not you think I am too grave upon the subject; there are great Swarms of little Flies which the Natives call *Malhoulakins: Houlack*, they tell me, signifies, in the Country Language, a *Fly*, and *Houlakin* is the Diminutive of that Name. These are so very small, that, separately, they are but just perceptible and that is all; and, being of a blackish Colour, when a Number of them settle upon the Skin, they make it look as if it was dirty; there they soon bore with their little Augers into the Pores, and change the Face from black to red.

They are only troublesome (I should say intolerable) in Summer, when there is a profound Calm; for the least Breath of Wind immediately disperses them; and the only Refuge from them is the House, into which I never knew them to enter. Sometimes, when I have been talking to any one, I have (though with the utmost Self-denial) endured their Stings to watch his Face, and see how long they would suffer him to be quiet; but in three or four seconds, he has slapped his Hand upon his Face, and in great Wrath cursed the little Vermin...

Walk along the path which cattle have trampled and made muddy in places, to near NN42100 23500 from where the two streams that flow down the hillside from the Bealach-eadar-dha Beinn can be seen. On a grassy strip of hillside between the two streams stands a huge boulder. Take the faint path, it climbs the hillside to the right of the second stream and the boulder.

One November climbing Ben More with Morag and two of his colleagues. An early start from Edinburgh... I crouch in the heather and snow... Thermos flask coffee... chocolate biscuits. I empty the contents of a plastic pill box into the palm of my hand. Wash them down with rucksack chilled water from a plastic bottle. I don't explain this handful of white tablets and red capsules. They don't ask.

A large bird of prey circles overhead as I climb up beside the stream. A rowan grows from a crack in a boulder. Ferns and moss edge the stream as it flows down over smooth black rock and tormentil grows among the grass by the path.

It's an easier climb up to the Bealach-eadar-dha Beinn than the steep climb directly up the north-west shoulder of the mountain from Benmore Farm. I have glimpses of the upper slopes of Ben More and Stob Binnein as they drift in and out of the mist. Ravens fly around the rocky crags on Stob Binnein's lower slopes. From high up near the bealach the huge boulders that dot the floor of Benmore Glen look like pebbles.

Both types of ladies' mantle grow by the stream here. The sides of the rocks are white with lichen, their tops capped with woolly fringe moss. A fox scat in the grass by the path is speckled with the remains of autumn berries.

The footpath ends at about 840 metres at another large boulder a short distance below the bealach. It's worth noting the position of this boulder in order to find the footpath easily on the way down. From the wide grassy Bealach-eadar-dha Beinn (862m) pick up a well-worn path and head north up the steep but easy south ridge of Ben More. Tucked in among rocks seamed with white quartz and green lichen are two ptarmigan, mottled grey and brown on top and white underneath. Just below the summit of Ben More, crags I had forgotten about loom out of the mist. These rocky steps can look slightly daunting in bad weather but can be bypassed or easily climbed over even by a man with a labradoodle on a lead.

Transits of Venus are rare astronomical events similar to solar eclipses of the moon. Eighteenth century astronomers had predicted that the planet Venus was set to pass between the Earth and the sun and would be seen as a dark spot moving across the face of the sun. By careful observation of this phenomenon astronomers hoped to measure the size of and distance to, the sun. During the 1760s there were two transits of Venus and groups of 18th century astronomers travelled to many remote parts of the world to make astronomical observations of the phenomena;

Midge Muncher

The midge has its enemies too. This plant, common butterwort, looks like a starfish and is
insectivorous. The leaves of are coated in a sticky substance that traps small insects like midges.

Captain Cook led an expedition sent to Tahiti and Nevil Maskeleyne, the
Astronomer Royal, who we will meet on Schiehallion, journeyed to St
Helena in 1761. An unknown group of astronomers travelled to the
Scottish Highlands and made the first recorded ascent of Ben More in
1769 in order to view the transit of Venus.

A few years later on 17 September 1776 a group of soldiers working
on General William Roy's military survey of the Highlands climbed the
hill and recorded its height barometrically. William Roy was born in 1726
in Lanarkshire and was most famous in his day for studying Roman Britain
but he also played an important role in the development of Scottish cartography and was a pioneer of the Ordnance Survey. Following the crushing
of the 1745 Jacobite rebellion the victorious Duke of Cumberland
ordered a military survey to be carried out of Scotland because the maps
he had access to during his 1745–6 campaign were so poor and General
William Roy as he now was took charge of this survey. John MacCulloch
who explored the Scottish hills in the early 19th century climbed Ben More
and commented; 'the ascent is so easy as to permit riding to the top.'

Go to the right along a little path on grass when you reach the first
crag if you don't want to climb over it. A short distance beyond is the
second crag which can be turned on the left. If bypassing the crags keep
close to them, don't drift off downhill. There is no difficulty and soon the
summit of Ben More (1,174m) with its trig point and cairn is reached.

Flecks of mica schist glisten on the ground by the cairn. Among the
rocks on the mountain's summit are patches of woolly fringe moss and tufts
of fir club moss. 'On high Benmore green mosses grow' wrote Sir Walter
Scott in *The Lord of the Isles*. The dogs wait patiently, tied to my rucksack
while I take photos and chat to a couple who know Alan MacRae from
Assynt from whom I got my old dog Cuilean when she was a puppy.

Ben More's north side contains a long-lasting snow patch which,
uniquely in the southern highlands, is named on the 1:25000 Ordnance
Survey map. It is called the Cuidhe Chrom, Gaelic for crooked wreath,
because of the shape which forms in late spring and sometimes lasts into
June. There is a Cuidhe Chrom on Lochnagar too. Look out for snow
buntings near the summit of Ben More; the altitude, long lying snow and
crags are the kind of habitat favoured by these visitors from the Arctic.

I watch as a long goods train carrying bauxite to the aluminium
smelter at Fort William crosses the girder viaduct in Crianlarich 3,000
feet below. Below the summit crags of Ben More the ridge drops down

to the Bealach-eadar-dha Beinn and through the mist a path can be seen climbing up the ridge to the summit of Stob Binnein. Lochans glint on the long south ridge of the mountain that rises from Inverlochlarig.

The summit of Ben More is nearly 4,000 feet high and feels it; a helicopter flies along Glen Dochart hundreds of feet below me. The mist has cleared and the dogs lead the way down. I pause for a last look at the mountains. In *The Scottish Peaks* WA Poucher described the view from Ben More;

> ... on a clear day the Cairngorms can be seen far away to the north-east... both Edinburgh and Glasgow can be picked out; while to the west Rhum and Jura can be distinguished on the glistening sea.

Mountains can be dangerous places; it was a winter ascent of Ben More that convinced WW Naismith, the 'father' of the Scottish Mountaineering Club, that Scotland's mountains needed to be treated as seriously as the Alps. The traditional route up Ben More takes a *directissima* line up the north-west spur of the mountain but is not as straightforward as it looks on the map. The path is faint in places and can be difficult to follow and in poor visibility it is easy to wander off route and end up on very steep ground. It can also be difficult to find the start of the path back down to Benmore Farm from the summit in bad weather so the north-west spur is not recommended as a descent route.

One of the earliest recorded mountaineering accidents on the Scottish hills occurred on Ben More. On 3 January 1874 Daniel Bower Mitchell a 27-year-old Dundee businessman slipped on ice and fell to his death during a winter ascent of the mountain. A search was carried out by local shepherds who located his body using sheep dogs. No stretcher being available in those days the victim was carried down the mountain on a ladder. An iron cross and plaque on the north side of Ben More marks the place where Mitchell's body was found.

More than a century later Ben More was the scene of a black day for Killin mountain rescue team. Sunday 1 February 1987 was a bright spring like day. During the afternoon the team was called out to Balquhidder to recover the body of a hill walker who had collapsed near Inverlochlarig. While there the mountain rescue team were diverted to Ben More following a report of a climber having fallen on the snow covered mountain. Members of the team set out up Ben More on foot to try to locate the climber. A Wessex helicopter was attempting to land on the mountainside to drop off another two members of the team to assist in the search of the hillside when the helicopter's rotor blades struck a rock. The aircraft crashed into the hillside and slid down the mountain towards the rescuers already on the hill, who were able to pull the crew of the helicopter clear before the aircraft burst into flames. But police sergeant Harry Lawrie was thrown from the helicopter during the crash and sustained fatal injuries. He is commemorated by an iron cross on the summit of Ben Ledi. The injured were treated at the scene and evacuated to hospital by a second helicopter.

But the team's job was not finished and they returned to the mountain at first light the following morning to recover the body of the female climber who had instigated the call out. According to Killin Mountain Rescue Team's website she was found at the foot of a steep snow slope with a new pair of crampons still in her rucksack.

Ben More Map

BEN MORE (1,174m)

Grade	***
Map:	OS Sheets 51
Distance/Ascent:	10km/994m
Starting height:	180m
Time to top:	3h +breaks
Public Transport Start/Finish:	Crianlarich
Car Start/Finish:	Glen Dochart

An ascent of one of the highest Munros in the Southern Highlands from the West Highland railway.

ROUTE:

1   From Crianlarich station walk down into village. Turn right along main road signposted *Stirling*. Walk E along pavement past Ben More restaurant to white painted Inverardran cottage.

2   Turn left and walk through cottage's parking area. Go through metal gate. Turn right along disused railway.

3   Follow footpath along track bed for about 2km to E end of Loch Dochart where there is a metal gate next to A85. Leave path here and walk a few hundred metres along grass verge A85.

4   Cross road near Benmore Farm to small wooden sign reading *To Ben More* NN41449 2594. *If driving begin walk here.*

5   Go through the undergrowth at the side of the road and over stile. Turn left along track.

6   Keep left at a fork in the path a short distance from the stile.

7   At the 300m contour climb over stile next to gate.

8   Stay on the track and walk south through Benmore Glen for about 1.5km.

9   Reach fallen down bridge NN41806 24061. Continue on footpath by Benmore Burn for another 1km.

10 Near NN42100 23500 two streams flow down from the Bealach-eadar-dha Beinn. Follow a faint path up the hillside to the right of a huge boulder and the second stream.

11 Footpath ends at about 840m at another large boulder NN43106 23496.

12 From the Bealach-eadar-dha Beinn (862m) follow path up south ridge of Ben More.

13 Go to the right along a little path on grass when you reach the first crag NN43325 24290 (1,147m) if you don't want to climb over it.

14 The second crag NN43303 24323 (1,168m) can be turned on the left.

15 Reach summit Ben More (1,174m) NN43283 24415.

16 Return by route of ascent.

PUBLIC TRANSPORT: train leaves Glasgow at 8.21am arriving Crianlarich

10.09am. Train departs Crianlarich 7.33pm arriving Glasgow 9.31pm (no suitable trains on Sundays). Allow 30 min to walk from Crianlarich to Benmore Farm. Full public transport details at www.travelinescotland.com or phone 0871 200 22 33.

CAR PARKING: is limited to the verge of the A85 near Benmore Farm. If driving from Crianlarich, Benmore Farm is on the right about 3km east of Crianlarich just after sign to Portnellan Holiday Lodges. Coming from Stirling; pass the Luib Hotel and after a series of bends pass a sign to Loch an Iubhair, then a large layby on the right and finally a sign for Portnellan lodges. Park on the verge of the A85 next to a small wooden sign reading *To Ben More* NN41449 25945.

DOGS: lots of sheep and some cattle on Ben More so abide by the Outdoor Access Code. Also a couple of stiles/fences that dogs have to be lifted over.

STALKING: www.outdooraccess-scotland.com then click on Walking and Stalking link.

WINTER CONDITIONS: ice axe and crampons needed. Return by route of ascent only.

Somewhere Else: The Real Food Café, Tyndrum.

CHAPTER THIRTEEN

The Battle for Rothiemurchus

So many summers and I have lived them too.

Norman MacCaig

THE RIVER SPEY HAS its source in the heather covered hills at the head of Glen Roy beyond the pass where General Wade's military road climbs the headwall of Corrieyairack in a dramatic series of hairpin bends. From the old stone bridge at Garva the Spey flows down past Newtonmore and Kingussie and through the Forest of Rothiemurchus home to pine marten, osprey and capercaillie. Beyond the forest the Cairngorm mountains rise, a blue wall above the ancient Scots pines.

The Victorian railway network reached Aviemore in 1863 30 years before the building of the West Highland Line to Fort William. As a result the village of Aviemore and surrounding area of Strathspey became an established 19th century tourist destination. Today the area forms part of Scotland's largest national park and it was here during the closing years of the 19th century that a battle between landowners and hillwalkers was fought over access to the high tops of the Cairngorms which foreshadowed 20th century right to roam legislation and in which Caleb was to play a role. This chapter tells that story.

'Twenty-five holidays had we spent near the Cairngorms...' wrote Caleb in 1907. Not for him the fashionable Clyde resorts of Rothesay and Dunoon. Caleb and Alice travelled by train to Aviemore each Easter and summer holiday. I see Caleb peering out of the steamed up train windows at dense mist, patches of snow and dripping fences as 'the clouds rested on the carriage tops' at Drumochter.

Summers were spent in a cottage near Loch an Eilein or at the hamlet of Inverdruie to the east of Aviemore, in the 1900s a remoter, quieter place than today. Sitting in the cottage at Inverdruie one evening Caleb and Alice hear a strange, roaring noise outside; '... what's that?' they ask; 'surely it's not another car'. As he cycled along the sandy track into Aviemore on those sunny summer mornings Caleb could not have conceived of today's A9 jammed with thousands of cars, buses and lorries.

Caleb and Alice made friends with local people over the course of those 25 summer and Easter holidays in Strathspey. Among their friends, Walter Dempster, the school teacher at Inverdruie, with whom Caleb would have had many shared interests and Alexander Campbell the shoe maker and postman at Aviemore who took the photographs of chambered cairns and hill forts that illustrated the articles Caleb wrote about archaeology.

Caleb came to know the countryside around Aviemore well referring in his writing to the 'ancient Monadh Ruadh' and the Rathad nam Meirlach (The Thieves' Road). During his first holiday in Strathspey Caleb fell under the spell of the Cairngorms most especially Braeriach and Loch an Eilein;

> ... great mountain mass, steep crag, narrow pass, forest of fir and birch, tangle of juniper and heather, rushing stream, and placid loch with its solitary island crowned by the ruins of an old castle.

Sometimes a loch forms a backdrop to life... for me it is Loch Etive... for Caleb it was Loch an Eilein. Today chaffinches flit among the old Scots pines on the shore of Loch an Eilein. People on mountain bikes cycle around the loch with its island and ruined castle as Caleb did at the dawn of the 20th century. Several cottages stand among the trees. Some are still lived in, another is now a visitor centre and shop where the old kitchen range still burns and wood smoke comes out of the chimney. It was to Loch an Eilein that Caleb came on holiday and standing in the cottage that is now the visitor centre I find myself wondering if this was where he stayed, spending evenings smoking his pipe by the kitchen fire, then wandering outside to look at the stars

TALES TOLD IN ROTHIEMURCHUS

At the beginning of the 20th century there was a reawakening of interest in folklore and man of the times that he was, Caleb developed an interest in Highland folk tales and the second sight. The locals told Caleb the old stories; 'usually at the close of the day when we were seated at the kitchen fire indulging in tobacco and gossip.' Afterwards he wrote them down as 'Tales Told in Rothiemurchus' published in *The Cairngorm Club Journal* in 1909.

Caleb and Alice first holidayed in the Strathspey area in 1891. The years from 1880–1925 encompassed what environmental historian Robert Lambert has dubbed The Battle for Rothiemurchus. During this period the Rothiemurchus Estate was the focus of a campaign mounted by the Scottish Rights of Way Society in response to requests for action from tourists, walkers and mountaineers who;

> ... came to see Rothiemurchus estate as a recreational gem, and a fundamental link in the access route to the high tops of the Cairngorms.

In its early days the Scottish Rights of Way Society (SROWS) was a hard hitting and confrontational organisation. Formed in 1884 the Society worked tirelessly for public access to the Cairngorms, forcing landowners to recognise the existence of public footpaths and rights of way on their estates. In the mid-1880s Loch an Eilein was the scene of a bitter access dispute between the SROWS and the Grant of Rothiemurchus family during which hillwalkers took direct action forcing open locked gates and throwing them off their hinges.

In 1903–04 the dispute flared up again when the new Laird of Rothiemurchus attempted to obstruct the 'driving road' from the south end of Loch an Eilein. The Edinburgh based SROWS was heavily dependent on activists on the ground who played a vital part in their access campaigns and it was by this route that Caleb who spent every Easter and summer in the area became covertly involved in the campaign.

On 18 August 1904 Caleb who was on holiday at Fearn Bank, Aviemore sent a letter to the Edinburgh home of CEW MacPherson of the SROWS which contained revealing information about the financial position of the Rothiemurchus Estate and the delicate relationship between the Laird and Donald Grant of the Royal Bank of Scotland's Grantown-on-Spey branch. One favourite method used by the SROWS to pressurise landowners to allow access was to threaten them with legal action. The information contained in Caleb's letter about the dire state of the Rothiemurchus Estate finances at that time would have been very useful to the Society. Knowing the Laird lacked the money to pay expensive lawyers' bills if the SROWS chose to launch legal action gave the Society the upper hand in the Battle for Rothiemurchus.

> I am writing this separately sending it to your home instead of to your office, because I don't want it to go into any hands but your own...

Popular rumour here, with which as a veteran visitor I am now some little acquainted, makes out that Donald Grant [the bank manager] has JP Grant [the Laird] under his financial control, so that DG is de facto proprietor. I heard the remark made once that DG could put JPG out at his will. It may be well for you to know this, but obviously it would not do for me to tell you! So burn this note.

Weather glorious for three days. No osprey yet.

CHAPTER FOURTEEN

Ben Vorlich

In the Beat of a Dragonfly's Wing

SEEN ON A WINTER'S AFTERNOON from Rob Roy's grave in the old churchyard at Balquhidder, Ben Vorlich appears a sharp pointed cone, white with snow and trailing a plume of spindrift from its peak. There are two Ben Vorlichs in Scotland and at least half a dozen explanations of the meaning of the name of the hill. The Ben Vorlich on Caleb's list is the one on the south shore of Loch Earn described as visible from Arthur's Seat at the 'left-hand end of Cramond Isle'. Standing at the southern edge of the Highlands Ben Vorlich (985m/3,232ft) and its twin Stuc a Chroin are the nearest Munros to Edinburgh.

Timothy Pont sketched Ben Vorlich and named it *Ben Vouirlyg* on his 16th century map of Scotland. In the 1790s Colin Baxter the minister at Comrie explained the name as *Benvourlich* meaning *the mountain of the great lake*; he wrote that Loch Earn is *great* in comparison to the other lochs in Strathearn.

Mh is pronounced *v* in Gaelic and an alternative suggestion is that the name comes from *Beinn Mhòr-Luig* meaning hill of the big hollow or corrie. *Scottish Hill Names* points out that *Beinn Mhòr-Luig is* close to the way the name of the mountain was pronounced by local people a century ago and it fits in with the scenery and the shape of the hill which does have big corries.

In July the little bays along the shore of Loch Earn are popular places to pitch a tent or park a camper van for a night or two. In his classic *History of the Celtic Place-Names of Scotland* published in 1926 WJ Watson wrote that Ben Vorlich got its name from these small bays on Loch Earn. The name was said to come from *Beinn Mhuir'lag* which literally translated means mountain of the sack shaped sea bags or sea bays which is strange as Loch Earn is a freshwater loch. It is thought this name came to be used to describe features of large inland lochs too, such as Loch Lomond, on the shores of which stands the other Ben Vorlich. Furthermore the farm at the foot of the mountain is called Ardvorlich which means the height above the bay, so the generally accepted explanation of the hill's name is the geographical one, the hill of the bays.

Climbing Ben Vorlich

Leave the A84 about half a mile south of Lochearnhead at a road junction signposted *South Loch Earn Road* and drive along the narrow single track road for about four kilometres. Go past the west gate of Ardvorlich House, the road runs along the shore of Loch Earn here and just before a little arched stone bridge there is a parking place. Old oak trees shade the road and Ben Vorlich can be seen beyond the meadow and woodland that surround Ardvorlich House. Walk along the road towards the little arched stone bridge. On the grass verge look out for a weathered gravestone on which is inscribed;

> Near this spot we
> re interred the bo
> dies of 7 Mcdonalds
> of Glencoe killed
> when attempting
> to harry Ardvorlich
> Anno Domini 1620.

The Seven MacDonalds were killed when the Stewarts returned home unexpectedly and were buried without ceremony. The stone marks the spot where their bones were found when the road was being built. A case of no rest for the wicked.

Cross the hump back stone bridge and immediately after it turn right and walk between gateposts topped with urns which may once have decorated the walls of Ardvorlich house.

The driveway to the house is lined with lime trees. Pied wagtails flit across a field of sheep. On the left is a walled garden built to supply Ardvorlich house with fruit and vegetables.

A sign directs hillwalkers to keep right, avoiding the farmyard. In summer swallows and house martins swirl about the roofs of the old farm buildings. Continue along the driveway past a hedge of rhododendron. At an arrow shaped signpost reading 'Hillwalkers', turn left away from the house past tall larches and a copper beech tree.

Ardvorlich House, all turrets and ivy covered walls, was built in 1790 by master mason Robert Ferguson and probably incorporates stonework from an earlier castle on the site. Centuries old home of the Stewarts of Ardvorlich it has a gruesome history and is the Darnlinvarach of Sir Walter Scott's novel *The Legend of Montrose*.

In *Highways and Byways in the Central Highlands* Seton Gordon the famous 20th century naturalist and writer describes climbing Ben Vorlich and afterwards staying the night at Ardvorlich House; 'the fire burned in the hearth and the piper played a tune', which certainly beats chips in Callander after a hillwalk. For many years a family talisman the Clach Dhearg, Gaelic for red stone, was kept at Ardvorlich. This crystal, secured with silver hoops and fitted with a chain, was said to have miraculous properties;

> If the stone were dipped in a pail of water and moved thrice… sun-wise, round the pail, the water would then have healing powers in the illnesses of cattle.

In the crystal wrote Seton Gordon 'a hidden fire' seemed to glow.

Cross a stone bridge over the Ardvorlich Burn. The track continues up Glen Vorlich on the right hand side of the stream. On the far side is a stone built powerhouse part of a small scale hydro-electric scheme recently constructed on the burn. Horses and a foal grazed in the tree dotted parkland behind the house. Go through a gate or climb the stile. There is a splendid old oak tree here. The track crosses a field and climbs uphill away from the stream. On the east side of Glen Vorlich cattle grazed among the trees and bracken. On a hot summer's day in July dragonflies hovered over the path and I could hear the chatter of grasshoppers.

I photographed a golden-ringed dragonfly near the Ardvorlich Burn that day. With its Gaelic name tarbh-nathrach cearcaill-oir the dragon fly is one of the most beautiful insects. Dragonflies are found near slow moving or still water. The adult dragonfly lays its eggs in the muddy sediment at the bottom of a pool or shallow lochan. The larvae of dragonflies live 2–4 years in the soft sediment which allows them to overwinter and survive summer droughts. The insects and plants around these pools provide the dragonfly with food and shelter. A dragonfly can beat its wings independently allowing it to fly backwards as well as forwards and this combined with its highly developed eyesight makes the dragonfly a superb predator.

And when you look at a dragonfly on a sunny day remember it lives for only a few short weeks of summer. The winter ice survived in the mud at the foot of the lochan, the summer's scorching drought… all there in the beat of a dragonfly's wings.

Purple and white fox gloves poke up through the bracken by the side of the stony track, high above the tree lined burn and heading straight towards the north shoulder of Ben Vorlich. The track crosses a low bridge of old railway sleepers and fords several side streams on their way to join the Ardvorlich Burn down in the glen. A larger stream is crossed by a wooden bridge. Rowans and birches grow among moss and lichen covered stones here. The stream pours over blue grey rocks worn smooth by the peaty water. Last time I climbed Ben Vorlich the burn had been spoiled by an ugly concrete intake, part of the 'micro' hydro-electric scheme which has scarred the east side of Glen Vorlich with a dirt track road. Just past the bridge a lone boulder stands among grass and bracken. Past the boulder the vegetation on the hillside begins to change; cross-leaved heath, marsh orchids and hare's tail cotton grass grow among the heather.

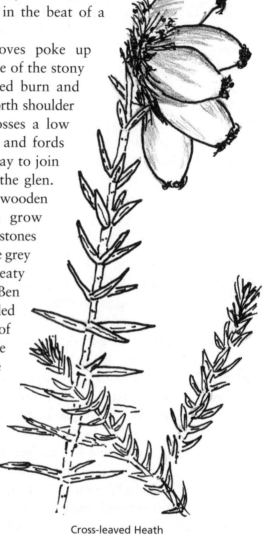

Cross-leaved Heath

The track becomes a well maintained path with carefully constructed rainwater gullies and flights of steps where tormentil grows in the gaps between the stones. Purple thistles grow among rocks speckled with orange and grey lichen and meadow pipits fly across the blaeberry covered moorland. To the north, across Loch Earn I can see Ben Lawers.

As height is gained the north ridge of Ben Vorlich becomes more defined; in Gaelic its name is Sgiath nan Tarmachan, the wing of the ptarmigan. Other hills come into sight among them Ben More and Stob

Meadow Pipit

Binnein are easy to recognise. Just above the 600 metre contour line ignore a walkers' path that forks to the right. Stay on the main path which becomes very wide, eroded and in need of repair – it is easy to follow and unless snow covered, difficult to lose.

FATHER BURN

At New Year 1918 a young priest called Ronnie Burn, keen to learn about winter mountaineering climbed an icy gully on Ben Vorlich with the legendary Scottish climber Harold Raeburn. Five years later in 1923 Ronnie Burn became the first man to complete all the Munros and subsidiary tops, 558 peaks over 3,000 feet in total; the first 'Compleat Munroist'. A tiny short legged, hunchback with a black beard Burn had a hard life. From a young age he lacked any real family and spent a miserable childhood at boarding school. In the years 1914–1927 Burn climbed on the Scottish mountains, almost always alone, walking very fast and covering huge distances even in mid-winter. In remote farmhouses and crofts such as Alltbeithe in Glen Affric and Loch a'Bhraoin in Wester Ross he sometimes had a taste of the home and family life he had never experienced. The local people called him Father Burn. Due to government spending cuts following the Wall Street Crash in America Burn lost his job as a lecturer at Glasgow

University and had to move south to live in Ipswich. Made homeless following the death of his father, by 1937 Burn was living as a down and out on the streets of Edinburgh's old town. His luck changed in 1938 when he got a job in Oxford but although he lived into his eighties Burn never climbed in the Scottish hills again. In 1967 when he was 79 he returned to Scotland for a last nostalgic journey around the Highlands... by car.

In summer purple patches on the sides of the glen show where the heather has been burnt to promote new growth. I stop by some strange shaped rocks on the hillside – below me the path winds across the moorland and down Glen Vorlich to Ardvorlich House among the trees by the shore of Loch Earn.

LOCHAN NA MNA

To the east of Ben Vorlich, Beinn Domhnuill sends out a long ridge above Glen Vorlich. High up on this ridge lies a lochan unnamed on the Ordnance Survey 1:50000 map but traditionally known as Lochan Na Mna or the lochan of the woman. This lochan is connected to a bloodthirsty incident in the 16th century. Drummond of Drummondernoch was the King's forester and his daughter was married to Stewart of Ardvorlich. One day Drummond caught some MacGregors poaching the King's deer and according to the gruesome punishment of the time cut their ears off with his knife. The MacGregors soon took their revenge. They captured Drummond, cut his head off and took it to his daughter's home at Ardvorlich. Keeping the head hidden they asked for food and in the manner of Highland hospitality in days gone by, Drummond's daughter put bread, cheese and oatcakes on the table and left the room. When she returned her father's head was on the table with the bread and cheese stuffed into his mouth. Traumatised and terrified the woman fled to the hills above Ardvorlich House and hid at the high shielings, near the lochan for ever afterwards known as Lochan na Mna. Meanwhile the MacGregors took the head to the church at Balquhidder where they placed it on the altar and swore an oath they would all take the blame for their deed.

The final section of the climb is up the steep scree strewn upper slopes of Ben Vorlich. I can see the trig point perched on the summit ridge above. Blaeberry grows among the boulders. Alpine-ladies mantle and common butterwort cling to the eroded scree and gravel at the edge of the path.

WHO OWNS BEN VORLICH?

The Stewarts of Ardvorlich, Ardvorlich Estate, Ardvorlich, Perthshire, FK19 6QE. The Stewarts of Ardvorlich have lived at Ardvorlich for over 500 years. The estate is still run by the family as a working sheep farm.

Follow the path as it leads increasingly steeply up the last part of the north shoulder to reach the trig point that marks the summit of Ben Vorlich. There are dramatic views from here to the broken buttress of Stuc a'Chroin across the Bealach an Dubh Choirein. Seton Gordon described how he;

> climbed the hill at sunrise on a May morning and, although the Lowlands were then hidden in haze, the view west... was clear and extended as far as the peak of Goat Fell on Arran.

The trig point on the west top is the highest point (986m) on the mountain but walk out along the ridge 100 metres to the east top (984m) for views south-east to Dumyat and the Ochils, the Wallace monument, the River Forth and Glen Artney where Sir Walter Scott's epic poem *The Lady of the Lake* begins with the lines;

> *The stag at eve had drunk his fill,*
> *Where danced the moon on Monan's rill,*
> *And deep his midnight lair had made*
> *In lone Glenartney's hazel shade;*
> *But when the sun his beacon red*
> *Had kindled on Benvoirlich's head,*
> *The deep-mouthed bloodhound's heavy bay*
> *Resounded up the rocky way.*

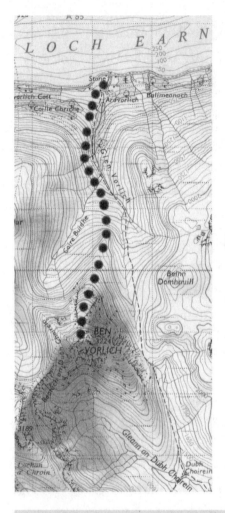

Ben Vorlich Map

BEN VORLICH (985m)

Grade **
Map: OS Sheets 51 and 57
Distance/Ascent: 9km/885m
Starting height: 100m
Time to top: 2h30min +breaks
Start/Finish: Loch Earn

A straightforward route on paths all the way. Rivals Ben Lomond as easiest ascent of a Munro in the Southern Highlands.

1   Leave the A84 about 1km south of Lochearnhead at road junction signposted *South Loch Earn Road* and drive along narrow single track road for about 4km.

2   A few hundred metres past the west gate to Ardvorlich House there is a parking place NN63210 23200.

3   Walk east along road. Immediately after road crosses stone bridge turn right through east gate of Ardvorlich House (signposted *Ardvorlich House*).

4   Keep right at entrance to farmyard and cross bridge over Ardvorlich Burn.

5   At an arrow shaped signpost reading *Hillwalkers* turn left away from Ardvorlich House.

6   Go through gate/over stile. Follow track across field and up Glen Vorlich on right hand side of Ardvorlich Burn.

7   Follow track across a low bridge of railway sleepers.

8   Keep right at a fork in the track NN63048 21820.

9   Cross wooden bridge.

10 Track becomes a well maintained footpath when moorland is reached.

11 At 624m NN62897 19817 ignore a walkers path that forks to the right. Stay on main path (easy to follow and unless covered in snow, difficult to lose).

12 Follow path up scree strewn upper slopes of Ben Vorlich as it leads increasingly steeply up last part of N shoulder.

13 Reach trig point that marks summit Ben Vorlich (985m) NN62900 18900.

14 Return by same route.

DOGS: there are signs asking dog owners to keep dogs under strict control/ on leads – there are a lot of sheep and lambs on Ben Vorlich. A barbed wire covered gate at NN63022 22064 is sometimes locked but there is a stile you can get dogs over.

WINTER CONDITIONS: ice axe and crampons needed. Steep and icy near the summit.

CHAPTER FIFTEEN

Ben Cleuch

Lady Alva's Web

Ένας πολιτισμός ανθεί όταν οι άνθρωποι φυτεύουν δένδρα
κάτω απο τα οποία ποτε δεν θα καθίσουν.

A civilization flourishes when people plant trees under which
they will never sit.

Greek proverb

IN THE 18th CENTURY the shopkeepers of Edinburgh's Lawnmarket sold
a type of heavy cloth they called Tillicoultry serge. The Tillicoultry Burn
which pours down from the Ochil Hills through a narrow gorge known
in Scots as a *cleugh* provided a useful source of power for the textile
mills of Tillicoultry at the beginning of the industrial revolution. The
highest point of the Ochils, Ben Cleuch (721m/2,365ft) cannot be seen
from Tillicoultry. It stands a couple of kilometres back from the steep
southern scarp slope of the Ochils but is well seen from the summit of
Arthur's Seat 30 miles away in line with the right-hand end of Cramond
Island, 55 degrees west of north.

The steep slopes of the Ochils, they rise up to 400 metres almost from
sea level at an angle of 35 degrees in places, give the hills a dramatic
profile, made all the more striking by the way they are set against the
flat plain of the River Forth. Some have interpreted the name Ben Cleuch
as hill of the ravine or narrow glen. The Scottish Mountaineering Club
guidebook *The Corbetts and Other Scottish Hills* (Ben Cleuch is a
Graham) gives the meaning of Ben Cleuch as 'gullied hill' from the Gaelic
ben meaning hill and *cleugh*, the Scots word for a gully. This explanation
is problematic though because Gaelic and Scots words are hardly ever
found together in hill names.

In 1783 the hill was known as *Benclach*, in 1790 as *Ben-Cloch*, in
1848 as *Benclach* and in 1869 as *Ben Cloich*. As recently as 1957 it was
mapped *Ben Clach* by the Ordnance Survey (see page 145). *Scottish Hill
Names* suggests these historical spellings all point to the Gaelic word
clach (genitive/possessive form *cloich*) which means a rock or stone. There

are distinctive rocks near the summit of Ben Cleuch and these stones uniquely identify this grassy hill for navigational purposes in a way that hill of the *cleughs* does not as many of the Ochils are riven by gullies.

The Scottish winters of past centuries were colder than today's and in 1836 Andrew Robertson wrote;

> ... at the bottom of a ridge of rock, near the summit of Bencloch, where it is sheltered from every wind, snow is frequently seen in the month of June. From the singular appearance of the narrow and extended sheet of snow, it has received the fanciful name of *Lady Alva's Web*.

Climbing Ben Cleuch

One approach to Ben Cleuch starts from the Woodland Park on the A91 between Alva and Tillicoultry. The Woodland Park was originally planted as an informal garden, part of the grounds of the demolished Alva House. Alva House is one of Scotland's lost country houses. Designed by the architect Robert Adam and originally the home of the Erskine family in the 18th century, Carolin Johnstone inherited it in 1890, but ran up such big debts that the sale of the estate could not cover them. By the 1920s the house had been abandoned and was used as target practice during the Second World War and reduced to ruins. From the entrance to the car park turn right (east) along the Hillfoots Link path to Tillicoultry past the fine old 18th century stables block with arched windows, all that remains of the old Alva House. Behind the Stables the trees of Wood Hill Wood (their branches bare of leaves in November) climb up the steep south facing slope of the Ochils.

Where the track turns right at a line of mossy boulders continue straight on along a footpath. Among the rushes at the edge of a field, an old stone sink, used as an animal trough would fetch £100 at the architectural salvage yard in Edinburgh. The buildings of Tillicoultry come into view, Knock Hill and the Pentlands in the distance.

Rhododendron grows high at the side of the path. This shrub introduced from the Himalayas in the late-18th century on account of its beautiful flowers is common throughout Wood Hill Wood but chokes out other vegetation if not controlled. Planted in the grounds of many Scottish country houses, it probably escaped from the garden of Alva House.

The path crosses a stream that flows down from one of the thickly

An early 20th century postcard of Alva House
[*The DiCamillo Companion Ltd*].

wooded, gorse and bramble filled cleughs so characteristic of the Ochil Hills. Where the path comes out of Wood Hill Wood and runs along the edge of Tillicoultry golf course a man appears walking three German Shepherds; Cuilean makes literally to turn tail and flee. It is the beginning of November. In the garden of a house on the edge of Tillicoultry a big heap of wood is stacked ready for bonfire night.

At a *Hillfoots Link* sign on the outskirts of Tillicoultry the track joins a tarmac road. Three grey squirrels running about on the ground here are quite bold until the Labradoodle barks at them and they shoot up a tall old tree beside the road.

The path emerges from bushes at a pink sandstone Victorian villa behind a stone wall with a row of tall evergreen trees in the garden and an electricity pole nearby. Go along a little lane into Scotland Place past a white painted cottage. Some of the old cottages in Tillicoultry were originally built for weavers.

Cross a footbridge with green painted iron railings over the Tillicoultry Burn near the Clock Mill. With the hills at the end of the street it's hard to see this as a dark satanic mill. The Ochils are reminiscent of the Lancashire mill towns and Welsh valleys in the way they rise straight up behind the streets of Tillicoultry and Alva.

Upper Mill Street is a quiet part of town today but at one time the foot bridge must have been busy as people hurried to work at six in the morning, toiling in the Clock Mill until seven at night in 1841. The mill manufactured blankets, plaids and tartan shawls. Built in 1824 it was initially powered by water from the Tillicoultry Burn. This stream was the source of Tillicoultry's wealth in the 19th century and led to the construction of many of the buildings seen in the town today. The fast flowing water once powered eight textile mills using a system of lades (water channels). A dam on the Tillicoultry burn in Mill Glen used to collect water overnight to power the mills. In the middle of the 19th century *The New Statistical Account of Scotland* recorded that 300 men, 120 women and 140 children were employed in the mills of Tillicoultry. Textile mills and coal mines remained the biggest employers of local people until the 1950s.

If using public transport the corner of the High Street (A91) and Upper Mill Street marks the starting point for climbing Ben Cleuch. At the top of Upper Mill Street where a pre-1960 road sign reads *The Glen* follow the east bank of the stream into Mill Glen. A newer signpost warns that the path passes above cliffs and that rocks can fall on it at any time. Anyhow I survived to write this account.

Go through a metal gate and shortly after pass the shallow cave known as the Lion's Den NS91387 97628. A small gully which passes underneath the Lion's Den indicates the actual line of the Ochil fault, the crack in the Earth's crust, movement of which over 300 million years ago gave rise to the steep southern scarp of the Ochil Hills. Elsewhere the Ochils Fault coincides approximately with the line of the old road along the base of the hills.

The path crosses from one side of the stream and then back to the other on a succession of bridges as it sneaks its way through Mill Glen. The day I climbed Ben Cleuch there were lakes in the flat fields around Stirling and the hills were holding a lot of rain water. The Tillicoultry burn was roaring down – white and fast flowing. To the left of the path a large quarry has gnawed into the flank of the hillside and a pinnacle ridge looms over the heaps of gravel and rocks. Whinstone was quarried here.

Go through a metal gate with a box labelled *Access and Safety Information* (empty). The name Mill Glen has a sleepy peaceful feel but in reality it is a deep ravine, its steep sides mossy and thickly wooded. Ivy hangs down the dripping walls of the gorge and ferns grow in cracks in the rock. Wild flowers and shrubs flourish under the trees and higher up dense thickets of gorse grow beneath crags. Mill Glen is too steep for sheep grazing and so it was left as woodland – the path by the Tillicoultry Burn with railings, flights of steps and concrete bridges was engineered in 1926.

The Ochils are not Highland hills, the Highlands do not begin until after the Highland boundary fault north of Strathallan but their steep slopes and deep gullies should be treated with respect. A few years back with two friends (both compleat Munroists and members of one of Scotland's oldest climbing clubs) I followed a circular route from Dollar to Tillicoultry outlined by a 'professional' mountaineer in his weekly column in a Scottish newspaper. Despite having the newspaper cutting with us and following its rather vague instructions carefully my two companions and I ended up stuck at the top of the cliffs of Tillicoultry quarry in the rapidly gathering darkness of a winter afternoon contemplating the unthinkable prospect of being benighted on the Ochils within sight and sound of the streets of Tillicoultry. Fighting our way through steep gorse and over fallen trees we ended up scrambling down a steep rubble and bramble filled cleugh in Wood Hill Wood. The moral of the story; beware of attempting to descend the sides of Mill Glen, there are crags, cliffs and sheer drops hidden by dense vegetation and always buy a guidebook written by someone who has actually done the walk.

Looking north up Mill Glen between cliffs and crags I can see the lower slopes of the Law, coloured orange by dead bracken. Beside a bridge high above the stream a holly tree grows straight out of a cliff. The path a ledge cut into the side of the gorge. Near the head of the glen where the Daiglen Burn and the Gannel burn meet there is a wooden bench. I stopped for food there once on the way down from Ben Cleuch (raining, too cold to stop for long higher up). A solitary rowan grows by the stream at the foot of The Law, still covered in red berries in November.

Just past the bench leave the engineered path and the railings at a hairpin bend and climb down to a wooden foot bridge over the Gannel Burn at the rocky base of the Law. Careful on this short descent – the rocks can be slippery; I manage with two dogs on leads pulling furiously to get at some sheep higher up the hillside. Immediately after crossing the Gannel Burn a short easy scramble leads to the grassy footpath up the bracken and gorse covered lower slopes of the Law.

It's a steep climb to the summit of The Law but in summer the path is fairly easy to follow up the grassy hillside. The mist is down on the top of The Law and Ben Cleuch but below me I can see the ox bows of the River Forth winding down to the two bridges at Kincardine. To the

The Law from Mill Glen
Law is a Scots word for a hill, equivalent to the Gaelic *beinn*. *Law* is mainly found
in the names of rounded hills with a slightly conical shape in the south and east of Scotland.
Law comes from an old English word *Hlāw*.

south extensive views open out across the flat plain of industrial Central
Scotland with Longannet power station and the smoking chimneys of the
Grangemouth petro-chemical complex in the distance. To the east the
Gannel Burn flows down a deep glen and on King's Seat Hill the russet
bracken spread like shadows across the hillside.

Near the 450 metre contour a large rock stands beside the path – local
hillwalkers call it *halfway boulder*. I stop, out of breath, legs aching and
look around. Below me Central Scotland is disappearing into the mist. The
hillside changes at this height – the steep sided cleugh of Mill Glen eases
back and the vegetation of the gorge, bracken and thorny gorse, gives way
to the tussocky grass and moss heath of the upper slopes of Ben Cleuch.

Low cloud. Mist. All I can see, the occasional lichen covered rock,
little orange fungi (three distinct types), tall clumps of soft rush and

(change of texture on the hillside) a lone patch of stones. The dogs bedraggled, cold and wet. Smir of misty drizzle. Droplets of water on blades of grass. The flicker of the GPS arrow. The floating compass needle. This was my world for an hour or two.

At about 600 metres you reach a fence (often a useful navigational aid on a hill) it can be followed to the top of the Law (638m) and onto the summit of Ben Cleuch. A path, boggy and eroded in places, runs beside the fence for most of the way and dips down to a shallow col north of the Law before climbing to the summit of Ben Cleuch (721m). The indicator donated by the *Daily Record* in 1930 lists the peaks visible from Ben Cleuch but has suffered from the mountain climate and despite restoration in 1990 is difficult to read in freezing cold mist. Ben Cleuch is one of the hills on Caleb's list from which you can see Arthur's Seat.

I'd picked up a couple of chocolate bar wrappers on the path; at the summit of Ben Cleuch a banana skin and orange peel were being effectively refrigerated and preserved by the altitude. On Arthur's Seat I often remove rubbish people have left behind – batteries from digital cameras, spent fireworks after Bonfire night, empty bottles and cans… disposable barbecues. Litter on hills is nothing new, Caleb described finding the Wells of Dee on Braeriach in 1899;

> … sorely disfigured by the debris of the lunch of previous visitors… defiled with decaying bones and soiled paper… We cleaned the place up as well as was possible, and cursed and prayed for the evil-doers.

It seems Ben Cleuch has been a popular climb for a long time. In the 1790s the minister at Alva wrote;

> The view from the top of Ben-Cloch is the most extensive and beautiful anywhere to be found, and is visited by all travellers of curiosity who delight in fine prospects.

And he goes on to describe the hill as; 'the summit of all the Ochills [*sic*]; and according to the observation of Mr Udney, land surveyor, is about 2,420 feet…' This accurate (for the 18th century) estimate of the height (only 57 feet out) suggests Mr Udney may have climbed the hill and measured its height barometrically. Thomas Grierson ascended the hill in 1849, possibly the first *recorded* ascent of Ben Cleuch and described the view from the summit in his bestseller *Autumnal Ramblings among the Scottish Mountains*;

... within sight on this occasion were Ben Lomond, the Cobbler, Ben Ledi, Stuc a Chroin, Ben Vorlich, Ben Cruachan, Ben Laoigh, Am Binnein, Ben More, Ben Chonzie, Ben Lawers, Schichallion and Beinn a'Ghlo.

The Victorian surveyors who climbed Ben Cleuch in 1863 abandoned plans to build a railway up the hill. But solitude was absent last time I stood on the summit of Ben Cleuch. Approaching from Dollar Glen the song of the skylarks was gradually replaced by the bleeping of reversing vehicles and mechanical clanking. When I reached the trig point I saw on the slopes of Burnfoot Hill to the north, huge excavators and lorries tearing open a thousand metre long strip of hillside the width of a motorway to construct a wind factory.

I gazed over my realm. On Ben Cleuch I was standing at the centre of Caleb's view of the hills visible from Arthur's Seat; Ben Lomond and Ben Ledi to the west. Stuc a'Chroin and Ben Vorlich to the north. Loch Leven and the Lomond Hills of Fife to the east. Arthur's Seat south across the Firth of Forth.

From the trig point (chilly, exposed) descend west to Ben Ever past the stones, unusual on the predominantly grassy Ochils, that give Ben Cleuch its name. These white lichen spattered rocks, are conspicuous approaching the summit from the south-west. Seen from Ben Ever the top of Ben Cleuch appears to be crowned with a ring of stones.

The long ridge of Ben Ever juts out over the flat plain of Stirling. The Ochils end suddenly and fields stretch out below, almost the view from an aeroplane. A couple of winters ago I climbed Ben Cleuch one icy December day. Freezing fog lay over the town of Alva at the foot of the Ochils and drifted up Mill Glen. Only the chimney of Longannet power station rose above the fog.

At the col to the west of Ben Cleuch cross a stile and leaving the fence behind walk along a grassy track south towards Ben Ever. The hillside here is criss crossed with sheep paths and faint vehicle tracks making it confusing in mist so navigation may be needed. By the time I reach the very indistinct summit of Ben Ever, just two small cairns on either side of the track above the deep gash of the Daiglen, the sky over Ben Cleuch has turned a dark shade of grey purple.

The name Ben Ever is a strange one – it could be derived from the Scots word *ever* or *over* meaning upper (hill) but the word order is wrong for Scots (it should be *Ever Bin*) and besides Gaelic and Scots words are not often found in the same name. The explanation the name is derived from the Gaelic word *eibhir* (granite) doesn't work either because the rock of the Ochils isn't granite. The origin and meaning of the name Ben Ever are shrouded in a toponymic mist. Likewise the track over Ben Ever marked on the Ordnance Survey 1:50000 is not as clear or easy to find on the ground as might appear from a casual glance at the map. Where it forks go right on a faint track which drops steeply downhill south west towards Silver Glen and the Nebit. The Nebit is a good Scots word meaning 'the nosed one'. At a sheep pen turn left (south) along a vehicle track. On the hillside here, in among the long grass, lie old wooden boxes, filled with fodder in winter to feed the sheep.

Follow the stony track along the flank of the Nebit, high above the burn that flows down to Silver Glen. A line of Scots Pines on the hillside marks the edge of Wood Hill Wood, believed to be one of the oldest plantations of trees in Scotland, laid out in the early 18th century by Sir John Erskine the laird of Alva House. Scots pine and open grassland with scattered larch near the top of the hill – ash, birch and oak in the middle and sycamore on the lower slopes.

WHO OWNS BEN CLEUCH?

There are probably over 100 different landowners who own bits of the Ochils. Dollar Glen is owned by the National Trust for Scotland, Hermiston Quay, 5 Cultins Road, Edinburgh, Scotland, EH11 4DF and Wood Hill is owned by The Woodland Trust. The National Trust for Scotland is the country's third largest landowner.

Again that feeling of stepping off the edge of the Ochils as the track hairpin bends down the steep hillside west of Silver Glen through rocks, gorse and short cropped turf. The mist drifts about Wood Hill Wood and the Wallace monument on Abbey Craig beyond the craggy outline of Dumyat. Perching on a dwarf tree growing out from a crag are two carrion crows. Down below lay the streets and houses of Alva. Strude Mill dominates the town and tells of Alva's industrial past; at each window of the mill there was once a handloom.

Leave the track at a bend signposted *Public Footpath* and go through a wooden gate into Wood Hill wood. Buzzards and green woodpeckers nest here and in spring bluebells cover the woodland floor.

On the way back to the Woodland Park and the start of the walk – where the Silver Burn pours down through the birch trees, just before a small footbridge across the stream – the sealed off entrance to a mine shaft (marked by a fence and warning signs) can be seen between ivy covered tree trunks.

The geology of the Ochil Fault turns up many minerals, usually low quality. The year is 1714 and plans are afoot in France to put Bonnie Prince Charlie's father, the Old Pretender, on the British throne as King James III of England and James VIII of Scotland. Just as the Jacobite rebellion (from the Latin *Jacobus* and meaning supporters of James) breaks out, Sir John Erskine of Alva discovers a promising vein of minerals here on his estate barely ten minutes walk from Alva House. In only a few months, 40 tons of silver ore, the biggest amount ever found in Britain, is mined and buried in barrels near the gate of Alva House for safekeeping. For a time the mine produces £4,000 worth of silver per week. Sir John Erskine accumulates an estimated fortune of £50,000 – a vast sum of money in the 18th century.

Sir John is a supporter of the Old Pretender and spends much of his time in Europe raising funds and gun running for the Jacobite rebels. He leaves his wife in charge of the mine, together with a manager James Hamilton. In her letters to her husband in France Lady Erskine assures Sir John that the estate is in good shape, the hedges are clipped, the ditches maintained and the crops sown. She avoids mentioning the mine directly, referring to it in only coded references; 'Mr. Nabit does not employ old H or any of his profession at present,' writes Lady Erskine in one letter; 'It is yet impossible to tell what money Mr. Nabit will be worth, his reputation amongst the common sort is so high that no body credits it.' The mysterious Mr Nabit is the Nebit, the hill under which the silver mine is situated. Lady Erskine of Alva sits at the centre of a web of intrigue.

The Erskines try to keep the find a secret but their mine manager James Hamilton has other ideas and takes samples of the silver ore to London to be tested by the Master of the Mint, Sir Isaac Newton, who finds them to be; 'exceeding rich'. By then the Jacobite rebellion is over and Sir John a wanted man in exile in France. The British government grants him a pardon on condition he gives ten per cent of the mine's proceeds to the Treasury in London.

The mine is worked for several more years but never again produces the riches of the early finds and gradually the seam gives way to copper and lead which are not economically viable to extract. Sir John spends his fortune on improvements to his estate, including, around 1720, the establishment of Wood Hill Wood, a living testament to the Greek proverb *a civilization flourishes when people plant trees under which they will never sit.*

And the 40 tons of silver ore buried in barrels near the gate of Alva House? Perhaps it was smuggled abroad to aid the Jacobite cause, in any event it disappeared and was never seen again.

It was the winter of 1988. The first time I climbed King's Seat Hill in the Ochils, Ben Cleuch was the original objective.

I'm sure the plan, a hillwalk with friends on a Sunday, seemed a great idea after a few pints of Younger's No.3 in the warm smoky fug of the Blue Blazer in Bread Street, Edinburgh.

The best laid plans... on the Sunday appointed to climb Ben Cleuch I woke up alone through a thumping head of empty glasses to Morag and Gra buzzing the entry phone on the tenement stair door again and again. David was given the camp name Morag in the 1970s because it fitted his reputation for stomping through the heather on the Scottish hills. Since developing a knee problem he's blossomed into a leather queen and hasn't been up a mountain in years but the name Morag has stuck.

Finally I got to the front door, Gra protested it had all been my idea in the first place to do a hill walk. I'd planned an early night but somehow ended up in The Laughing Duck or maybe it was the Blue Oyster Club. A fringe of dark hair, white T-shirt, Levi 501s. Trade? That happened many times. Back in the day.

More drink taken. Then home with a cute stranger to the flat I rented in Stockbridge on the corner of Dean Park Street where it joins Comely Bank Road. Circles closing. Ecstasy of his cock in my bum... blood... shit... cum. And particles of virus too, replicated a billion times over the decades from the hot African night in Leopoldville to a cold Scottish city.

And we climbed a hungover King's Seat slithering on patches of snow in the long grass.

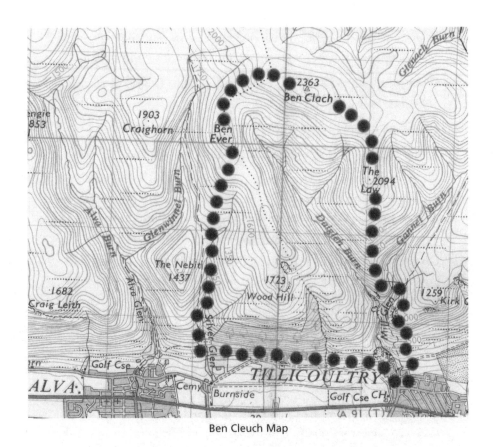

Ben Cleuch Map

BEN CLEUCH (721m)

Grade   **
Map: OS Sheet 58
Distance/Ascent: 10km/670m
Starting height: 70m
Time to top: 2h +breaks
Start/Finish: Alva/Tillicoultry

A circular route starting with an exciting walk through a dramatic gorge and passing a silver mine.

ROUTE:

Ascent

1   Park in Woodland Park car park NS89836 97492 on A91 between Alva and Tillicoultry (signposted *Woodland Park*).

2   At entrance to car park go east along track towards Tillicoultry (part of Clackmannanshire Countryside Path Network's Hillfoots Link).

3   Where track turns right at line of mossy boulders continue straight on along footpath.

4   Follow path along edge of field then golf course.

5   At the edge of Tillicoultry a tarmac road is reached at a *Hillfoots Link* sign.

6   Turn right along tarmac road then almost immediately left along footpath through undergrowth and bushes for short distance to emerge at pink sandstone Victorian villa with electricity pole nearby.

7   Go along a little lane into Scotland Place. Keep straight ahead and cross footbridge with green railings near the Clock Mill NS91459 97291.

8   Turn left along Upper Mill Street.

9   At top of Upper Mill Street follow east bank of stream into Mill Glen signposted *The Glen/Public Path Tillicoultry Glen*. **Start walk here if using public transport.**

10 NS91387 97628 Go through a metal gate and follow path up Mill Glen crossing from one side of the stream and then back to the other on a succession of bridges.

11 Ignore faint paths heading off up hillside and keep following engineered path until head of Mill Glen where Daiglen and Gannel burns meet.

12 Just past a bench leave engineered path as it switches back in a hairpin 236m NS91208 98199 and descend towards wooden slatted bridge over Gannel Burn. Care should be taken on this short descent as rocks can be slippery.

13 Immediately after crossing Gannel Burn a short easy scramble leads to grassy footpath that climbs through bracken steeply up the Law.

14 At about 440m pass halfway boulder NS91093 98896.

15 At 610m NS91025 99498 follow fence to the top of the Law (641m) NS91025 99648 (stone shelter).

16 Follow eroded path beside fence down to shallow col 619m NS91022 99866 north of the Law.

17 Follow fence to summit of Ben Cleuch (721m) NN90276 00633 (trig point).

Descent

18 From trig point follow fence west to broad col between Ben Cleuch and Ben Ever.

19 Cross stile and leave fence behind. Take grassy track south towards Ben Ever.

20 Reach indistinct summit of Ben Ever NN89334 00080 (two small cairns).

21 Follow grassy path south downhill to shallow col between Ben Ever and Wood Hill.

22 From col take right hand fork in path NS 89479 99791 which drops steeply down towards Silver Glen and The Nebit.

23 At sheep pens turn left along track below The Nebit.

24 With Wood Hill Wood in sight follow series of hairpin bends down steep hillside.

25 At bend in track NS89129 97686 (signpost reading *Public Footpath*) LEAVE track and follow path a few metres to a wooden gate into Wood Hill Wood.

27 Follow path as it crosses Silver Burn on a little foot bridge. (Ignore left turn that goes steeply uphill near here).

28 Pass field on right before you reach the Woodland Park car park and start of walk.

29. If using public transport follow Hillfoots Link path back to Tillicoultry (*directions 2–7*)

NAVIGATION: hillside around Ben Ever is criss crossed with sheep paths and faint tracks – confusing in mist (take care with route finding).

PUBLIC TRANSPORT: Frequent buses from Stirling (bus station close to Stirling railway station); ask bus driver to let you off at the Holly Tree Pub on the High Street (A91) in Tillicoultry, walk up Upper

Mill Street and start the walk from the Clock Mill (Steps 9–29 then 2–7). Full public transport details at www.travelinescotland.com or phone 0871 200 22 33.

DOGS: A bit of an awkward walk with a dog due to locked gates (some covered with barbed wire), stiles and fences in Silver Glen. Path in Mill Glen is ok for dogs though big drops in places. Lots of sheep on open hillside from head of Mill Glen on.

Something Else: if having a pint after the walk you might want to try a Harviestoun cask ale or filtered bottled beers which are brewed in Tillicoultry.

CHAPTER SIXTEEN

The Memory of Fire

BEING CAUGHT IN A MAJOR FIRE sears itself into the human mind so that years after the last charred piece of wood has been cleared away and the smell of smoke has faded, still the memory of fire is burnt into the cells of the frontal cortex. So it was with Caleb and the Rothiemurchus Forest Fire which broke out one August morning in 1899. Through his writing even a century later we can feel a lingering trace of the searing heat of the flames scorching the burning heather and catch a faint smell of charred wood across the decades.

On Thursday 24 August 1899 Caleb cycled into Aviemore to meet the midday train. He admires the new station buildings and the brightly dressed ladies; in that order. Aviemore station had been rebuilt in 1898 when the direct railway line from Aviemore to Inverness via Slochd summit was constructed (before then trains between Perth and Inverness went via Forres and Nairn). While strolling along the platform Caleb notices a plume of smoke rising from the forest to the south of the village.

From his favourite vantage point on the footbridge over the railway line (where he had sketched the panorama *The Cairngorm Mountains As Seen From Aviemore Railway Station* the summer before) Caleb guesses the fire must be near Loch an Eilein. Several groups of estate workers set off to tackle the blaze and abandoning the friends he had gone to meet to their own devices Caleb races off on his bicycle to help fight the fire.

Arriving at Loch an Eilein to find the heather ablaze Caleb uses a large sheath knife he often carried with him to cut branches of juniper to use as beaters. While Caleb and the estate workers, enveloped in clouds of thick, stinging smoke are beating back the flames a shooting party arrives at the Loch. The huntsmen had noticed a small fire nearby while they were having lunch but did not know what to do. To Caleb's disgust one of the men in the shooting party refuses to help with the fire-fighting. Later Caleb was to blame the spread of fire on the shooting party's lack of action. Caleb hated hunting and would have been dismayed

---

TIMBER FLOATING AT ROTHIEMURCHUS

During the 19th century wood cutters used dams on lochs and controlled flooding of rivers to move timber downstream from the Forest of Rothiemurchus. Workers toiled up to their waists in water to clear log jams. The arrival of the railways led to timber floating falling into disuse but in April 1904 Caleb watched as this ancient activity was briefly revived in Rothiemurchus following tree felling in the wake of a forest fire. He later described what must have been a dramatic sight as; '... the big logs were swept down to the fall and plunged with sullen bump into the pool below, thereafter nodding their way down stream.' In 'Timber Floating at Rothiemurchus' published in *The Cairngorm Club Journal*, Caleb wrote about helping unjam the logs where they were stuck on the gravel river bank behind the old Free Kirk in Inverdruie. Caleb enjoyed the physicality of timber floating; 'the work affords good, hard exercise, bringing into play all the muscles of the body.'

---

to find men with guns in the vicinity of Loch an Eilein where ospreys nested. In 1899 there was little effective protection for rare birds and Edwardian 'sportsmen' shot pretty much what they liked including endangered species.

Caleb paints a vivid picture of the fire as it raged through the night, the beaters silhouetted against the glow as they fought the flames. He was still there at midnight on Thursday 24 August and was back the next day Friday 25th to fight the blaze again. That night a big thunderstorm and accompanying heavy rain followed by three wet days doused the flames for good. An inquiry by the local Procurator Fiscal into the cause of the fire concluded the most likely cause was a burning match or wad from a shotgun dropped by the shooting party, though the hunters indignantly denied any responsibility for the blaze. A day or two later under the headline SCOTCH MOUNTAINS ON FIRE *The Daily Mail* printed a wildly inaccurate report of the fire at 'Lochanecklan'.

A few days later walking across the burnt ground where the flames had raged Caleb came across a strange memento of the fire. For a moment Caleb's perception tangles with his fears for the Loch an Eilein ospreys and he thinks he sees; 'the charred remains of some poor bird that had met its death in the blazing heather'. Then picking the object up he realises it is a piece of fir root. Caleb sketched the charred piece of wood with its strange resemblance to a bird and used it to illustrate the article he wrote for the January 1900 edition of *The Cairngorm Club Journal* entitled 'The Rothiemurchus Forest Fire'.

CHAPTER SEVENTEEN

Ben Lawers

Regeneration

Thousands of tired, nerve-shaken, over-civilized people are beginning to find out going to the mountains is going home; that wilderness is a necessity...

JOHN MUIR, 1901

THE FIRST MOUNTAIN I climbed after being diagnosed with HIV was Suilven in the north-west Highlands of Scotland. Six months later I climbed Ben Lawers one cold November day and I date my fight back against a disease once routinely referred to in sections of the press as the gay plague, from around that time. On Caleb's list Ben Lawers is described as visible from Arthur's Seat at the left-hand end of Inchcolm Island and is most easily seen when white with snow in winter.

Andersons' Guide to the Highlands and Islands of Scotland describes Loch Tay as;

> encompassed by a chain of mountains ,rising towards the west and centre, into bare and lofty heads, of which Ben Lawers, the most elevated of the Perthshire hills, towers pre-eminent.

Ben Lawers is the highest mountain in Scotland south of Ben Nevis and at 1,214 metres the only Arthur to approach 4,000 feet in height. Ben Lawers (3,983ft) is unique among the Arthur's in that another Munro, Beinn Ghlas, has to be climbed on the way to its summit.

Ben Lawers and its surrounding hills are mainly grassy and characterised by great sweeping slopes, high summits, connecting ridges, crags and lochans. Geologists know Ben Lawers as the upside down mountain because the rocks of Ben Lawers were originally laid down in an ancient ocean as a series of flat limestones and sandstones that over time were folded and turned upside down by the collision of continents.

According to the Scottish Mountaineering Club the only real cliffs are above Lochan nan Cat and these are; 'vegetatious, of more interest to the botanist than the climber'. Botanists discovered the unique arctic-alpine mountain plants for which Ben Lawers is famous in the 18th century.

Some of the rarer plants that exist on the mountain only survive because they grow on cliff ledges inaccessible to grazing sheep and deer. Rare wild flowers will not be seen growing at the side of the path. A combination of factors including local climate, altitude, geology and type of soil are the reason why alpine gentian, alpine woodsia and alpine mouse-ear are found on Ben Lawers but not on other Scottish mountains. These plants are the reason why in 1950, the National Trust bought Ben Lawers in order to conserve rare species of national and international importance.

One explanation of the name Ben Lawers is that it comes from the Gaelic *ladhar* meaning hoof or claw. This suggestion fits well with the pronunciation of Ben Lawers today and as *Scottish Hill Names* points out fits the mountain's topography of 'great ridges and spurs sweeping round like talons to enclose corries'. Perhaps a link exists too between *ladhar* (claw) and *Lochan nan Cat* (lochan of the wildcats) which lies in the corrie below the mountain's summit.

But... there is another Gaelic word *labhar* (pronounced lavar) and meaning loud. A couple of years ago I climbed Ben Lawers in thick mist, after a spell of wet weather; all was silent but for the sound of a stream roaring down the hill below me. In his book *In Famed Breadalbane* William Gillies suggests Ben Lawers means 'the sounding one' from the Burn of Lawers which is very loud when in flood. Over time the name extended from the burn to the district around it and to the mountain and today this is the generally accepted meaning of the hill's name.

The hydro-electric dams constructed in the 1950s on Ben Lawers left the burns depleted and played a part in the mountain streams being less 'loud' today than historically. There are several other 'loud' or 'noisy' hills in the Highlands – Lochnagar meaning loch of noise, is one – hill names that are a memory of a quieter world before there were cars on the roads and aircraft overhead, and in the Highlands the streams were one of the noisiest features of the mountains.

Climbing Ben Lawers

Driving along the side of Loch Tay on the way to climb Ben Lawers I think of Caleb on holiday in Killin in September a hundred years before. The slopes of Ben Lawers have been cultivated from earliest times because of the fertile soil provided by schist and limestone rock and are rich in prehistoric remains. In 1912 Caleb reported his 'Archaeological

Gleanings from Killin' in the *Proceedings of the Society of Antiquaries of Scotland*. Near the hamlet of Morenish where the lower slopes of Ben Lawers sweep down to the shore of Loch Tay, Caleb sketched a cup and ring marked limestone rock. Although he and his companion knew roughly the location of the rock; 'even with the assistance of a local farmer we had much difficulty in finding it, and had searched many hundreds of yards of ledges before Mr Haggart rediscovered it.'

To climb Ben Lawers take the A827 from Killin to Aberfeldy and about six kilometres east of Killin turn left up the byroad signposted *Ben Lawers*. Park about two kilometres up this road at the National Trust pay and display car park situated at a height of about 400 metres. At the start of this road signs warn *No Gritting Or Snow Clearance Carried Out. Use Alternative Route In Winter Conditions*. I have got stuck here twice in winter so park lower down the road if it's snowy.

In the summer of 2010 the Ben Lawers visitor centre stood forlorn and abandoned by the car park bringing back memories of nature tables and 1970s display boards about the ice age. The building has since been demolished due to financial cutbacks at the National Trust. In 1950 the National Trust was able to purchase Ben Lawers because of a large sum of money donated by Percy Unna a past president of the Scottish Mountaineering Club. Unna laid down guidelines to keep land owned by the National Trust wild. He rejected man-made developments which might spoil the Scottish landscape and his principles became known as 'The Unna Rules'.

I open the car door to a vista of high mountain scenery. I can see Loch Tay down in the glen but the tops of the grassy mountains that encircle the car park, Beinn Ghlas, Meall Corranaich and Meall nan Tarmachan (of Tarmachan ridge fame) are in cloud.

The path to Ben Lawers is signposted and starts at a drystone wall topped with turf. Cross moorland in summer bright with yellow bog asphodel and the pink flowers of cross leaved heath. Sections of boardwalk carry the path over pools where the surface of the water has a naturally oily sheen. Look out for newts in the bog pools under the boardwalk – on a hot summer's day lizards can sometimes be seen basking in the sun on the wooden planks. Given the severity of winter in the Scottish hills it may seem strange that the lizard, a cold blooded amphibian can survive here; from October to March lizards hibernate underground in holes and crevices where the temperature stays above freezing.

Go through a gate in a deer fence and follow the path signposted *Ben*

Lawers up the west bank of the Burn of Edramucky. The area around the burn was fenced off by the National Trust in 1990 to exclude sheep and deer and to allow the restoration of vegetation destroyed by grazing. A wide variety of plants and wild flowers flourish here because erosion by the stream has exposed bedrock; minerals in the rock are dissolved into the water which enriches the soil at the sides of the burn and provides nutrients not available to plants on the open hillside.

Stags horn moss, lichens, blaeberries, cow berries, moss campion and yellow mountain saxifrage flourish by the path. There is devil's bit scabious too; between August and October its purple-blue flowers herald the approach of autumn. The Gaelic name of this plant, greim an diabhail, translates as devil's bite and is derived from its root, which looks as if it's been chopped off. In days gone by the plant was used for dyeing cloth and tradition has it that the devil bit off the tip of the root in revenge for the plant's benefits to humanity.

Near the path mountain pansies grow among a square of stones, the remains of one of the many shielings that once lined the banks of the Burn of Edramucky. It is likely the first ascent of Ben Lawers was made from these summer shielings located at around 2,000 feet, from where it is an easy walk over Beinn Ghlas to the summit of Ben Lawers. On 17 September 1776 an unnamed group of soldiers carrying out General William Roy's military survey of Scotland made the first recorded ascent of Ben Lawers and measured its height using a barometer. During the 19th century Robert Christison was the Queen's Physician in Scotland and a keen mountaineer. He climbed Ben Lawers as a young man during a heat wave in 1826. Sixty-five years later in 1891 when John Macharg climbed the mountain in wintry October weather, he was down in time to catch the steamboat *Lady of the Lake* from the pier at Lawers village which took him to Killin and the train back to Glasgow. Ben Lawers was the original Scottish ski centre and in the 1930s the first downhill ski races were held in Coire Odhar below Beinn Ghlas.

Follow the path above the stream to where it dips down to cross some stepping stones and continues along the east bank of the Burn of Edramucky. Birch and rowan trees grow by the burn and its steep banks are patterned with mountain ferns, green cladonia lichens and purple strips of heather. In summer Alpine ladies mantle and bluebells grow among the grass.

The day I climbed Ben Lawers in the rain the Burn of Edramucky was roaring down. There is an old story that Loch Tay was formed from a lockable spring which a milkmaid inadvertently left open after she had fed and watered her cows in the west corrie of Ben Lawers. Today the level of streams on the mountain varies depending on the requirements of the Breadalbane hydro-electric scheme. A small dam on the Burn of Edramucky diverts the waters through a tunnel and into Lochan na Lairige about a mile north of the car park from where the water descends a vertical distance of 415 metres (the greatest drop of any Scottish hydro-electric scheme) to Finlarig power station on the shores of Loch Tay.

Beyond the upper gate in the fence the path climbs the grassy south ridge of Beinn Ghlas. Over centuries the grassland that covers most of Ben Lawers has replaced the native trees, shrubs and tall flowering plants that once grew on these hills. In summer there is a dramatic difference between the wild flowers, long grass with seed heads and small trees within the deer fence and the impoverished grassland outside it – caused by the grazing pressure of 200 years of sheep farming on the mountain. Human activity combined with climate has tended to produce in the Scottish Highlands what pioneering ecologist Frank Fraser Darling called 'a devastated landscape' and a 'wet desert'.

Shortly after the gate go right when the track forks at a large boulder. The path climbs up through grass spiked with thistles. Looking back I can see the path snaking down the hill and the hydro board road cutting across towards Lochan na Lairige.

SECOND SIGHT

Around the middle of the 17th century the Laird of Lawers married a daughter of the Stewarts of Appin. She became known as the Lady of Lawers. Tradition tells that a group of Appin Stewarts known as Na Combaich, the Companions, came to the House of Lawers as an escort for her. According to William Gillies's book *In Famed Breadalbane* the Lady whom the Companions escorted had a strange gift – she was a seer who could predict the future and she was to make many prophecies, among them one about the Highland Clearances foretelling; '... that the jaw of the sheep would drive the plough out of the ground; that many holdings would become one holding; that the home-steads on Lochtayside would yet be so far apart that one cock would not be able to hear his neighbour crow...' Another of the Lady's prophecies yet to come true fore-sees a new ice age when; '... Ben Lawers would become so cold that it would chill and waste the land around it for seven miles...'

In the summer of 1878 Malcolm Ferguson sent 30 labourers to work to build a giant cairn to add 20 feet to the height of Ben Lawers and take it over the 4,000 feet mark. The National Trust seems to have carried out a scarcely lesser task with the construction of the path up Ben Lawers. Almost a flight of steps in places with elaborate rainwater gullies, it equals the stalkers' paths built by wealthy landowners on the Scottish mountains in the 19th century. The National Trust have worked hard to combat erosion of the path up Ben Lawers caused by thousands of hill-walkers wearing away the thin vegetation and exposing the soil to rain. On the ridge between Beinn Ghlas and Ben Lawers boulders have been strategically positioned to divert hillwalkers away from eroded ground that is being restored. It has taken years of work to heal the scar of the old eroded path – the new path cost £100 a metre to build at high altitude.

Cuilean, the Labradoodle and I climb higher; the mountain seems all steep grass slopes, stony path and sheep in the mist. The dogs startle a flock of five ptarmigan who rattle up skywards.

The path abruptly reaches the eroded summit of Beinn Ghlas (1,103m) where a small cairn perches right on the edge of a vertigo inducing drop. From Beinn Ghlas the path continues north-east along the broad easy angled ridge to Ben Lawers. Alpine ladies mantle grows here and many of the rocks by the path are grey green with lichen and moss. These so called 'lower plants' are less well known than the flowering plants and ferns of Ben Lawers but the mountain is one of the most important sites in Scotland for lichens and it is possible new species may still be discovered here.

FERGUSON'S CAIRN

A native of Morenish, a hamlet between Killin and Ben Lawers, Malcolm Ferguson was a successful Glasgow businessman who was devoted to the area around Loch Tay and wrote a book *Rambles in Breadalbane* describing its scenery and people... In 1878 Malcolm Ferguson had a band of work-men build a monumental cairn on the summit of Ben Lawers '45 to 50 feet in circumference and about 20 feet high' capped with a massive block of white quartz to take the mountain over 4,000 feet. For their labors the workmen were each paid with a handsome bound volume of Gaelic poetry. Today nothing remains to be seen of Ferguson's cairn which in the words of Muriel Gray was; '... probably sabotaged by a disgruntled worker who got home to find he'd already read this particular volume of Gaelic poetry.'

The path, sandy and eroded in places, leads along the ridge dropping gently to about 1,000 metres near a tiny lochan at the wide col below Ben Lawers. The paths winds up through little crags and rocks above the col then climbs a wide grassy slope to the triangulation pillar that marks the summit of Ben Lawers (1,214m).

Just before the top a little hollow makes a good lunch place on a cold day. Cuilean checks it thoroughly for leftover sandwiches, something she makes a habit of doing on top of mountains since finding a half-eaten bridie behind a rock on Stuchd an Lochain, her first Munro, when she was a pup. Beyond the trig point the ridge disappears into the mist towards An Stuc and the crags on the north side of the mountain called in Gaelic, Creag an Fhithich, the crag of the raven.

Followers of the Wolf Packs

At the end of the 16th century ravens (fitheach) were still common in Edinburgh but numbers declined as the streets became cleaner and the last pair nested on Arthur's Seat in 1837. Ravens were once widespread in the countryside too but sheep farmers and later gamekeepers persecuted them ruthlessly and by the start of the 20th century ravens were only to be found in the remotest areas of Scotland. In the words of Stuart Benn; 'The long rough miles being the best defence against gun, trap and poison.' Today ravens have recolonised much of the area they used to occupy including Holyrood Park in Edinburgh in the last decade.

Historically in Scotland ravens were followers of wolf packs, but now the wolves are gone from the Scottish mountains the raven follows a more deadly predator; man. Ravens shadow deer stalkers and have learned that the sound of a rifle shot means a deer disembowelled by the hunter on the hillside, and a feed from the still warm grallochs.

In literature the raven is often seen as a bird of ill omen. As she plots to murder the King of Scotland Lady Macbeth soliloquises; 'The raven himself is hoarse that croaks the fatal entrance of Duncan under my battlements.'

In 1879 Ben Lawers was Sir Hugh Munro's first summit at the age of 23; Munro's first Munro...? Seton Gordon climbed Ben Lawers in the autumn of 1940 and described the view from the summit;

… brilliant sunshine flooded the Lowlands, and the air was so clear that on the far eastern horizon the distant North Sea was visible beyond the Firth of Tay… Far below us, yet at no great distance to the north, were the green slopes of Glen Lyon where St Adamnan, when the world was young, stayed the advance of the plague with his staff.

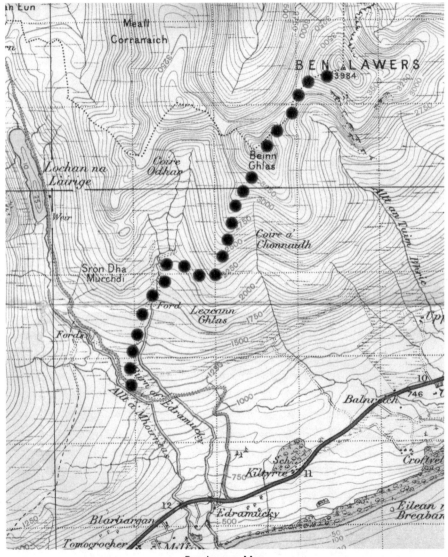

Ben Lawers Map

BEN LAWERS (1,214m)

Grade   **

Map: OS Sheet 51

Distance/Ascent: 10km/950m

Starting Height: 400m

Time to top: 2h45min +breaks

Start/Finish: Ben Lawers car park near Killin

A straightforward route on a path which in summer at least, in words of the 1991 SMC Munros Hillwalkers' Guide 'cannot possibly be missed'.

ROUTE:

1   From A827 about 6km east of Killin turn left up byroad signposted *Ben Lawers*. Walk starts 2km up this road at National Trust pay and display car park (400m). Start lower down road if snow.

2   Leave car park by path that starts at drystone wall topped with turf (signposted *Ben Lawers*). Go through gate. Cross road. Path continues on other side of road.

3   Go through gate NN61480 BNG39207 in deer fence and follow path signposted *Ben Lawers* up w bank of Burn of Edramucky.

4   Cross stream at stepping stones and continue along the path on E bank of Burn of Edramucky Burn to upper gate in deer fence.

5   Go through gate and shortly after keep right when track forks at large boulder (669m) NN61645 BNG39233.

6   Follow path NE up s ridge of Beinn Ghlas to small summit cairn of Beinn Ghlas 1,103m NN62523 BNG40437. Paved sections of path can be slippery in wet or icy weather.

7   From Beinn Ghlas path continues NE along broad easy angled ridge to Ben Lawers dropping gently to about 1,000m at wide col NN63004 BNG41101 below summit of Ben Lawers near tiny lochan (unmarked on map).

8   Follow path through some little crags and then up wide grassy slope to trig point at summit Ben Lawers (1,214m) NN63500 BNG41400.

9   Return by same route.

At the summit of Arthur's Seat

Ben Venue from Loch Katrine

Ben Vorlich from Balquhidder

Stob Binnein from Ben More on a September morning

Ben Lawers and An Stuc from Meall Garbh

Beinn Ghlas, seen here from the old shielings by the Burn of Edramucky, has to be climbed on the way to Ben Lawers

Lizards can sometimes be seen basking in the sun on the wooden walkway at the start of the Ben Lawers path

Like living stones. Ptarmigan on the Ptarmigan ridge of Ben Lomond

Carvings on rocks at the summit of Schiehallion

A golden-ringed dragonfly near the Ardvorlich Burn

Big skies and a feeling of space… approaching the summit of Beinn a'Ghlo

Lochnagar from the Old Brig o' Dee

The Stuic from Cac Carn Beag

John Knox's Pulpit, West Lomond Hill

Cuilean at the top of Arthur's Seat.

DOGS: no problems with dog access here. We met about four different dogs which is far more than usual on a Scottish hill. You can safely let your dog off the lead inside the deer fence near start of walk but on the rest of the mountain there are lots of sheep so keep your dog under close control/on a lead unless you're confident it won't chase sheep.

WINTER CONDITIONS: ice axe and crampons needed.

Somewhere Else: the Ben Lawers Hotel, Lawers village
(at Ben Lawers road end go left/east along A827 for 7km.)

CHAPTER EIGHTEEN

Meall Garbh

The Shieling Life

MEALL HILLS HAVE AN IMAGE PROBLEM, a reputation among mountaineers for being dull, uninspiring hills. One author from Skye writing in the 1920s went so far as to as to describe *meall* hills as 'heaps or almost shapeless lumps'. Dictionaries translate *meall* as a lump, knob, heap, eminence or mound but in Gaelic, as well as referring to hills, the word can also mean swellings, banks of clouds and buttocks.

Garbh means rough or stony; the Gaelic speaking people who named the Scottish mountains had a good eye for topography, there are many hills called *meall garbh* (pronounced myowl gaarv) in the Highlands. Listen to the word garbh; it has a sound of rough walking... over peat hags and heather and stones.

Peter Drummond has calculated there are more *meall* (around 1,600) in Scotland than there are *beinn* (1,200) yet there are three times as many *beinn* as *meall* in the tables of Munros and Corbetts (i.e. the higher Scottish peaks). In the hundred highest Scottish mountains there are only four *mealls* and of these the Meall Garbh on Caleb's list is the highest coming in at number 33. In his list of Scottish mountains visible from Arthur's Seat, again consisting mainly of the higher hills, there are two *mealls* but 12 *beinns*. Caleb described Meall Garbh (1,118m/3,668ft) as the east peak of Ben Lawers situated 43½ degrees west of north, 58 miles from Arthur's Seat and to be seen beyond the left-hand end of Inchmickery Island.

The two *mealls* visible from Arthur's Seat are both in Perthshire but while the rounded *meall* in chapter 23 of this book (Meall Dearg in Glen Cochill) is typical of the genre, Meall Garbh of the Lawers range, with its cliffs dropping hundreds of feet down to Lochan nan Cat is not. Conclusion; not all *mealls* are boring lumps or as Jim Crumley once put it, there is no such thing as a dull hill, only dull people.

Climbing Meall Garbh

Begin at the Horn Carver's Cottage just outside Lawers village on the A827 Killin to Aberfeldy road along the north side of Loch Tay. The Horn Carver's Cottage is a pretty whitewashed building with red roses growing up it. A car with a foreign number plate is parked outside and an American woman is buying a horn carved trinket as I go in to pay the parking charge. Loch Tay shines blue across the fields and my mind turns to Caleb in September 1911 with just six years of life left him, cycling along the road from Killin to sketch a cup marked rock at Craggantoul.

Take the track that goes to the right of the Horn Carver's Cottage where a sign reads *Machuim Farm Private Road*. In a field next to the track Highland cattle gaze at us as we walk past; they look like distant relatives of Cuilean. When the track turns sharp right go straight on, up a path keeping to the left of an old stone farm building with a corrugated iron roof. A short stretch of muddy path leads to a barn where a terrier comes rushing out barking to greet Cuilean and the Labradoodle. When large scale sheep farming arrived in Breadalbane 19th century farm buildings like these at Machuim (pronounced ma'wheem) replaced the old black houses that once lined the shores of Loch Tay.

The path is shaded here under the trees and there are glimpses through the leaves and undergrowth of the Lawers Burn tumbling down. In past centuries this old path above the wooded banks of the stream was used to access the shielings where livestock were taken to graze during the summer months. The walk to these upland pastures from the black houses on the shores of Loch Tay was called the imrich. To the west of the Arthur Ben Venue in the Trossachs a pass called the Bealach na h-Imriche recalls this journey made every summer before shielings were abandoned in the 1800s as livestock grazing methods changed and sheep farms were established. WH Murray imagined the day early in June, when the people set out to spend the summer at the shielings;

> Early on the day appointed, the townships were as busy as ant-heaps, with the women scuttling around collecting churns, three-legged stools, bowls, jugs, and tubs for the dairy work; pots and griddles for cooking; spades, ropes, axes, great bundles of dead bracken and straw for bedding, and sticks to repair the roofs and kindle fires in the shieling huts; sacks of meal and bags full of cheese and bannocks... When everyone was ready, they would load the ponies' and their own backs with all the gear

and set off – sheep first, cattle next, and then the ponies… The women, free at last from all too familiar hearth… broke into song, as if leaving their cares in the world below.

Climb over or squeeze through an old gate fastened shut with barbed wire. The sides of the Lawers Burn are thickly wooded and in summer the path becomes overgrown with bracken and ferns. From time to time a break in the trees gives a glimpse down to Loch Tay.

Reach a stile where wild raspberries grow among Scots pines, silver birch and rowan. Tall larches stand on the far side of the burn. The stile is fitted with a sliding wooden 'dog flap' and the path continues through long grass and bracken in summer dotted with fox gloves and Scottish bluebells. There are dragonflies in the woods and I can hear grasshoppers singing.

Dipper

A second stile gives access to the open hillside and a sign marks the boundary of the Ben Lawers national nature reserve. It's tricky getting both dogs through the 'dog flap' once they've spotted the sheep on the other side of the fence.

A buzzard flies overhead as I follow the path across short grassy turf high above the Lawers Burn tumbling over its smooth round boulders. Looking down the hillside towards Loch Tay, signs of the past; old walls, ditches, overgrown roads to peat cutting banks and shielings.

Across to the east I can see a dry stone dyke, a plantation wall, encircling the summit of the little hill of East Mealour. The construction of a dyke around 'Easter Mailer of Lawers', and its subsequent planting with trees, is recorded in the Breadalbane Estate accounts for 1789. Most of the trees were felled over the years and only a few isolated pines remain. A shepherd stands at a gap in the old wall whistling to call an unseen sheep dog. I hurry on by with Cuilean and the Labradoodle.

On the banks of the Lawers Burn there are many relatively well pre-served old shielings close to the path. Sheep graze over them and stonechats perch on the ruins. Like neighbouring Ben Lawers, the first ascent of Meall Garbh probably started from one of these summer shielings located at a height of 2,000 feet from which it is an easy walk to the summit.

The shieling huts or bothies were built of turf and stone. Grass and moss have grown over the walls on the outside but the shape of a dwelling is still recognisable. The ruins of these buildings are relics of transhumance when cattle, sheep and goats were moved to hill grazings accompanied young people who lived at the shielings all summer to guard their livestock from foxes, eagles and the odd far roaming wolf.

Recently archaeologists from Glasgow University excavated a rectan-gular shieling hut below Meall Garbh and some nearby ruins, including part of a small stone dairy or store. Based on bits of pottery found they pro-duced evidence for the use of the site in the 16th and 17th centuries. Inside the shieling on the floor of trampled earth a fire spot or hearth was found, tucked just inside the doorway and much needed. Wild camping in a tent at 600 metres, even in summer, can get very cold at night. Stone pot lids were also found, the kind of object usually discovered on prehistoric sites but clearly used on Meall Garbh for the storage of dairy products such as butter and cheese, which documentary sources record were made at the shielings. At other sites in the Highlands remains of illicit whisky stills have been found secretively located amongst the shieling ruins.

Many shielings were built on sites with fine open views. For the people who stayed on the mountain to tend the livestock, it must have been like a summer holiday albeit a working one. Some of the most beautiful Gaelic songs and poetry were written about the shieling life. The doorways of some of the Meall Garbh shielings face down to Loch Tay and it's easy to imagine people in the gloaming of a fine June evening sitting round the fire as it burns low beneath the darkening slopes of Ben Lawers.

Walking along the path by the burn I remember climbing Meall Garbh and its neighbouring Munro Meall Greigh in winter 10 years before. To prevent drug resistance developing anti HIV medication has to be taken at the same time each day... at work, in Athens airport or half way up a Scottish mountain. Back in the late 1990s the future was still a frightening place for people with HIV. At that time I took a drug called ritonavir to control the virus. The drug came in liquid form and had to be measured using an oral syringe. Crouching down in the snow by the Lawers Burn to rinse the syringe, the foul taste of the medicine still in my mouth, I watched as a dipper flew low along the stream; that day the water and the dipper's back were the only dark colours in a white world.

Look out for a waymarker at about 440 metres; leave the well maintained path near here before it reaches a footbridge (don't cross the stream) and climb a little way uphill to walk along the top of the high embankment above the steep sided Lawers Burn. Sheep tracks through grass dotted with thistles and tormentil make the going easier and there are fine views to Meall Garbh, An Stuc and Ben Lawers.

Continue along the east bank of the stream to near a small dam on the Lawers Burn. The dam is part of the Breadalbane hydro-electric scheme completed in 1961. Signs of the different uses man has made of the mountains over the centuries lie all around on Meall Garbh; from upland grazing at the shielings to hill sheep farming to hydro-electricity to Munro bagging.

WHO OWNS MEALL GARBH?

The National Trust for Scotland, Hermiston Quay, 5 Cultins Road, Edinburgh, Scotland, EH11 4DF.

From near the dam strike up the hillside aiming for the col at 830 metres between Meall Greigh and Meall Garbh. A deer fence erected by the National Trust but not marked on the OS map, starts at a height of about 700 metres and can be followed north almost all the way to the col. In summer the difference between the sheep grazed grass outside and the variety and size of plants and shrubs thriving within the fence is dramatic.

From the boggy ground of the col where cotton grass waves in the breeze, a path beside another fence can be followed west, nearly all the way to the summit of Meall Garbh, up steep grassy slopes speckled with tormentil and wild thyme. The summit ridge is reached at about 1,070 metres with the view opening out as height is gained. Just before the summit of Meall Garbh ignore a path that branches left onto a little out-crop with white quartz rocks and a cairn (NN64614 BNG43780). This is not the top despite the well-worn path that leads to it.

Instead continue to follow the fence to a corner where it turns down-hill and then climb a short distance south-west to the small summit cairn of Meall Garbh (1,118m) which perches on the crest of a mossy ridge carpeted with alpine ladies mantle.

From the summit of Meall Garbh there are views of Loch Tay, Glen Lyon, Loch an Daimh and north to Ben Nevis and the Mamores. To the south are the neighbouring peaks of Ben Lawers and An Stuc which was promoted to Munro status in 1997 by the Scottish Mountaineering Club. Hamish Brown climbed along the ridge from Ben Lawers to Meall Garbh in 1974 on his way to becoming the first man to complete all the Munros in a single trip. In *Hamish's Mountain Walk* he wrote that the descent of An Stuc in a white out using a tent pole as an ice axe was the most dangerous part of the whole expedition.

At the summit of Meall Garbh I take some photos, clip Cuilean and the Labradoodle to the fence and munch a sandwich watching two hang gliders circle in the air above the ridge, just happy to still be in the world and here on the mountain.

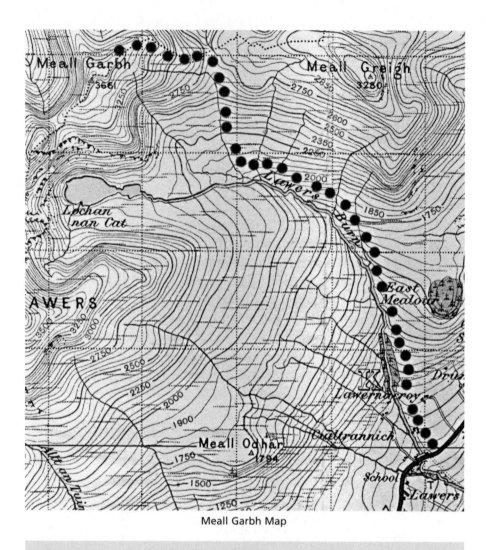

Meall Garbh Map

MEALL GARBH (1,118m)

Grade   ***
Map: OS Sheet 51
Distance/Ascent: 12km/938m
Starting Height: 180m
Time to top: 2h 45min +breaks
Start/Finish: Lawers village on north side of Loch Tay

A hill walk on a high Munro that starts with an historic path to the summer shielings. Requires careful navigation in poor visibility.

ROUTE:

1 Start at the Horn Carver's Cottage (NN68017 BNG39950) just outside Lawers village on A827 Killin to Aberfeldy road. Limited parking is available here (£5 charge). Hillwalkers are welcome to use the car park at nearby Ben Lawers Hotel on the understanding they spend money in the hotel afterwards.

2 Take track that starts on right of Horn Carver's Cottage (sign reads *Machuim Farm Private Road*).

3 When track bends sharp right go straight on, up path to left of farm building (signposted *Path to Hill*).

4 Go through gate by a barn (*Hill Path* and an arrow painted on iron tank).

5 Climb over old gate fastened shut with barbed wire.

6 Cross a footbridge with metal handrails. Walk along path overgrown with bracken to reach deer fence and cross a stile.

7 Reach a second stile that gives access to open hillside (sign indicates you are entering Ben Lawers national nature reserve.)

8 Look out for a waymarker (440m) NN67364 BNG41934 with arrow; leave the path near here before it reaches a footbridge (don't cross the stream) and climb a little way uphill to walk along top of high embankment on E side of Lawers Burn.

9 Walk along E bank Lawers Burn until you see small dam near NN66100 42800.

10 From near the dam aim for col (830m) NN65744 BNG44024 between Meall Greigh and Meall Garbh. In misty weather careful navigation will be needed.

11 A deer fence not marked on OS map starts at 700m near NN65832 BNG43367 and can be followed N almost all the way to the col.

12 Leave deer fence at NN65686 BNG43796 where fence turns E and walk a short distance N to the col.

13 From col follow path W beside sheep fence.

14 Path reaches summit ridge NN64935 BNG44115 at about 1,070m.

15 Near summit do not take path that branches left to a cairn NN64614 BNG43780 near white quartz rocks.

16 Instead continue to follow fence. Just before true summit, path leaves fence at NN64466 BNG43796 (at a corner with thick reinforced fence-post where fence turns N/right and goes downhill).

17 Path climbs a short distance SW to the small summit cairn of Meall Garbh (1,118m).

18 Return by the same route.

DOGS: lots of sheep on open hillside after woodland ends at second stile. One awkward gate fastened with barbed wire but both stiles have 'dog flaps'.

WINTER CONDITIONS: ice axe and crampons needed.

Somewhere Else: the Ben Lawers Hotel, Lawers village.

CHAPTER NINETEEN

Swimming with the Osprey

He was at his best on the heather or the ptarmigan ground above it. The nature of the rocks, soil, and plants, the direction of the wind, the aspect of the sky, the patch of late-lying snow, birds heard or seen, the red deer, the hill fox – all these arrested his attention and set his mind a-work, framing problems and attempting solutions.

SO WROTE HENRY JOHNSTONE of his friend and colleague CG Cash and this chapter will focus on Caleb's role in the development of nature conservation in Scotland.

Caleb was fascinated by the natural world and ahead of his time in his hatred of cruelty to wild animals. The tenor of human attitudes to the natural world during the 19th century is exemplified by the Glen Garry estate records. Over a period of three years 98 golden eagles, 18 ospreys and innumerable buzzards, red kites, harriers and sea eagles were slaughtered by the estate's gamekeepers. This pattern was repeated across Scotland. By contrast Caleb loved wildlife and disliked hunting and fishing, he was an early environmentalist and his ideas about nature conservation have become mainstream today a hundred years later.

Caleb kept records of the weather and used a barometer to make his own forecast in the days before accurate weather forecasts were available. Like the grandfather of Scottish naturalism Seton Gordon, CG Cash had an interest in the long lying snow patches of the Cairngorms. Adam Watson has continued to study these snow patches up to the present day. Since the mid-1800s the snowfield at the head of An Garbh Choire on Braeriach has disappeared in only five years 1933, 1959, 1996, 2003 and 2006. Today these patches of near perpetual snow are conspicuous indicators of climate change and have generated much research. In their fascination with the lingering snowfields of the Cairngorms CG Cash and Seton Gordon seem to have instinctively understood the danger of global warming.

One summer Caleb guided a botanist friend to An Garbh Choire of Braeriach. They scrambled (Caleb later wrote he found it scary) up by the

Falls of Dee while collecting plants. Caleb carried a vasculum on hill walks, a flattened tin cylinder lined with moistened cloth, used by botanists to keep field samples fresh by maintaining a cool, humid environment. He was interested in the plants to be found in the Cairngorms – whole days were spent in An Garbh Choire searching for rare Alpines, marvelling at the foot long roots of moss campion that anchor the plant to the gravel of the Cairngorm plateau.

Caleb was also a keen amateur ornithologist who used field glasses to spot both birds and distant mountains and once recorded seeing 33 black grouse in one day. In an article for *The Cairngorm Club Journal*, written in 1904 Caleb describes taking Alice to see an eagle's nest. Demonstrating awareness ahead of his time of the threats facing birds of prey Caleb keeps the location of the nest a secret and changes the names of surrounding hills in 'At Creag Na H'Iolaire'. The text is illustrated with photos taken by a teenage Seton Gordon who would go on to produce the first book of the 20th century in praise of the Cairngorms inspiring later writers like Nan Shepherd, Desmond Nethersole-Thompson, Adam Watson and Jim Crumley.

CALEB HEARS THE SONG OF THE CAPERCAILLIE

The capercaillie is a huge woodland grouse found in native Caledonian pinewood (a rare and vulnerable habitat) and in commercial conifer plantations where it feeds on berries and the buds and shoots of the Scots Pine. The male capercaillie is big, I have seen one only once, and it looked like a turkey scuttling across the track into the trees. The ptarmigan and the capercaillie are the only birds known by their Gaelic names. The Gaels named the capercaillie after its song calling it the horse of the woods for the clip clop sound they heard when it sang.

Caleb heard the song of the capercaillie, one of the weirdest in the world of birds in the Forest of Rothiemurchus in the spring of 1905. Later in *The Cairngorm Club Journal* he wrote about his encounter with the bird near the present day ski road through Inverdruie in the days when capercaillie could be seen in the woods on the outskirts of Aviemore. In 'The Capercailzie In Rothiemurchus' there are glimpses of Caleb's summers in the lost world of Strathspey in the 1900s; Mr Dempster the schoolmaster with his field-glass, the children throwing sticks at the capercaillie, the butcher's cart and the tinkers.

As well as observing wildlife Caleb contributed to a limited extent to the development of nature conservation in Scotland. He was present at the very beginning of human attempts to protect the osprey. Trying to protect a bird of prey marked a major change in human attitudes to the natural world. Half a century later in July 1954 this gradual shift in attitudes would culminate in the declaration of the Cairngorms National Nature Reserve.

Writing at the same time as pioneers of the environmental movement such as John Muir and Seton Gordon, Caleb sought to draw attention to the plight of the osprey in Scotland. By the early years of the 20th century this iconic bird of prey had been persecuted to the brink of extinction by men who stole its beautifully patterned eggs for their dusty collections and gamekeepers who shot the birds because they hunted fish.

'The cock osprey in the picture may be seen hovering on high, looking for finny prey in the water below… The hen bird is to be descried sitting at the edge of her nest on the right-hand turret.'

Caleb had first encountered these big brown and white birds with their characteristic slow flapping flight and spectacular hunting skills in 1894 when he spent August at a cottage on the shore of Loch an Eilein in

Strathspey. For centuries the osprey had nested on a tower of the ruined castle on the island that gives Loch an Eilein its name. Caleb became captivated by the ospreys circling above the loch hunting for fish. He observed the way the birds would hover and then hurtle suddenly from a height, feet first, to catch a brown trout in talons specially adapted for grasping and carrying slippery fish. Each morning Caleb swam in the loch; 'As I was in the water the bird would fly above me uttering its screaming cry' he wrote. Over the following decade each spring towards the end of March Caleb looked for the return of the ospreys to the loch after their long migratory flight from West Africa.

Robert Lambert has traced changes in attitudes to nature and the use of land in the Cairngorms and in his book *Contested Mountains* writes that CG Cash;

> found in the ospreys at Loch an Eilein a sense of the spirit and serenity of the natural world in the face of such human indifference to the suffering of wild creatures.

In April 1900 Caleb returned to Edinburgh after spending Easter in Strathspey. In a letter to the Laird of Rothiemurchus Caleb expresses concern about an osprey nest at Loch Gamhna near Loch an Eilein and the threat posed to it by egg collectors;

> The tree is easily approached, and would be quite easily climbed and I think it well to let you know of this, that the birds may be protected if possible. I at once went to keeper Cox and told him, but I have told no-one else at Rothiemurchus following on that my own feeling of what was best and Cox's advice. But I fear the new nest is too obvious and too easily accessible to remain unmolested.

Caleb was there on the shores of Loch an Eilein in the summer of 1895 when OAJ Lee took some of the first photographs of ospreys in Scotland. In 1907 Caleb published an article in the popular and widely read journal *The Scottish Naturalist* entitled *History of the Loch an Eilein Ospreys* in which he recounted how he had begun observing and making notes on the ospreys in 1894; 'I little thought then that I was perhaps writing the requiem of these noble birds...'

The article which also appeared in *The Cairngorm Club Journal* is a poignant account of the persecution of the osprey during the 19th century which Caleb so deplored. It describes how the Victorian egg collector

Lewis Dunbar swam out to the ospreys' nest on the island castle in Loch an Eilein to steal their eggs; '... I climbed up to the top of the ruin, and was just at the nest, I put out my hand to catch the hen, but when she felt me she gave a loud scream, and flew away...'; how the floating of rafts of felled timber on the loch caused the ospreys to abandon their nest and how they were shot by Victorian 'sportsmen'.

Caleb recorded that in 1897 two birds nested on the castle and probably two young were hatched. In 1902 a single osprey came to the castle nest on 4 April but remained alone and mateless. Earlier in the 19th century in a letter to another egg collector William Dunbar (brother of Lewis) had written; 'I am afraid that Mr St John, yourself and your humble servant have finally done for the ospreys.' And Caleb's article ends with the words;

> Since 1902 no osprey has been seen at [Loch an Eilein]... This finishes my story-a story of such ruthless persecution and of such altogether inadequate protection that the wonder is that the ospreys have survived so long. It will be a matter for serious regret if we lose these birds, but lose them we shall – even if we have not already lost them – unless this persecution is prevented...

I imagine Caleb, a lonely figure in Edwardian clothes standing on the shore of Loch an Eilein on a sunny April morning around 1904. The green water of the loch shimmers in the sunlight. The Cairngorm mountains rise blue and hazy beyond the edge of the forest. I see him look out across the water to the island with its ruined castle, wondering if the ospreys will ever return. After 1907 there were occasional rumours and reports of ospreys being seen in Strathspey but Caleb lived the last decade of his life fearing the osprey to be extinct in Scotland.

Since the 1950s a conservation programme has allowed ospreys to partially recolonise their ancestral breeding grounds and today there are about 225 nesting pairs across Scotland. Writing of the osprey's migration in 1902 Caleb posed questions half a century ahead of his time; 'Do the same birds come back in successive years? What becomes of the young ones?' he asked 'How it is that numbers do not increase?' Questions that would not be answered until the 1960s.

In 1903 Caleb predicted the return of ospreys as a breeding bird to Scotland writing that if ospreys did come back to Loch an Eilein they should; 'be protected even more carefully than in the past' and a systematic record should be kept of such points as dates of arrival, of hatching, and of departure. This could probably be done by arrangement between the Keeper and the tenant of Loch Cottage.

When a pair of ospreys built a nest at nearby Loch Garten in the 1950s the RSPB followed Caleb's proposed scheme almost to the letter.

In 1963 a pair of ospreys returned to nest again in Inshriach forest close to Loch an Eilein. Though they haven't yet recolonised their old nesting site on the castle, today more than a hundred years after Caleb kept his lonely vigil at the loch side ospreys can again be seen at Loch an Eilein. Sometimes in April when the long lying snow beds of An Garbh Choire on Braeriach are beginning to melt I think somehow, somewhere Caleb knows the ospreys have returned.

CHAPTER TWENTY

Ben Chonzie

Mountain Hares

*A hare over water meaning the verb 'to be' in the
sense of 'existing'.*
ANCIENT EGYPTIAN HIEROGLYPH, [*Wikipedia*]

IT BEGAN WITH JOHN MacCULLOCH early in the 19th century. After
climbing Ben Chonzie he wrote; 'there is not much interest in the view
from the summit.' A century later in 1910 Caleb described Ben Chonzie
as a 'flattish dish-cover' shape when seen from Edinburgh and over the
decades that followed the mountain acquired a reputation for being a
dull hill. Hillwalking guidebooks tend to be disparaging about Ben
Chonzie but why not pick on one of the Geal Charns instead? 'Can this
hill lay claim to be the dullest Munro in the land?' asks Cameron
McNeish and *The Ultimate Guide to the Munros* goes further (albeit
tongue in cheek) describing the hill as; 'an over-sized compost heap that
makes philately seem an attractive sport'. But for me, each time I've
climbed the hill, the sight of sometimes dozens of mountain hares,
poised, alert and clearly visible among the rocks below the summit has
made Ben Chonzie seem far from a dull hill.

WHO OWNS BEN CHONZIE?

Much of Ben Chonzie lies within the
boundaries of the Invergeldie Estate
which in 2004 was owned by James F.
Priestly, Head Bourne Worthy House,
Bedfield Lane, Headbourne Worthy,
Winchester, England.

HILLS SEEN FROM EDINBURGH

49 Comely Bank Road, Edinburgh,
July 11, 1910

SIR,

In your issue of this date, 'W.T.M.' asks whether Ben Chonzie can be seen from the neighbourhood of Edinburgh. Assuredly it can.

If 'W.T.M.' will ascend Arthur's Seat on a clear day, and look beyond the east part of the island of Inchcolm, he should see the flattish dish-cover shape of Ben Chonzie in the distance.

I should like to say that I have drawn up andprinted a table of most of the 'tops' that can be seen from Arthur's Seat.

I am,&c.
C.G. CASH

From letters to *The Scotsman* newspaper 16 July 1910.

Ben Chonzie rises to 931 metres or 3,054 feet above sea level and is described on Caleb's list as being north of Comrie and to be seen from Arthur's Seat in line with the right-hand part of Inchcolm Island. On Timothy Pont's map drawn in the 1590s Ben Chonzie appears to be named Hill of Turret after nearby Glen Turret. It was at Comrie at the mouth of Glen Lednock that the legendary Roman Ninth Legion suffered a disastrous night attack by the Caledonians and Irvine Butterfield suggested the name Ben Chonzie comes from Beinn a'Chaoneidh, hill of weeping, and a reference to the dead from the battle buried in Glen Turret.

Often the geology or plant life of a mountain gives clues as to the meaning of its Gaelic name. The summit of Ben Chonzie is blanketed in moss and the explanation most guidebooks today give of the name is 'hill of moss'.

In 1900 Caleb wrote a series of articles for *The Scotsman* newspaper about the progress of the Ordnance Survey of Scotland that was then being carried out. Gaelic names were being re-examined as part of the revision of Scotland's maps and Caleb described the system used; first a Gaelic speaking employee of the Ordnance Survey asked locally about place names. Names there was any doubt about were then submitted to the Place Names Committee of the Royal Scottish Geographical Society in Edinburgh (not a committee that included Caleb presumably, coming from the East Midlands he must have struggled with Gaelic). Caleb wrote that few Gaelic speakers or scholars were involved in the Place Names Committee unlike in Wales where Welsh speakers advised the Ordnance Survey on place names. Nothing, worries Caleb, is done about Norse names.

Sometimes surveyors confused Welsh and Gaelic names. This lingers on in the way local people in Crieff and Comrie sometimes call Ben Chonzie by its alternative name Ben y Hone. However the letter 'y' is not part of the Gaelic alphabet and it is thought that the first Ordnance Survey which 'mapped' these spellings was carried out by a surveyor who originated from Wales where 'y' is equivalent to the Gaelic 'a'.

In *Scottish Hill Names* Peter Drummond calls Ben Chonzie a 'terrible Anglicisation... often pronounced as it is spelt in English... of the gentle Gaelic *beinn na còinnich* (mossy mountain).' As Caleb pointed out many employees of the Ordnance Survey could not speak Gaelic and were ill suited to collecting names and this led to mistakes on maps;

> It is necessary that a man who collects... Gaelic names should have both a natural and a literary acquaintance with the language. It is pretty certain that a man who takes only an Englishman's ear... will make blunders; and too many of them have appeared on the Ordnance Survey maps...

The legacy of the Place Names Committee lives on today in the ugly Anglicisations of Gaelic words which still litter the Ordnance Survey maps of the 21st century.

Climbing Ben Chonzie

At the Deil's Cauldron restaurant on the A85 in the centre of Comrie turn up Monument Road following signposts to *Glen Lednock*. Drive about 6km north through Glen Lednock to reach a parking place near Coishavachan. The glen is pretty with craggy pointed hills rising above rich farmland and mature trees. One of these hills, the aptly named Balnacoul Castle has several rock climbs on it. The road through Glen Lednock follows the line of an old drove route from Loch Tay to Crieff and before the Highland Clearances Glen Lednock supported 21 small farming communities.

From the parking place take the track signposted *Public Footpath to Ardtalnaig* that leads towards the houses at Coishavachan. I climbed Ben Chonzie during a settled spell of sunny weather in June and bought fresh hen and duck eggs from the white painted house. A man in a tractor was cutting hay in a meadow by the road and a pied wagtail perched on the fence watching me as I put my boots on.

When I got back to the car after the walk a very shy three-month-old border collie puppy was being introduced to a flock of lambs for the first time in a nearby field. The woman with the puppy made it stay at her feet while the lambs ran away so in time the pup would learn only to chase sheep on command. Then a taxi arrived bringing the children back from school in Comrie and a little girl set off up the road towards Invergeldie with the puppy on a lead trailing along behind.

From the houses at Coishavachan follow the track through a field of sheep and along the edge of a windbreak of pine trees. Pass a dry stone walled sheep fank then cross a wooden bridge over the Invergeldie Burn. The track climbs the hillside on the west side of the burn through pastures where bracken is starting to take hold. Soft rush and thistles grow among boulders scattered by the sides of the track. Sheep and lambs graze nearby concealed in the deep bracken.

Sheep's wool and droppings litter the track which climbs gently uphill and where it draws close to the birch trees that line the course of the Invergeldie Burn, a steep eroded gravely bank is home to a colony of sand martins.

The houses at Invergeldie are hidden by the pine plantation. In the distance the rounded hills of Perthshire rise gently beyond brown moor land dappled with green. A dragonfly flies across the track. The June sun is hot and grasshoppers chatter in the grass. The hillside near the track may once have been cultivated for crops rather than just hill grazing. There are bright green areas of grass and the overgrown remains of dry stone dykes where sheep graze over walls once built to keep them out.

Go through a gate and a short distance beyond it ignore a grassy path that leads over to Ardtalnaig on Loch Tay. Keep to the main track which dips down to cross the bed of the Invergeldie Burn below a small dam where moss grows on the 50-year-old concrete.

The water level of the burn is often low as its waters have been tapped to feed Loch Lednock reservoir part of the Breadalbane hydro-electric scheme. Kellan's first (childhood) memory of hydro-electric development in the Highlands is of waiting and waiting in a seemingly endless traffic jam at the Pass of Brander where the road is being built out over the loch as part of the Cruachan Dam scheme. When the line of cars finally begins to move his face is pressed against the window of the Hillman Imp as the car edges across clanking metal plates below which through the gaps his nine-year-old eyes can clearly see the grey waters of Loch Awe.

Sandmartin

The track climbs away from the stream in a big hair pin bend uphill through the heather towards the green shoulder of Ben Chonzie that rises above the moor land. The route is clear as the track climbs the lower slopes of Ben Chonzie beside a little burn. Ferns grow on the heather covered banks of the stream and in summer there are wildflowers among the grass; yellow alpine ladies-mantle and purple-pink wild thyme. Nearby marshy ground is dotted white with cotton grass. Small wetland areas like these, rich in insect life, provide important feeding for dunlin, snipe and golden plover.

On the moorland below Ben Chonzie the instantly recognisable traces of grouse shooting can be seen in the form of patches of muirburn covered in dead twigs of burnt heather and stone grouse butts by the stream where the 'guns' conceal themselves as the grouse are driven towards them. They are usually enclosures six to eight feet square with waist high dry-stone walls and one entrance, facing away from the direction the beaters and grouse are expected. Grouse shooting has become less common in recent times because of a decline in the number of grouse and many grouse butts are no longer in use.

Just past the grouse butts a sign reads *Conservation Area Wild Birds Nesting Please Keep Dogs On Leads*. Ben Chonzie is designated a site of special scientific interest because of; 'its nationally important assemblage of upland habitats… rare plants and breeding birds'. Look out on the mountain for peregrine falcon, golden eagle, buzzard, red grouse, ptarmigan, raven, and ring ouzel. On ledges on the east facing cliffs of Ben Chonzie above Glen Turret many calcium loving plants grow including alpine cinquefoil, mountain pansy, twisted whitlow-grass, globe-flower, wood cranesbill, water avens, wild angelica, common valerian and meadowsweet.

The slopes of Ben Chonzie are striped with bands of heather and large squares of blaeberry interspersed with marshy ground spiked with rushes and dotted white with cotton grass. The bell heather is just beginning to flower and two orange brown northern eggar moths flutter across the track. Higher up the track becomes very stony and Cuilean, finding the going uncomfortable, searches out the little footpaths that run along the edge of the track created by hillwalkers avoiding the stony rubble. Ladies-mantle, tormentil and wild thyme grow among the lichen covered rocks that lie in the heather. Looking west beyond Balnacoul Castle the hills of the southern Highlands begin to appear, Ben More and Stob Binnein prominent among them, Ben Lawers, An Stuc, Meall Garbh and Ben Vorlich too.

THE FIRST RECORDED ASCENT OF BEN CHONZIE

The first documented ascent of Ben Chonzie was made by John MacCulloch (1773–1835) who was probably Scotland's first peak bagger. MacCulloch was born in Guernsey, but his father came from Galloway and childhood holidays were spent in Scotland. John MacCulloch studied medicine at Edinburgh University and was appointed geologist to the Trigonometrical Survey, an early exercise in mapping the Scottish Highlands. MacCulloch made scientific trips to Scotland every year between 1811 and 1821 during which time he climbed a number of Scottish mountains and later wrote about his exploits in *Highlands and Western Islands of Scotland* published in 1824.

In September 1896 an article in the Scottish Mountaineering Club's Journal described a day on Ben Chonzie and suggested;

> the most pleasant time to ascend this hill is about the middle of the month of July, for then the whole hill is under a thick carpet of ripe berries, which one can gather in handfuls at every step. When a friend and I made the ascent from Comrie on 18th July... The crowberries were in millions and millions, the blaeberries in thousands and thousands, cranberries in hundreds and hundreds, and the cloudberries in dozens and dozens.

As the track climbs higher heather gives way to grass. Near the 700 metre contour ignore a couple of walkers' paths that branch off to the left. A short distance to the south of the track a well built cairn stands above the crags of Creag Gharbh. I walk out to it through ankle deep heather, blaeberry and the distinctive broad leaves of cloudberry wondering why it was there. I'm still none the wiser although you can see the town of Comrie from the cairn so perhaps that is why it was built. Comrie sits astride the Highland Boundary Fault which separates the sandstones of the central valley of Scotland from the older harder rocks of the Highlands. Movement along the fault line sometimes gives rise to minor earthquakes. Records began in 1789 when the first seismograph in Britain was set up at Dunira and *The Old Statistical of Scotland* makes mention of earthquakes.

Though usually only strong enough to rattle the window panes in Comrie, one tremor thought to be around 4.9 on the Richter scale became known as the Great Quake of 1839 and caused alarm when 20 shocks in 24 hours caused cracks to appear in the walls of houses and sent chimney pots crashing to the ground. The dam on Loch Lednock at the head of the glen is reinforced against earthquakes and local people used to speak of close sultry weather during periods of prolonged rain as earthquake weather.

Continue along the track as it climbs steeply uphill to end at a cairn on a level plateau at a height of about 800 metres. From the cairn walk north along a faint grassy path for about half a kilometre to reach a fence. The summit plateau of Ben Chonzie is blanketed with wind clipped heather and blaeberry covered heath. The stubby heather crunches under walking boots. On the hillside near the fence is an area of rocks and boulders. I look carefully and on the skyline see two poised crouching shapes with pointed ears; mountain hares. Ben Chonzie is famous for them. I tie the dogs to a rusty iron fencepost and try to take photos but the Labradoodle's yelping scares the hares away.

Mountain Hare

For Robert MacFarlane hares are totemic wild animals. He writes of 'the ghostly beauty of their winter pelage' and how when watching a hare make its curved run in a steep snowfield you can understand why the Egyptian hieroglyphic, of a hare over a zigzag of water, means the verb 'to be' in the sense of 'existing'.

Mountain hares are known by many names; in Gaelic they are called *maigheach-gheal*, in Scots *tormalkin* and in English sometimes blue hares or in winter white hares. In Latin the hare is *lepus timidus* meaning timid or frightened. Pliny called them snow hares and believed they went white from eating ice. Smaller and more ancient than the brown hare, at the end of the last ice age, 10,000 years ago when the glaciers retreated, mountain hares were left marooned on islands of high ground.

One day about 10 years ago climbing in winter in the Monaliadh mountains Cuilean went off chasing madly after hares for hundreds of metres. The strength of a young border collie was impressive to watch as she ran at full speed through what to her were shoulder high snow drifts. Even as a young dog she was never able to match a hare for speed and I put her on the lead to prevent her chasing hungry mountain hares, forcing them to use up precious energy needed to survive the long dark Scottish winter.

Some early travellers in Scotland left descriptions of mountain hares; an animal some had never seen before. In 1754 Edward Burt wrote;

> It is no uncommon thing, when the mountains are deep in snow, for us to see hares almost as white as snow... but although we have hunted several of them for a while, yet always without success, for they keep near the feet of the hills, and, immediately on being started, make to the heights, where the scent is lost, and they baffle all pursuit.

A large bird of prey circles over the hillside. The hares sense its shadow on the ground and stay among the rocks. That day I see only three hares, many fewer than on a previous visit in winter. Eagles and buzzards are not the only threat the hare must contend with. Mountain hares are still hunted in Perthshire. One cold, wintry Tuesday morning in February in the mist on nearby Auchnafree Hill I came upon a group of Eastern European sounding men in land rovers with rifles and Labradors. The men put up their guns when they saw me and a surly grey haired gamekeeper came across and muttered something about access. In his hand he held the still warm body of a mountain hare he'd just shot. The hare's white winter coat had failed to save it and was stained with red.

Continue to follow the fence north-west for about 500 metres until it turns north-east and follows the broad and in places stony ridge another half kilometre to the summit of Ben Chonzie (931m) with its cairn and stone shelter. The mountain takes its name from the mosses that grow on its summit, among them woolly fringe moss which consists of soft finely branched tufts which look pale turquoise when dry and yellow green after rain. The plant both looks and feels woolly and has a lightly frosted appearance.

Return by the same route. On the way back retrace your route of ascent carefully remembering that successful navigation requires concentration. A few years ago two friends of mine were on the top of a snow covered Ben Chonzie in thick mist. After lunch at the summit cairn, still deep in conversation they set off back down the hill. It wasn't until they came out of the mist and found themselves above a loch they hadn't passed on the way up (Loch Turret) that the realisation dawned they had made a major navigational error. In the gathering dusk of a winter's afternoon they were faced with the salutary prospect of a 17 mile walk from Glen Turret round to Glen Lednock by road. Luckily for them the chivalrous owner of a well-known climbing shop, who happened to be on the hill that day, came to their rescue and gave them a lift back to their car at Coishavachan.

The day I climbed Ben Chonzie it was clear and compass bearings were not needed. From the summit I recognised the Cairngorms by the large snow patches that remained on them at the end of June after the long snowy winter. Across Loch Turret I could see Auchnafree Hill and faraway the Lomond Hills of Fife. Ben Lawers, An Stuc and Meall Garbh were prominent along with Schiehallion, Beinn a'Ghlo, Ben Vorlich and Stob Binnein. The long hot spell of weather was breaking and already the top of Ben More was disappearing into the clouds.

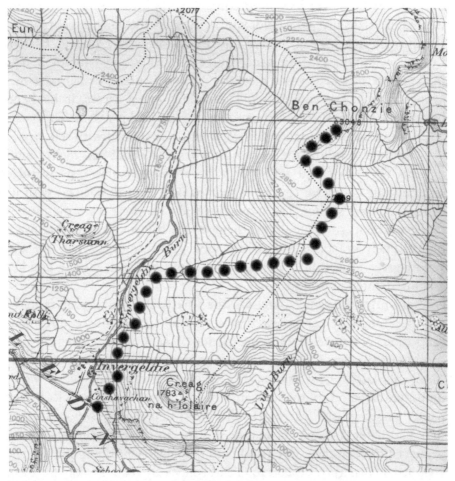

Ben Chonzie map

BEN CHONZIE (931m)

Grade   **
Map: OS Sheet 51
Distance/Ascent: 13km/715m
Time to top: 2h45min +breaks
Starting Height: 215m
Start/Finish: Parking place near Coishavachan in Glen Lednock

Look out for mountain hares on a straightforward ascent of one of the easiest Munros in the Southern Highlands.

ROUTE:

1   At Deil's Cauldron restaurant on A85 in centre of Comrie turn up Monument Road (signposted *Glen Lednock*). Drive about 6km N through Glen Lednock to reach parking place NN74304 27274 near Coishavachan (where signpost reads *Public Footpath to Ardtalnaig*).

2   From parking place take track signposted *Public Footpath to Ardtalnaig* that leads towards houses at Coishavachan.

3   In front of houses at Coishavachan turn right (waymarker with arrow) and go through gate by garage. Turn left and follow track along edge of pine trees through field.

4   Pass sheep fank then cross wooden bridge over Invergeldie Burn and go through another gate. Follow track as it climbs hillside on W side of burn.

5   Go through gate NN74578 28703. Just past gate ignore grassy track that goes left. Keep to main track which dips down to cross Invergeldie Burn below small dam.

6   Keep left (uphill) at fork in track just past dam.

7   Ignore track that branches left across stream near some grouse butts.

8   Near 700m contour ignore cairns and walkers' paths that branch left off main track.

9   Continue along track steeply uphill to cairn NN77082 29268 on level plateau at about 800m.

10 From cairn walk follow faint grassy path on bearing of 14 degrees N for about 500m to reach fence near NN77274 29820.

11 First follow fence NW (left) for about 500m then follow it as it turns
   NE for another 500m along broad ridge to summit of Ben Chonzie
   (931m) NN77317 30844 (cairn and stone shelter).

DOGS: lots of sheep on Ben Chonzie.

WINTER CONDITIONS: a good hill for a first winter outing (ice axe and
   crampons needed).

CHAPTER TWENTY ONE

Schiehallion

The Attraction of Mountains

and what was the toast?
schiehallion! schiehallion! schiehallion!
From Canedolia an off-concrete Scotch fantasia by Edwin Morgan

TWENTY YEARS AGO MURIEL GRAY wrote that she loved hillwalking alone but sometimes missed having someone else there so she could; '... enjoy the standard argument at the summit about the identity of the peaks you can see... or... be the first one to correctly name the pointy little sod all on its own on the far horizon'. She went on to say; 'in such a squabble the answer is always Schiehallion.'

Schiehallion. One of Scotland's most famous hills. In folklore the mountain was believed to hold magical powers and iron age people left an ornamental stone cup high on its slopes. A look at a map shows that Schiehallion stands at the centre of Scotland and 18th century scientists climbed the mountain to weigh the world. Today the mountain is owned by a charity that exists to protect wild land and has a North Atlantic oil-field named after it. Schiehallion (pronounced sheehalyan) rises to 1,083m/3,553ft and on Caleb's list of Scottish mountains visible from Arthur's Seat it is described as lying 35 degrees west of north in line with the east breakwater at Granton.

In the 1790s Duncan McAra spelt Schiehallion's name *Thichallin* which he wrote; 'signifies the Maiden's Breast, its form being quite round'. This explanation of the name comes from the phrase *sine chailinn*, breast of the maiden, but is problematic because in Gaelic the usual word for a breast is *cioch*, as found in hill names all over the Highlands.

In July 1838 Robert MacDonald named the mountain *Sith-Chaillin*; 'from its being the supposed place of resort of the maiden or queen of the fairies.' This is close to the modern spelling and today guidebooks give the meaning of Schiehallion as 'the fairy hill of the Caledonians' from the Gaelic *sìth chaillean*. The Caledonians were a tribe known to the Romans and Perthshire was their stronghold. The town of Dunkeld takes its name from *Dùn Chailleann* meaning the fort of the Caledonians.

Sìth is pronounced 'she' and means fairies or 'peaceful people' (possibly in contrast to other tribes who were more aggressive and warlike). There are *sìthean*, fairy or pointed hills are all over Scotland and the word is found in names like Glenshee. Perhaps the first people to climb Schiehallion belonged to the Caledonian tribe for whom the mountain may have held some crucial significance.

Schiehallion lies between the two great geological faults in Scotland; the Highland boundary fault and the Great Glen fault. The size and shape of Schiehallion and nearby Loch Rannoch and Loch Tummel date from the last ice age 10,000 years ago. The summit of Schiehallion consists of quartz, a pale grey-white crystalline rock. The lower slopes consist of schist rocks rich in mica. After climbing Schiehallion the back seat of the car sparkles with tiny silver shards of this rock carried in on the dogs' paws. Andrew Greig gave a character in his novel *In Another Light* the nickname Mica because she was... 'bright and shiny and a bit flaky...'

Climbing Schiehallion

East Schiehallion estate is owned by the John Muir Trust. The Trust tries to manage land with minimal intervention, leaving things to nature and;

> through conserving, campaigning and inspiring people seek(s) to ensure that wild land is protected and that wild places are valued by all members of society.

In the past the John Muir Trust has been criticised for accepting money from the oil company BP. Formed in 1983 it takes its name from the Scots born pioneer of the modern environmental movement John Muir (1838–1914), one of the first people to call for the conservation of wild places and who urged people to; 'Do something for wildness... make the mountains glad'.

A single track road signposted *Schiehallion Road* leaves the B846 between Coshieville and Tummel Bridge and goes round the north side of Schiehallion to Kinloch Rannoch. Drive about three kilometres along this road until you come to a stone cairn with a memorial plaque that stands at the entrance to the Braes of Foss car park. The path to Schiehallion starts in woodland at the back of the car park.

The John Muir Trust asks that you keep your dog close by to minimise disturbance to wild life. There were a lot of dogs going up Schiehallion the day I climbed it with the Labradoodle and Cuilean including a wee

Westie that had to be carried over the scree and boulders at the top of the mountain. Be warned though; Cuilean was off the lead to cross the boulder field on the way down when three sheep appeared from nowhere. Fortunately for the sheep I spotted them before the dog did or we'd probably still be up there. There aren't supposed to be sheep on Schiehallion but evidently incursions do occur!

As the path comes out of the trees it crosses a footbridge over a burn near a tall pine that stands alone at the edge of the straight man made boundary of the plantation. Beyond is moorland patched with brown dead bracken, green grass and purple heather.

Near the path faint traces remain of the people who lived and culti- vated the lower slopes of Schiehallion from the first millennium BC until about 200 years ago. Between the end of the forest and the second wooden bridge, a few metres to the west of the path among the bracken, is a lichen covered boulder NN75260 55310 with cup marks on it. The carvings on this stone may have been made two or three thousand years ago. The purpose of cup marks is not known – theories as to their meaning include art, maps, signposts or religion.

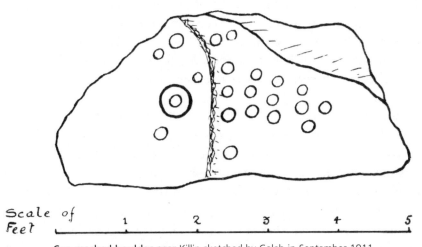

Scale of Feet   1   2   3   4   5

Cup marked boulder near Killin sketched by Caleb in September 1911

The bracken at the sides of the path was turning from green to brown when I climbed Schiehallion one cloudy September morning. Yarrow grows by the side of the path, bog myrtle where the ground is marshy. From here Schiehallion appears as a long whale back of a ridge rather than the triangular peak featured in *The Scotsman* calendar.

A few hundred metres further along the track, on the same side as the cup marked stone (just before the path goes over the brow of a little hillock to the east of a sheep fank), there is evidence of 18th century farming on Schiehallion. About 100 metres to the west of the path and uphill from it at NN74977 54920, among the grass and heather, are the remains of field boundary walls, four oblong buildings and a corn drying kiln. These ruins once formed part of a *ferm toun* and two families may have lived here. The houses probably had turf walls and animals were kept at one end of the building while the people lived at the other. Today only wheatears live among the ruins and the name of this settlement that stood in the shadow of Schiehallion has been forgotten.

The footpath crosses an old track near a sheep fank where bracken grows among fallen down stone walls. The track leads to another ancient settlement, the hut circle marked on the Ordnance Survey map at Aonach Ban. A sheep fank or pen is where a shepherd would temporarily corral his sheep allowing him close access to them, for shearing for example. Towards the end of the 18th century sheep rearing increased in importance and became East Schiehallion estate's principal activity. The older *ferm touns* near the mountain had by that time been abandoned.

The path climbs above the sheep fank up to the broad ridge of Schiehallion through grass dotted with bluebells and tormentil. Over 60 species of upland birds have been recorded on Schiehallion and important breeding species include hen harrier, merlin, ptarmigan, black grouse and ring ouzel.

About 20,000 people a year climb Schiehallion and by 1999 the footpath had become a 'mountain motorway', an ugly scar on the hillside. In a five year project at a cost of £800,000 the John Muir Trust set out to realign the path onto a more sustainable line and repair the scar of the old 'mountain motorway'. The 3.4km of 'new' path, built by contractors and volunteers, has been in use since 2003 and is a stalkers' type path; narrow, with a steady gradient, and a gravelly surface of locally sourced material. This kind of path is much easier to walk on and less slippery than, for example the Ben Nevis path, which is paved with large stones for long sections.

The line of the old path can be seen from the car park, a visible but fading scar on the hillside. To repair the damage the John Muir Trust reseeded the ground and constructed low barriers across the old path, formed from rocks and topped with turf to prevent further damage from water run-off. The old 'mountain motorway' path was itself quite recent, dating only from the opening of the Braes of Foss car park in the 1970s.

When I climbed Schiehallion engineering work was in progress beside the Allt Mor stream. A quick check on Google revealed this to be the construction of an intake for the small scale Keltney Burn hydro-electric scheme. The lonely farmhouse at Braes of Foss stood out white against the green forest and brown moorland with Loch Tummel a sheet of blue among the trees. A heath bumble bee whirred over the heather and low blaeberry bushes as I followed the path higher up the ridge. Little Loch Kinardochy, formed when retreating glaciers carved out 'kettle holes' and a popular venue for curling in the early 19th century can be seen among the trees of the Tay Forest park.

Schiehallion became a sporting estate in the 19th century, part of the old estate of Kynachan bought by the Marquis of Breadalbane in 1834. Documents record 'the shootings of Schiehallion' being let to various tenants. Traces of grouse butts remain near the path, they probably date from about 1870. The opening of the Highland Railway's branch line to Aberfeldy five years earlier made selling grouse to city restaurants financially viable.

At about 870 metres the scree begins as the path reaches a cairn where it ends abruptly at a 'deflection bar' of stones, the point where the old 'mountain motorway' reached the ridge. A faint path worn by generations of hillwalkers trying to find the easiest way through the scree and boulders continues west along the ridge. For the remainder of the route to the summit of Schiehallion a line of cairns marks the way through the quartz boulders and scree. However these cairns are separated by quite long distances

Merlin

and navigation may be needed in poor visibility. Be careful not to lose the line of cairns among the other piles of rock. At about NN 72615 54599, a short distance from the end of the constructed path a horseshoe shaped cairn is reached. This cairn is thought to stand on the site of one built in 1774 and is known as the Maskeleyne cairn.

Sometimes the stars are closer from a mountain top. Schiehallion was the site of one of the most famous experiments in the history of science when 18th century astronomers and mathematicians came to Schiehallion to weigh the world. Their experiment used Sir Isaac Newton's discovery of gravity to calculate the weight of planet Earth and in the words of the memorial plaque on the roadside cairn at Braes of Foss car park this; '… became the first determination of Newton's Universal Gravitational Constant.'

Around this time scientists were beginning to understand the pull that massive objects exert on bodies of a smaller size. Newton had theorised that a large object such as a mountain would attract a plumb line by a measurable amount from the vertical, owing to the gravitational force of the mountain itself. From this the weight of the mountain could be calculated and hence the weight of the world. In September 1774 *The Scots Magazine* reported;

> Mr Maskeleyne, Astronomer-Royal, and Mr Ruben Burrow, have, at the desire of the Royal Society, been employed a good part of last summer, on Shichaillin, a very high mountain near Loch-Tay, making observations to determine the attraction of mountains.

Far from being some scientific wild goose chase, the experiment on Schiehallion was vital to Britain as an exporter of goods with a growing empire that depended on accurate navigation by merchant ships. Until the mystery of the attraction of mountains could be solved, maps were hopelessly inaccurate as they did not allow for the fact that mountains and differing densities of the earth's crust distort surveyors' plumb lines and produce serious errors in the measurement of latitude.

Initially Charles Mason a surveyor, remembered today for the Mason-Dixon line in North America, was sent to Scotland to recce likely looking mountains and to choose one suitable for the experiment, ideally it should be a steep sided cone. Schiehallion fitted the bill and was duly selected. The mountain was chosen for its accessibility and relative isolation from other mountains which would simplify calculations.

Reverend Nevil David Maskeleyne, Astronomer Royal to his Majesty King George III, was the man chosen by the Royal Society to conduct experiments on Schiehallion in 1774. Maskeleyne was in his early 40s, an excellent astronomer with a house in London and a taste for the good things in life. For Maskeleyne an expedition to the Highlands must have been fairly unappealing and he later wrote;

> My going to Scotland was not a matter of choice, but of necessity. The Royal Society... made a point with me to go there to take the direction of the experiment, which I did, not without reluctance, nor from any wish to depart from my own observatory to live on a barren mountain, but purely to serve the Society and the public, for which I received no gratuity, and had only my expenses paid for me.

A distant Schiehallion from Loch Tummel

Maskeleyne sailed by boat from the south of England to Perth. It is indicative of the state of the roads in the 1770s that the Astronomer Royal travelled by land for only the last 30 miles of his journey. By July 1,774 a locally recruited workforce had levelled platforms for observatories on the north and south faces of Schiehallion at a height of about 2,000 feet. A wooden tower was built to protect the expedition's zenith sector telescope from the weather and plumb lines were suspended on each side of the mountain.

Maskeleyne was to spend four months on Schiehallion working firstly from a stone and timber bothy (probably similar to a shieling hut) on the south side of the mountain and then at one on the northern slopes. Most of his assistants were housed in tents. Maskeleyne's 'uncommon experiment' on Schiehallion generated much interest and the Astronomer Royal was visited by the local gentry and academics from Edinburgh, Glasgow and Aberdeen Universities. Maskeleyne's work was prolonged from July to mid-November because of bad weather and he recorded; 'all the people of the country agreed it was the worst season that had ever been known.' Another of Maskeleyne's letters is headed; 'From the Observatory, in the south side of Shihallien, July 18 1774'. In it the Astronomer Royal complains it has been a week since he first; 'saw a star in the Sector (so bad has the weather been)'.

But Maskeleyne remained optimistic noting patches of blue sky and that; 'the clouds fly much higher than before.'

Maskeleyne began his experiment by making hundreds of observations of the stars from the mountain to record the true vertical, a measurement he needed in order to be able to record the sideways pull exerted by the mountain on the plumb lines. Schiehallion moved the plumb lines by just one six-hundredth part of one degree, a tiny amount but detectable by

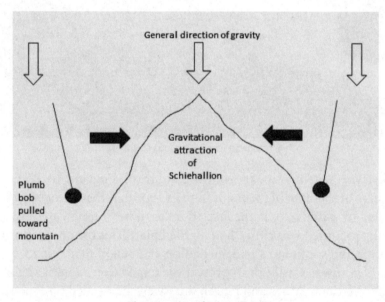

The Attraction of Mountains

the scientific instruments of the 1770s. Work all carried out on exposed hillside at 2,000 feet in between periods of wild weather.

All that now remained was to calculate the mass of Schiehallion and extrapolate from that the weight of the world. Maskeleyne did this with the help of (truculent Yorkshire) mathematician Reuben Burrow and Charles Hutton. They produced a surprisingly accurate figure, considering the limitations of 18th century scientific equipment, for the mass of the earth. Today this figure is around 5.9 billion trillion tonnes, only around one per cent different from the figure derived by Maskeleyne from his experiment. The expedition to Schiehallion cost the Royal Society £597 16s and was considered then and with hindsight to have been a great success.

Beside the A9 on the site of an old hotel stands the House of Bruar, the retail experience known as the Harrods of the Highlands. A white harling covered building beside a car park houses the Clan Donnachaidh centre. Inside is a small museum and in one of the glass cases, a violin. The well-known Shetland fiddler Aly Bain played this instrument at Blair Castle and commented on the beauty of its tone. The violin was originally purchased by Nevil Maskeleyne.

Maskeleyne's wine bills for his voyage to St Helena to observe the transit of Venus in 1761 still exist today and make impressive reading. To celebrate the end of his expedition to Scotland Maskeleyne hosted a wild party on Schiehallion. One Duncan Robertson, a cook and cleaner, was sent to Kinloch Rannoch for supplies of whisky and played the fiddle at the farewell party. But things got out of hand and Maskeleyne's bothy where the party was taking place caught fire and burned to the ground and the fiddle was destroyed. 'Never mind, Duncan,' Maskeleyne is said to have told the fiddler; 'when I get back to London, I will seek you out a new fiddle and send it to you'. Maskeleyne was as good, indeed better than his word and a few months later Duncan received a package wrapped in brown paper. Inside was a black leather bound case containing a beautifully crafted violin. Duncan composed a tune in honour of the new fiddle he called *A'Bhan Lunnainneach Bhuidhe*, the Yellow London Lady.

Fifteen hundred feet below the summit ridge of Schiehallion lies Gleann Mor; it forms a sort of moat on the south side of the mountain. Gleann Mor is a green glen because of a band of limestone there. Schiehallion supports a variety of upland habitats and a richer botanical life in contrast to surrounding hills, because of its underlying limestone. Limestone areas provide good grazing and can often be identified at a distance by the presence of lush green grassland.

The ridge narrows towards the summit and there are views across to Beinn a'Ghlo and Ben Vrackie and a white dot that is Blair Castle. The pointed summit of Farragon Hill can be seen and a dirt track road on the nearby Corbett Meall Tairneachan leads to a barites mine.

Fir clubmoss grows in little clumps in between the bare blocks of shattered quartz below the summit of Schiehallion. Some of the rocks have what looks like a red lichen growing on them and I notice ptarmigan droppings on the stones. Ptarmigan droppings appear identical to those of red grouse but can be distinguished according to the altitude where they are found. The words Meall nan Tarmachan marked on the OS 1:25000 map on the north side of Schiehallion are another indicator of the presence of these birds on the mountain.

Mountaineering is unique among sports for the rich body of literature it has inspired. *Hamish's Mountain Walk* was a big influence on Kellan's parents' generation. He remembers them reading it during a summer holiday in a caravan in Argyll in the 1970s. Both are teachers and Hamish Brown's stories of taking groups of working class kids from Braehead School in Fife to climb Munros and stay in remote bothies prove something of an inspiration to them. As a child the bit of the book that makes the greatest impression on Kellan is being told Hamish read novels as he tramped along the seemingly endless miles of forestry roads during his 'walk'.

Muriel Gray wrote a laugh out loud account of climbing Schiehallion early in her hillwalking career in a foul mood and while suffering from a filthy hangover; she made the first recorded ascent of Schiehallion to culminate in smashing a flask of tomato soup over her boyfriend's head at the summit cairn. Muriel Gray's much loved book about the Munros *The First Fifty* was a big influence on women mountaineers when it was published 20 years ago. A friend Ruth describes the book being passed from tent to tent on the slopes of Foinaven as the rain poured down, everyone in hysterics at the bit about going into an outdoor shop. Kellan's mother, who compleated the Munros ten years ago at the age of 61, always orders a bottle of Becks in the pub after a hill walk because that's what Muriel Gray ordered in the Inchnadamph Hotel after climbing Ben More Assynt.

Ptarmigan droppings appear identical to those of red grouse but can be distinguished according to the altitude and terrain where they are found as here on Schiehallion among rocks near the summit and well above the heather line.

The last section of the climb to the summit of Schiehallion is across a boulder field; tedious, difficult walking, over what one guidebook describes as 'ankle wrenching rubble'. Eventually the little outcrop that forms the summit of Schiehallion is reached, a small cairn stands on lichen covered rocks near the remains of a trig point.

A cold wind blows from the west over the summit but it is sunny and sheltered on the east side. Hamish Brown described the view; 'on a clear day you can see from North Berwick Law to Lochnagar to Ben Nevis from the summit of Schiehallion'. Closer by I could see Ben Lawers, Ben a Chuallaich, the Drumochter hills and the Lomond Hills of Fife. The big white building on the lochside is the hotel at Kinloch Rannoch. The small loch visible from the summit of Schiehallion is Dunalastair water. The much larger sheet of water is Loch Rannoch. At its far western end, the first Munroist Archibald Aeneas Robertson was the minister at Braes of Rannoch church for several years at the beginning of the 20th century.

The first *recorded* ascent of Schiehallion was made by General William Roy who measured the mountain's height barometrically while on a visit to Maskeleyne in July 1774. It is not known if Maskeleyne himself climbed to the top of Schiehallion but unnamed members of his expedition made the ascent in order to erect a cairn at the summit.

In his book *Weighing the World* Edwin Danson writes of how navigators today once again look to the skies to fix their position. At the top of Schiehallion I glance down at the Foretrex 101 GPS on my wrist. Push the sequence of keys for *trac bac*. An egg timer appears, then a reassuring arrow pointing the way back to the car. Science and technology have moved on since Maskeleyne's 18th century experiments yet even the high orbiting *Navstar* satellites of the US Defense Department's Global Positioning System cannot resist the attraction of mountains.

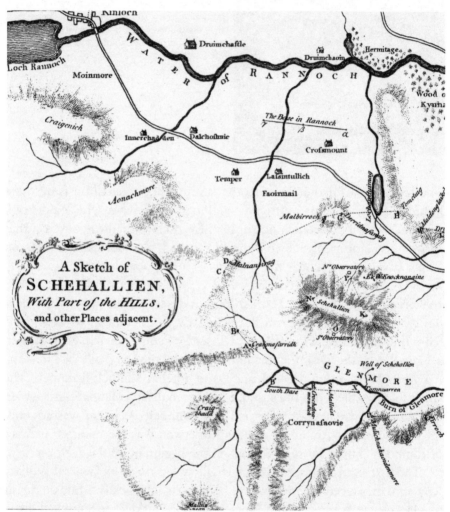

A map of Schiehallion drawn at the time of the weighing the world experiment and published in 1778. While mathematician Charles Hutton was calculating the mass of Schiehallion as part of Maskeleyne's experiment he made the discovery that if you draw lines on paper linking points of the same height on Schiehallion then the brain can interpret these to give a three-dimensional shape of the mountain: Hutton had invented contour lines.

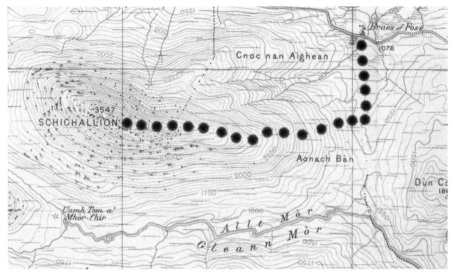

Schiehallion Map

SCHIEHALLION (1,083m)

Grade ✳✳
Map: OS Sheet 42 or 51
Distance/Ascent: 10km/752m
Starting Height: 331m
Time to top: 2h 30min +breaks
Start/Finish: Braes of Foss car park near Kinloch Rannoch.

An ascent of one of Scotland's iconic mountains.

ROUTE:

1   Take single track road that leaves B846 between Coshieville and
    Tummel Bridge (signposted *Schiehallion Road*) Drive about 3km along
    road. At stone cairn with plaque turn left into car park NN75260
    55800 (signposted *Braes of Foss*). Pay and display (£2): toilets are
    closed in winter.

2   Footpath to Schiehallion starts at rear of car park by picnic bench and
    sign reading *No Overnight Parking*. A short distance along path go
    through gate by information board.

3   Follow path out of trees, over a couple of footbridges and across
    moorland to reach old sheep pen.

4   Ignore faint track at sheep pen and continue to follow constructed path up heathery flank of Schiehallion.

5   At about 870m constructed path ends at cairn NN73029 54540.

6   A fainter path continues west along the ridge through scree. For remainder of walk along ridge to summit of Schiehallion follow line of cairns. Take care crossing boulder field.

7   Reach little rocky outcrop that forms summit of Schiehallion (1,083m) (small cairn) NN71399 54754.

8   Return by same route.

WINTER CONDITIONS: Straightforward winter route though be careful at summit if rocks are ice covered/slippery, there is a steep drop on the south side. Ice axe and crampons needed.

DOGS: good hill for dogs – the John Muir Trust ask that you keep your dog close by to minimise disturbance to wildlife and sometimes a few sheep stray onto Schiehallion.

Somewhere Else: The Motor Grill on the A9 at Ballinluig.

CHAPTER TWENTY TWO

Theatrum Orbis Terrarum

Maps give you seven-league boots – allow you to cover miles in seconds. Using the point of a pencil to trace the line of an intend-ed walk or climb, you can soar over crevasses, leap tall cliff-faces at a single bound and effortlessly ford rivers.

ROBERT MACFARLANE, Mountains of the Mind

AN ABERDEENSHIRE FARMHOUSE. I sit and write at a simple old wooden table. I put a log on the wood burning stove. This morning I filled the basket from a 30 foot long log stack built to last a northern winter. Scots pines stand by the edge of the fields. On the way to the woods there are chickens and a duck pond. A buzzard flaps across the ploughed earth. Bennachie on the distant skyline. As I write in early February, snow drops are out along the grassy verges of the byroads around Wedderhill Farm. Out the window I see grey granite buildings, some roofless, some ruined. The walls of the farm are built of irregularly shaped blocks of grey granite. Only the corner stones and lintels have been shaped to rectangles by a stone mason.

The countryside of rural Aberdeenshire is dotted with slate roofed grey granite farm houses like this. Sometime during the 1890s a displenishing sale was held at one. A displenishing sale took place when someone retired from running a farm, or died while still in business. Their stock-in-trade would be sold by auction. Household furniture and other personal pos-sessions were sometimes included too. A friend of Caleb was present at one such a sale of the contents of an Aberdeenshire farmhouse. He was probably someone Caleb knew from the Cairngorm Club many of whose members lived in the Aberdeen area.

When the sale was advertised no mention was made of any books but when the auction reached the contents of the kitchen Caleb's friend was surprised to see included a pile of large books with grubby white vellum covers. He knew nothing of historic atlases but realised they were old and possibly valuable, bought them for a small amount of money and gave them to Caleb who later wrote; 'My own copy of Blaeu's Atlas ran a risk somewhat comparable to that of Pont's maps,

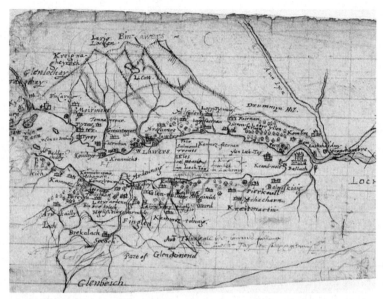

Caleb played an important role in conserving the maps of Scotland drawn
by Timothy Pont in the 16th century. Pont's maps like this one of Ben Lawers may have
inspired Caleb to draw mountain panoramas and compile lists of hills.

[*National Library Scotland*]

for it passed into the hands of people who did not understand its value,
and it probably escaped the fate of waste-paper by a mere chance.'

The cobbled High street of Old Aberdeen, the university quarter of
the city, with its little granite houses seems a long way from the traffic of
Union Street and the oil support vessels lined up in the harbour. Behind
a low wall on the lawn in front of Kings College Bishop Elphinstone lies
on his tomb. Among the University of Aberdeen's most treasured posses-
sions is the copy of the Theatrum Orbis Terrarum once owned by Caleb.

I want to see the atlas, Caleb's treasured book, for myself. It has to
be brought out of storage and I must wait until the afternoon. When I
return to King's College library after lunch and go into enquiries, it is
waiting for me, the Theatrum Orbis Terrarum, the Google Earth of the
1650s. Five giant volumes, much bigger than I had expected lying on a
trolley. Each book looks two feet long by two feet wide. I've never
opened a book this old before, nor seen a book bound in vellum. As
Caleb described, the white covers look soiled and the thick paper pages
are stained yellow in places as if rain had leaked through the farmhouse
roof. The librarian has me carry volume five, the one that covers Scotland

across to a table; it is so heavy she doesn't want to lift it. The librarian arranges foam triangles under the book to support it and a white weighted cord to keep the pages flat.

I open the first volume and read the handwritten inscription *Clarissimo Viro Roberto Gordonio A Strathloch, In Perpetuae Signum Amicitiae Atlantem Hunc D.D. J. Blaeu.* The inscription is as Caleb described it in his article in *The Scottish Geographical Magazine* in 1901. This is the copy of the Theatrum Orbis Terrarum given by its publisher Jan Blaeu to Robert Gordon of Straloch and once owned by Caleb. Lost at some time and found again at the sale at the Aberdeenshire farmhouse. How did this rare and valuable book, given as a gift to a famous scholar and man of learning, Robert Gordon, come to end up being sold in among the kitchen stuff at a sale sometime in the late 1890s? To be acquired by chance by a school teacher and geographer, the son of a foundry worker... it was almost as if the atlas found Caleb.

As I gingerly turn the pages, I see Caleb carefully lift this volume down from its place on his bookshelves in the flat in Comely Bank. I imagine the evenings spent perusing the atlas, thinking... contrasting its maps with those of the Ordnance Survey. Cherubim decorate the margins of the pages... *architecto Timotheo Pont* inscribed on several of the beautifully drawn maps of a Scotland that is instantly recognisable. The pages of text are in Latin, descriptions of Scotland, its people... In the wake of the 15th century information revolution Amsterdam became a world centre of publishing and map making. The five volumes of the Theatrum Orbis Terrarum published by Jan Blaeu around 1654 are considered today to be the first true modern atlas and made Scotland one of the best mapped countries in 17th century Europe.

Caleb collected historical maps and atlases (he once exhibited a rare and valuable map of India dated 1632 in his classroom at the Edinburgh Academy). When the Theatrum Orbis Terrarum was published by Jan Blaeu the maps of Scotland included in the atlas were copies of maps drawn by Timothy Pont (c.1573–1614) in the 16th century. The acquisition of the Theatrum Orbis Terrarum led Caleb to become interested in the maps of Timothy Pont. In the 1900s Blaeu's printed atlas was well enough known but the study of Timothy Pont's manuscript maps only really began with CG Cash's pioneering work.

In Caleb's day Pont's maps were kept in the Advocates Library (before becoming part of the National Library of Scotland collection in

1925). Caleb made an extensive study of the manuscript maps and in the opening years of the 20th century recognised that Timothy Pont's maps were unique and invaluable.

Caleb outlined the history of the Pont maps in an article for the *Scottish Geographical Magazine* published in 1901 in which he described the maps as the first topographical account of Scotland. This article and a second which included a detailed catalogue of the maps ordering them from north to south drew unprecedented attention to Pont's maps. Jeffrey Stone wrote that the accessibility of these two articles; 'ensured that Cash would become perhaps the most influential of Pont's many biographers'.

Caleb realised the way the maps were being stored in the Advocates Library was damaging them and drew attention to how they were being frequently and inappropriately handled. Caleb thought it imperative that the maps be mounted and conserved, writing that they were; '... undergoing a process of slow but sure destruction.'

Conservation of the Pont maps was carried out by the Keeper of the Advocates Library a few years later and Caleb was closely involved in the process, carrying out important work classifying and describing the maps whilst they were being conserved and remounted. Today when Caleb is remembered it is for his work on the maps; saving Timothy Pont's maps for future generations was Caleb's greatest achievement. In the words of Jeffrey Stone, 'we are indebted to Cash above all for rescuing the maps from impending destruction by mis-use'.

Maps are not mirrors to the world. Maps are maps of omissions and sometimes the experience of maps is about the gaps, the things left out. Caleb's interest in cartography extended to contemporary maps of Scotland too. One summer Caleb noticed the Ordnance Survey's newly issued One-inch to the mile, 2nd edition map of Grantown had removed half a mile of road near Loch an Eilein even though; '... the road exists in its entirety, and is in daily use.' The missing half mile of road in Strathspey prompted Caleb to check Ordnance Survey maps of the Edinburgh area where he spotted more gaps – the North British railway at Granton marked as single track when it was in fact a double passenger line and the Caledonian mineral line from Crewe Toll to Granton wrongly marked as a double passenger line.

Maps should always be understood in the context of their making. Early Ordnance Survey maps were supposed to distinguish between churches with spires as opposed to towers (I reach for the nearest map on the desk, Cape Wrath it turns out to be) revised 2008, and see, a reflection of the decline of religion, today it's between *current or former place of worship with tower* and *current or former place of worship with spire, minaret or dome*. St Mary's Episcopal Cathedral, the Church of Scotland Assembly Hall, the Barclay Free Church and the Tron were then as now among the most prominent spires in Edinburgh; 'It is amazing to find these churches are not marked as possessing spires;' wrote Caleb in the Science and Nature column of *The Scotsman* newspaper in 1901; 'that, indeed, neither of these buildings is even marked as being a church at all.' Caleb wrote to the Ordnance Survey at their headquarters in Southampton. Throughout his life he offered 'friendly criticism' of the Ordnance Survey, an organisation of which he was a 'keen but appreciative critic'. Examination of the 3rd edition of the one-inch to the mile maps shows that many of the mistakes Caleb pointed out were subsequently corrected.

In 1900 the Ordnance Survey was still run by the British Army just as it had been when General William Roy was first sent north to compile reliable military maps of the Highlands in the wake of the Jacobite rebellion of 1745. Writing in *The Scotsman* Caleb described how another war (the Boer War in South Africa) was having a negative effect on the work of the Ordnance Survey as it took soldiers and officers away from the re-survey and revision of the maps of Scotland that was underway in the 1900s.

Mapmaking had come a long way from Pont's sketches in the 16th century. Caleb was interested in the technical aspects of Edwardian map making and printing, something he perhaps inherited from his father the brass finisher. An interest in copper plates and photo-zincography; in how hachures (short lines of shading used to provide information about slope and steepness of hill features) were engraved on one plate and contour lines on another. Caleb treated the readers of *The Scotsman* to a detailed explanation of the techniques involved in producing maps. For Edinburgh was then home to one of the country's largest map making companies Bartholomew and Sons. That day on the summit of Arthur's Seat, Caleb looked down on the glass roofs of Thomas Nelson's Parkside Works on the edge of Holyrood Park. Printing was a major industry in Edinburgh during the first half of the 20th century... in the 1970s 11-year-old Kellan visits his Scottish grandfather Tommy in the cramped Dickensian like printers' workshop where he has worked all his life.

Ordnance Survey maps were where Caleb's passion for mountaineering, geography and topography intersected. While climbing in the Cairngorms Caleb noticed more cartographical inaccuracies and omissions, maps of the hills around Loch Einich one mountaineer complained in *The Cairngorm Club Journal*; 'have long been a bother to hillmen'. The January 1899 edition of the journal included a sketch by Caleb of the summits of the Sgoran Dubh ridge above Loch Einich with the correct names and heights of the tops clearly marked.

Caleb was genuinely keen that Ordnance Survey maps should become 'really complete and satisfactory'. Characteristic of the man of action he was, in August 1899, having learned the Ordnance Survey were in the Cairngorms carrying out a revision of Scotland's maps, Caleb joined the Superintendent Surveyor of the Ordnance Survey for a day. They drove along Glen Einich; '... having an interview on the way with some road-mending ghillies, who had vague notions as to the functions and powers of Ordnance Surveyors.'

At a point in the glen where the track crossed a stream they set up a table and Caleb ensured the positions of the tops of Sgor Ghaoith and Sgoran Dubh Mor would be accurately marked on the Ordnance Survey maps of the future. To carry out further mapping Caleb and the Ordnance Surveyor then climbed Sgor Ghaoith from Loch Einich returning along the Sgoran Dubh ridge and passing the rocky tor known as the Argyll stone.

That August afternoon in 1899 when Caleb and the Superintendent Surveyor of the Ordnance Survey stood by the Argyll Stone they formed one link in a long chain of surveyors and mapmakers that reached from Timothy Pont in the 15th century who mapped Scotland for reasons shrouded in mystery, through General Roy and his soldiers ordered to compile military maps of the Highlands after Culloden and on, to a future of aerial surveys, satellites, global positioning systems and digital mapping.

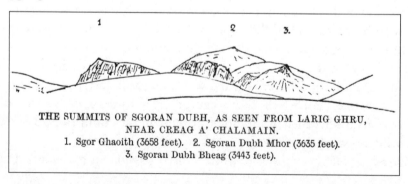

THE SUMMITS OF SGORAN DUBH, AS SEEN FROM LARIG GHRU, NEAR CREAG A' CHALAMAIN.
1. Sgor Ghaoith (3658 feet). 2. Sgoran Dubh Mhor (3635 feet).
3. Sgoran Dubh Bheag (3443 feet).

CHAPTER TWENTY THREE

Meall Dearg

Bless Not General Wade But Mr Cash

IT IS EDINBURGH'S TOPOGRAPHY that gives the city its spectacular urban landscape. One hundred years ago CG Cash used several of the capital's landmark buildings as guidelines to identify the Scottish mountains visible from Arthur's Seat. The Cooperative Wholesale Society's Chancelot roller flour mill in Dalmeny Road, Bonnington with its four faced clock tower and distinctive brick chimney was a conspicuous feature on the skyline of late Victorian Edinburgh. In the 1880s roller flour mills were transforming milling; up until then all flour had been ground using millstones. When Caleb stood at the summit of Arthur's Seat compiling his list of mountains the splendid sandstone built Chancelot Mill, completed five years earlier in 1894, must have been almost as prominent a sight on the skyline of North Edinburgh as Fettes College. Caleb used the mill as a guideline for Meall Dearg (690m/2,263ft) on the north side of Strathbraan, 48 miles and 31 degrees west of North from Arthur's Seat.

The Dalmeny Road building was demolished around 1970 when the present day Chancelot Mill opened at a site on the edge of Leith Docks. It took me two years of dog walking and gazing at the hills visible from Arthur's Seat for the realisation to dawn that today's Chancelot Mill could not possibly be in line with Meall Dearg. Looking out across the skyline of 21st century Edinburgh Meall Dearg can be seen in line with the Palace of Holyroodhouse.

There are two *meall* hills on Caleb's list, one a Graham; Meall Dearg north of Strathbraan and the other a Munro; Meall Garbh of the Ben Lawers range. Meall Dearg rises gently on the west side of Glen Cochill south of Aberfeldy where General Wade's military road to Dalwhinnie skirts the hill's heathery eastern slopes. Meall Dearg is a typical *meall* type hill, situated as it is in Perthshire where the hills often have what Peter Drummond in *Scottish Hill Names* calls the 'lumpy bumpiness of middle age'.

Andrew Dempster's hillwalking guidebook *The Grahams* describes Meall Dearg (pronounced myowl **dye**rak) as; '... a fairly non-descript little hill [with] few redeeming features.' Mealls are often described in these kind of terms; typically they are rounded hills with a reputation for being dull and uninspiring. Joined with *beinn*, *carn* or *meall*, the word *dearg* is found in the names of more than one hundred Scottish hills. On the eastern slopes of Meall Dearg I searched in vain for red rocks or scree, for in Gaelic *dearg* is the colour of a kestrel's wing, blood-red tinged with crimson.

The Victorian Chancelot mill on Caleb's list may be long gone but before this book is published new manmade landmarks will be visible from Meall Dearg, rising above the forest on the east side of Glen Cochill – the giant turbines of the Griffin wind factory.

Climbing Meall Dearg

From Dunkeld I drive west along Strathbraan on the A822 for about 12km and then turn north on the A826 following signposts to Aberfeldy.

At the foot of Meall Dearg in Glen Cochill a prehistoric burial site called White Cairn is marked on the Ordnance Survey map. Today the tumbled stones of White Cairn hardly rise above the heather and cannot be seen from the road. Curlews fly low over the moorland here uttering the whistling cry that once gave them their name.

Look out for a small unsurfaced parking place about half a kilometre north of White Cairn after the road emerges from the forest and climbs up onto open moorland. The parking place is at a height of about 330 metres making Meall Dearg one of the easiest Arthurs though it is rough going underfoot and navigation will be needed to find the summit in bad weather.

Cross the road, go through a gate in the fence and head west across rough, boggy moorland over clumps of soft rush, sphagnum moss, white hare's-tail cotton grass and drier patches of deep heather. The east side of Glen Cochill is blanketed by the Tay Forest's blocks of conifers while Meall Dearg appears as a long ridge rising above the moorland on the west side of the glen. The lower slopes of the hill are dotted with boulders which stand out among the patches of muirburn. Charred twigs of burnt heather crunch underfoot and the dogs find it scratchy and uncomfortable on the paws. Muirburn is the deliberate setting alight of the heather; in the central and eastern Highlands moorland is burnt in small strips to encourage the growth of tender new shoots of heather that red grouse like to feed on.

After about 500 metres, cross General Wade's military road where it cuts a straight line across the moorland. Following the Jacobite rebellion of 1715 English troops stationed in Scotland found it practically impossible to police the country because of the lack of a road network across the Highlands. In those days most journeys were made on narrow footpaths and deer tracks or by boat. Major-General Wade was ordered by King George I to build a network of military roads and forts across the Highlands. In all Wade was to build 250 miles of roads and 28 major bridges, his soldiers working in teams of 100 men with half a dozen officers. The roads were built using hand tools and gunpowder where needed. Between May and October if the weather was kind each team was expected to complete about 150 metres of road per day. Wade built his roads to a standard width of about five metres, similar to a B road today, using locally sourced gravel, stone and rock. Hence the old saying in Scotland;

Had you seen these roads before they were made
You would lift up your hands and bless General Wade.

Wade began work on a road linking Crieff, Aberfeldy, Tummel Bridge, Trinafour and Dalnacardoch in the spring of 1730. This road followed an old drovers' route to the Crieff cattle markets and climbs through Glen Cochill passing below Meall Dearg. Wade completed the 44 miles between Crieff and Dalnacardoch near Dalwhinnie during the summer months of that year. A decade and a half later the road was to play an important role in the 1745 Jacobite uprising. General Wade's road building was so appreciated by the British government that the National Anthem includes a verse written in his honour;

Lord, grant that Marshall Wade
May by thy might aid
Victory bring.
May he sedition hush
And like a torrent rush,
Rebellious Scots to crush.
God save the Queen!

Continue west across rough moorland through low growing clumps of cowberry and blaeberry with its pinkish bell flowers, aiming directly for the summit of Meall Dearg and steering to right or left of some small crags. The lower slopes of Meall Dearg are checked with grey brown patches of muirburn and the green of new heather growth. Higher up the hill, grass predominates with here and there cushions of green and red sphagnum moss. Among the moss grows lichen of the cladonia family in dense clumps of fine branches. Mountain hares with white tails shoot across the hillside and skylarks sing in the sunshine. I soon reach flatter ground which turns out to be a false summit but on the skyline I can see the trig point marking the top of Meall Dearg.

In May cloudberry throws up beautiful white flowers from the damp, peaty hillside of Meall Dearg. I first saw this plant growing high up on the misty ridge of An Sornach above Glen Affric. I took a photo and when I Googled it loved the fact it was called cloudberry.

Ring ouzel

Cross or steer around a small area of peat hags which cut shallow trenches into the heather at the foot of the final rise to the summit. After a short climb I reach the grass and stone covered top of Meall Dearg (690m) with its concrete triangulation pillar.

THE EARTH MEASURERS' TRIANGLES

In bad weather on the hills a trig point appearing out of the mist is always a friendly sight. These triangulation pillars constructed by the Ordnance Survey between 1935 and 1962 are one of the most widespread traces of human activity on the Scottish hills. From any one trig point in clear weather it is possible to see the site of at least two other trig points and so define the triangles which used to form the basis for map making. Today the triangulation method of surveying so familiar to Caleb has been rendered obsolete by satellite based GPS measurements. Edwin Danson calls trig points forlorn monuments that 'mark the apexes of the earth measurers' triangles'. A metal sign on Meall Dearg's trig point reads *This monument forms part of the Ordnance Survey National GPS Network*. The network of triangulation pillars is no longer actively maintained, except for a few trig points like this that have been reused as part of the Ordnance Survey's network of GPS base stations as land surveyors and geodesists once again look to the skies to fix their position.

On a clear day there are fine open views from the summit of Meall Dearg to Farragon Hill; Loch na Craige can be seen in the conifer forest and Schiehallion is a whaleback shape to the north beyond Loch Hol. The more I climbed the Arthurs the more familiar became the view of Caleb's line of mountains along the Highland edge from Lochnagar and Beinn a'Ghlo in the east to Ben Lawers and Ben Lomond in the west.

Head north from the trig point for about 500 metres then descend the indistinct north eastern 'ridge' of Meall Dearg. Below I could see the A822 road through Glen Cochill and the lonely house at Scotston with its wind break of trees. General Wade's military road cuts a fainter older line through the moorland on the opposite bank of the River Cochill. On the way back it's the same rough going encountered during the climb up Meall Dearg. A roe deer takes off down the hillside startled by the dogs, I am surprised by how much wildlife I see on this relatively unvisited hill. Animals must tend to keep away from busy footpaths on more frequently climbed mountains.

WHO OWNS MEALL DEARG?

Meall Dearg is part of the Lochan Estate owned by Tay and Torridon Estates Ltd & Culfargie Estates Ltd, Tarrylaw, Balbeggie, Perth, PH2 6HJ.

BONNIE PRINCE CHARLIE

It is ironic that the first military force to make effective use of Wade's network of military roads, paid for by the Treasury in London was Bonnie Prince Charlie's Jacobite army. On the 2 February 1746 pursued by an English army led by the Duke 'Butcher' Cumberland, the Young Pretender halted at the Drummond Arms Inn at Crieff for a Council of War with his generals. Some historians consider the 2 February to be the day, more than even the retreat from Derby that doomed the Jacobite rising. The Council at Crieff was a momentous one for Bonnie Prince Charlie because at it the fateful decision was made to head north through the hills and to abandon North East Scotland with its sea ports such as Montrose, thus ending any possibility of reinforcement by French troops landed by boat. And so Charles Edward Stuart and the Jacobite army marched north from Crieff through Glen Cochill passing Meall Dearg on their way to Aberfeldy and Dalnarcardoch and defeat two months later on the Moor of Culloden.

Go down the broad ridge keeping parallel to the forest edge finding a way between the lichen covered boulders that lie among deep heather and blaeberry bushes aiming to join General Wade's military road about half a kilometre after it emerges from the forest.

On the east side of the River Cochill a line of pylons marches above the conifers. Soon they will be joined by the giant wind turbines of the Griffin wind factory towering over the trees. At a height of about 380 metres, General Wade's military road is reached. Turn right (south) along it. A large bird of prey circles overhead as I tramp along the road once walked by red coated troops headed for the north from Crieff. The charred heather stalks by the sides of the track make it seem as if soldiers have just passed that way and scorched the earth.

Follow the track gently downhill for about two kilometres until it joins the main road at a gate near White Cairn about 500 metres from the start of the walk. A prehistoric burial cairn with the remains of an outer circle of stones arcing around its south side, when White Cairn was excavated nothing was found but a few fragments of pottery.

The moorland around here is dotted with hut circles, the remains of shielings, boundary walls and other signs of old agricultural use; little more than overgrown rectangular mounds in the heather where sheep graze. The slopes of Meall Dearg rise beyond the stones lying in the grass where people once made their homes.

Caleb explored another stone circle of white quartz rocks (the origin and purpose of which remains a mystery to this day) in nearby Glen Quaich on the west side of Meall Dearg during August 1910. He wrote up his notes in Edinburgh during the mild, wet and snowless winter that followed and in April 1911 his *Archaeological Gleanings from Aberfeldy* were published in the Proceedings of the Society of Antiquaries of Scotland.

The last part of this route along the military road makes for easy walking after the deep heather and rough going on the upper slopes of Meall Dearg. In the 18th century General Wade's roads made journeys across Scotland's rugged landscape quicker. One hundred and fifty years later it fell to Caleb to construct an easier path through the mountains of books, manuscripts and maps relating to Scotland's topography. His last book was a reference source, a kind of dictionary of Scottish geography. When it was finally published in 1917 under the self-deprecating title *A Contribution To The Bibliography Of Scottish Topography*, one reviewer, Lord Guthrie, President of the Royal Scottish Geographical Society, wrote that a student consulting the Bibliography and; '... thinking of the previously uncharted sea, will hold up his hands and bless, not General Wade, but Mr Cash.'

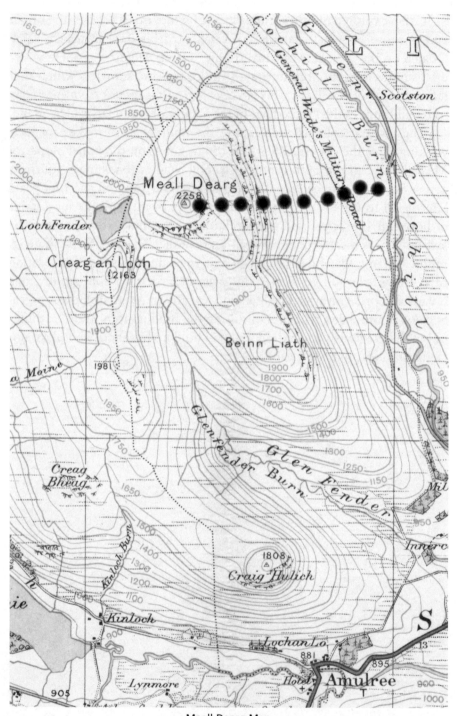

Meall Dearg Map

MEALL DEARG (690m)

Grade	**
Map:	OS Sheet 52
Distance/Ascent:	7km /360m
Starting height:	330m
Time to top:	1h 30min (3h for whole circuit) +breaks
Start/Finish:	Glen Cochill south of Aberfeldy

A short hillwalk in rough, remote country. Includes a section of General Wade's military road. Navigation needed to find the summit in poor visibility.

ROUTE:

1 From Dunkeld take A822 W for 12km then turn right onto A826 following signposts to Aberfeldy. Look out for parking space after A826 emerges from forest onto moorland. Parking place NN90811 41757 is ½ km north of White Cairn on right hand side of road opposite Z bend sign just before bridge over the Cochill Burn (space for about 4 cars).

2 Cross the road and go through gate and head W across moorland.

3 After about 500m cross General Wade's military road near NN90278 41557 and continue W up E slopes of Meall Dearg avoiding some small crags.

4 Reach flatter ground which is a false summit.

5 Cross small area of peat hags to reach foot of final rise to summit of Meall Dearg (690m) NN88670 41491 (trig point).

6 Head N from trig point for about 500m then bear NE to descend indistinct NE 'ridge' of Meall Dearg.

7 Go down the broad ridge keeping parallel to forest edge aiming to join General Wade's military road about 500m after it emerges from the forest.

8 Reach General Wade's military road at about 380m and turn right (south) along it.

9 Follow track gently downhill for 2km to a gate near White Cairn where it joins A826.

10 Go through gate and turn left along A826. Walk about 500m along the relatively quiet road to return to parking space and start of walk.

NAVIGATION: map and compass work will be needed to find summit in mist.

DOGS: there are a lot of sheep on the lower slopes of Meall Dearg particularly near White Cairn.

STALKING: grouse shooting and deer stalking sometimes takes place on Meall Dearg between 12 August and 20 October (not on Sundays).

Somewhere Else: The Watermill, Aberfeldy; coffee and cake and bookshop.

CHAPTER TWENTY FOUR

Beinn Dearg

Mr Scrope of London

MOUNTAIN NAMES SOMETIMES reflect their geology. Beinn Dearg is a pointed hill rising above a sea of flat or rounded hills, a solitary granite peak surrounded by a large area of schist hills. Hills named *dearg* are often found where hard granite rock intrudes through layers of grey schist. Near the summit of Beinn Dearg is an area of reddish coloured scree that gives the mountain its name. Dearg (pronounced **dyerak**) is a blood-red colour with a hint of crimson and linked to *meall, carn* and *beinn* is found in the names of many Scottish hills.

Beinn or *ben* is the most common Scottish hill word and there are nearly 1,000 listed on Ordnance Survey maps. Often the highest Scottish mountains are the *beinns* or *bens. Beinn* (pronounced bYn) is the Gaelic spelling of *ben.* In Welsh the name for a hill is *bann,* in Breton *ban* and even the Serbo-Croat word *brdo* may be a distant relation of *ben.* Scottish emigrants took the word *ben* overseas with them – there are Ben Nevises in New Zealand and Hong Kong and a Ben Macdui in South Africa.

Standing nine miles north of Blair Atholl, Beinn Dearg is the remotest of the Arthurs. The mountain is one of a trio of hills on Caleb's list visible from Arthur's Seat to the left of the steep scarp of Bishop Hill in Fife. Beinn Dearg rises to 1,008m/3,307ft on the west side of Glen Tilt 69 miles from Arthur's Seat and 22 degrees west of north.

In the 1820s William Scrope rented Bruar Lodge at the foot of Beinn Dearg. In his book *Days of Deerstalking*, Scrope sets the scene in true 19th century style;

> Huge, lofty, and in the district of Atholl, second only in magnitude to Ben-y-Gloe, Ben Dairg, or the red mountain, stands dominant. At the right entrance of the pass, the little white and lonely dwelling, called Bruar Lodge, lies a mere speck beneath it... Down winds the river Bruar through the glen, sometimes creeping silently through the mossy stones, and at others raving, maddening and bearing all before it, so that neither man nor beast may withstand its violence.

Climbing Beinn Dearg

Centuries before General Wade built his military road through Glen Garry and over Drumochter, the route later followed by Thomas Telford's Great North Road which became today's A9, travellers between Atholl and Badenoch used an ancient highway called the Minigaig. The most straightforward route to the foot of Beinn Dearg follows this old hill track for part of the way.

The early Scottish mountaineers used train and bicycle to get to the hills. It would be an adventure to take a bike and climb Beinn Dearg on a long summer's day by train from Edinburgh or Glasgow but you'd have to be up very early. According to Scotrail's timetable a train leaves Edinburgh at 6.32am arriving in Blair Atholl at 8.55am. Bikes are carried free but must be booked in advance. The last train back from Blair Atholl is at 9.50pm allowing plenty of time to climb the hill and fix a puncture. Or better still you could stay in the Allt Sheicheachan mountain bothy at the foot of Beinn Dearg and not have to hurry.

From Blair Atholl follow road signs for Old Blair and use the car park signposted *Glen Tilt Parking*. It is possible to cycle all the way to the foot of Beinn Dearg. A gate about three kilometres from Old Blair where the track leaves the forest has a padlock on it. When I climbed Beinn Dearg researching this book on a Saturday in June the gate was unlocked but on a previous visit it was padlocked and we had to lift our bikes over a stile next to the gate, not easy if cycling alone. The track climbs steadily uphill so there's a lot of bike pushing on the way to Beinn Dearg but you get a great hurl on the way back down.

An estate house stands opposite the entrance to the car park with carved wooden eaves and a tree trunk holding up its porch. The first three kilometres of the route are way marked with black arrows, it follows part of the Banvie Burn walk shown on the information board in the car park.

A high stone wall runs along one side of the road and tall trees shade it. Keep right at the driveway to Gardener's Cottage, following the road as it climbs gently uphill through fields of cattle and sheep. Rooks flap from tree to field and back in meadows which in springtime are bright with daisies and buttercups.

In a field to the right of the road stand two dead trees, branches bleached and stark. A grassy rise nearby is called Tom na Croiche, the knoll of the gallows and a stone built obelisk among the trees marks the site of the last public hanging in Atholl which took place in 1630. Over the rooftops of Home Farm I can see the pointed top of Ben Vrackie and the path up the shoulder of Carn Liath, first of Beinn a'Ghlo's three Munros. The Home Farm was built to supply Blair Castle and today produces organic lamb and beef sold through a mail order business.

From the road there are glimpses into the grounds of Blair Castle where a lead statue of Hercules resting on his club rises above the walled gardens. A Saint Andrew's cross fluttered on the flagpole of the white turreted tower of the historic fortress of the Earls and Dukes of Atholl. It was to Blair Castle that Bonnie Dundee was carried, mortally wounded, after his victory at the battle of Killiecrankie. The rich farmland around Blair Castle stands in marked contrast to the bleak heather moorland higher up. Travellers going south along the Minigaig from Kingussie in past centuries must have been glad to reach the shelter of the woods above Old Blair.

THE MINIGAIG

For part of the way the track to the foot of Beinn Dearg follows the line of an ancient highway called the Minigaig. This once important path from Kingussie to Blair Atholl declined in use after the opening of General Wade's military road over Drumochter. The Minigaig is 15 miles shorter than the A9 route through Glen Garry but climbs much higher; north of Bruar Lodge the Minigaig pass reaches a height of 836m/2,745ft and in winter it was a dangerous route that claimed many victims including a company of soldiers who lost their lives in a violent storm crossing the pass on their way to Ruthven barracks in 1745.

Cattle drovers used the Minigaig in order to avoid paying the tolls levied on the road through Drumochter. In 1829 the toll man at Drumochter reported that 300 cattle and horses had passed through Glen Bruar. Cattle drovers liked the Minigaig because of its directness and the lush grazing at places along the route. Despite the attempts of landowners and game keepers to obstruct them, the Minigaig Pass continued to be used by drovers until about 1900 when cattle droving died out as transportation of livestock switched to the railways.

Where the tarmac ends at a cross roads continue straight ahead through the woods following an unsurfaced track along the north-east side of the Banvie Burn. There are various way marked paths around here but the track to Beinn Dearg follows the stream through the forest. Rhododendron bushes hug the sides of the steep gorge. Beech trees line the track and last autumn's leaves still lay on the ground. As I walk wearily, back from Beinn Dearg a brown hare sits in the middle of the track here. As I get closer it lollops lazily away into the fields and I feel Caleb's untiring step on the path behind me.

In early June after the long winter the leaves of the trees are still a very young bright green. Walk past but do not cross, the moss covered Rumbling Bridge built in 1762. When the Banvie Burn is in spate you can hear the rumbling of boulders being moved by the rushing water in the gorge below the bridge.

A prophetic signpost reads *Long Route* and points the way through the immensely tall fir trees that grow on the steep banks above the brown peaty water of the Banvie Burn. Pine cones have fallen on to the track and crunch under my boots as I pass.

Just before a gate at the edge of the forest, guarded by a solitary Scots Pine, leave the way marked route where it turns left down to an old stone bridge. Through the gate the landscape changes suddenly as the track emerges from the trees onto bleak open heather moorland home to black grouse.

A green tiger beetle scuttles across the path and disappears into the heather and rough grass. The Gaelic word for heather is *fraoch* and I see a lot of Scotland's most widespread dwarf shrub on the way to Beinn Dearg. White heather is thought to be very lucky and after climbing Braeriach in August 1900 Caleb wrote; 'there was but one side of regret about the day's proceedings – we saw no white heather.'

To the west of the track a few birch trees stand by a burn where a little waterfall flows into a brown peaty pool. Where strips of heather have been burnt, the hillsides are a patchwork of tawny shades. The sandy track climbs up to a cairn marking the spot where Lady March and the 7th Duke of Atholl 'fair enjoyed' a picnic in Victorian times. An old tweed cap hung from the cairn the day I climbed Beinn Dearg. North of Lady March cairn the track dips down to cross the Allt na Moine Baine, the stream of the white moss, at a concrete bridge. It was a hot day and the dogs pulled towards every stream and puddle.

WHO OWNS BEINN DEARG?

Beinn Dearg is owned by the Trustees of Atholl Estates, the Blair Charitable Trust and the Bruar Trust c/o The Factor, Atholl Estates Office, Blair Atholl, Perthshire, PH18 5TH. The Blair Castle Charitable Trust owns and manages the huge former estate of the Duke of Atholl and is one of the biggest land-owners in Scotland.

Continue up the east side of the Allt an t-Seapail, the stream of the chapel. Pronounced as it is in English, the name commemorates the township that used to stand about one kilometre south-west of here where the Allt an t-Seapail meets the Banvie Burn. Bail an t'Sepail or Chapel Town was cleared about 1850 and now red deer graze among the ruins where people once lived.

Common butterwort grows among the grass at the edge of the track. A buzzard circles over the heather and a big herd of red deer grazes heads down on the skyline over towards Glen Tilt. To the south-west I can see knobbly Farragon hill and pointed Schiehallion. The Minigaig stretches on and on across the high moor land past many rounded peaty hills and little ridges. I remember reading Tolkien; 'the Brown Lands rose into bleak wolds, over which flowed a chill air from the East.'

One kilometre 400 metres north of the bridge over the Allt na Moine Baine a patch of bright green short cropped turf on the west side of the track at NN8448 0 70746 marks the site of the Fuaran Bhadenoch, the Well of Badenoch. The well is one metre in diameter and lined with stones. To find it look for a stone slab, like a simple gravestone, a few metres to the west of the track. In the past there were many wells like this beside old roads, often equipped with a stone cup to drink from.

A little further north along the Minigaig from the Fuaran Bhadenoch, Beinn Dearg comes into sight at last, its pointed top easily recognisable to the east of the track, but still looking discouragingly far away. The track curves ahead through the heather to cross a stream by a wooden bridge. On the moorland I see wheatears and skylarks and curlews. These hills of the eastern Highlands have a feeling of space and big skies.

Past the wooden bridge a milestone stands by the track with a '5' carved on it – five miles to Blair Atholl. There may be other milestones by the Minigaig but this was the only one I found. Beinn Dearg disappears from sight again as the track drops down to cross the Allt Sheicheachan.

The top of this rise is a good place to leave bikes as the track beyond the bothy is rough and climbs steeply uphill. As the first Munroist AE Robertson himself a keen cyclist wrote;

> Don't be afraid your bike will run away, or be stolen in your absence! Turn him loose to browse in the heather, and he will be waiting for you when you return.

Allt Sheicheachan Bothy

Originally built in 1881 as accommodation for estate workers, today the cottage at Allt Sheicheachan is a mountain bothy, one of about 100 shelters maintained by the Mountain Bothies Association. Bothies are not holiday cottages, staying in a bothy is more like camping without a tent... and anyone can turn up as the grumpy man from Sheffield I shared a bothy with in Wester Ross discovered as he was woken up each morning by a labradoodle licking his face...

Walk down the track towards the welcoming chimneys of the Allt Sheicheachan bothy. The Allt Sheicheachan flows into Glen Bruar and from near the bothy the road to Bruar Lodge can be seen winding along the west side of the Bruar water. The lodge was built in 1789 and named Cabar Feith, deer's antler. The most famous tenant of Bruar Lodge was Mr William Scrope of London who rented it for 10 years from 1824. He was a friend of Sir Walter Scott and used to send the bard haunches of venison. By way of a poetic thank you Walter Scott replied;

Thanks, dear Sir, for your venison, for finer or fatter
Never roam'd in a forest, or smoked in a platter.

Glen Bruar has another literary connection, in 1787 Robert Burns visited the Falls of Bruar, at that time surrounded by open moorland, and was inspired to write *The Humble Petition of Bruar Water* in which the river addresses the 4th Duke of Atholl ;

Would then my noble master please
To grant my highest wishes,
He'll shade my banks wi' tow'ring trees,
And bonie spreading bushes.

Planter John as the duke was nicknamed granted Burns' wishes and planted larch and Scots pine by the river and today the area around the Falls of Bruar is leafy woodland, a mix of conifer and broadleaved trees.

Behind the bothy cross the Allt Sheicheachan and follow the track along the north-west bank of the burn. Once an old stalker's path now widened to a track, the heather has been slow to reclaim the bulldozed embankments. Tadpoles though have found a home in the drainage ditches at the side of the track.

THE FOOL OF THE PEAT MOSS

Dotterel nest high on the flat rounded summit of Beinn Dearg. Their Gaelic name *amadan-mointich*, 'the fool of the peat moss' refers to their tendency not to fly away once detected. Their English name is derived from a Middle English word meaning 'easily caught' itself related to the Portuguese word that gave us 'dodo'.

In the past dotterel were regarded as a delicacy and the *London Art of Cooking* published in 1811 includes a recipe for dotterel. On the bookshelves above my desk there is a tattered old paperback *Cordon Bleu Cookery* published in 1963. It doesn't include any recipes for dotterel but you'd be cooking up trouble today with the one on page 288 for capercaillie.

Ladies mantle and tormentil grow on the grassy banks of the stream. I climbed Beinn Dearg after a long spell of dry weather, all the burns were low except the Allt Sheicheachan still fed by melting snow patches high up on Meall Dubh nan Dearcag. A short distance north of the bothy between the path and the burn, among the heather and blaeberry are low stone walls NN83652 73879, the remains of summer shielings.

When the track reaches a ford across the Allt Sheicheachan don't cross the stream but continue straight ahead on a narrow stony stalkers' path that climbs Meall Dubh nan Dearcag. Follow the path up the heathery hillside with wide views opening out across a landscape of brown and tan rounded hills.

The track up Beinn Dearg is easy to follow in summer and although three footpaths are marked on the map, on the ground only the well tramped, eroded path to the summit of Beinn Dearg is clear. Above the 800 metre contour the path becomes fainter as it climbs the broad ridge north across dwarf heath and the red scree that gives the hill its name. As I climb crane flies drifting low over the heather and deer grass brush against my bare legs.

At a height of 931 metres, a short distance before the true summit of Beinn Dearg there is a cairn. William Scrope's book *The Art of Deer*

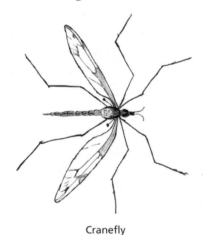

Cranefly

Stalking includes a detailed description of the summit area of Beinn Dearg with its; 'sundry large uncomfortable stones' and specifically mentions the false summit that must be passed before the top of Beinn Dearg is reached. It seems reasonable to infer that while he was the tenant of Bruar Lodge, Scrope made what was probably the first recorded ascent of Beinn Dearg around 1824.

A ptarmigan flies up, perhaps it is trying to distract the dogs so I put them on the lead just in case there is a nest nearby, hidden amongst the rocks. The weather forecast had threatened thunder but I'm on my way back, well past Lady March cairn, almost at the forest, before the first heavy drops of rain fall.

Just below the scree that covers the summit of Beinn Dearg I cross an area of boulders and patches of gravel among cushions of dwarf heather and alpine clubmoss; a natural rockery on the mountain top. To the east of the stony top of Beinn Dearg (1,008m) with its shelter and trig point I look across to the Corbett Beinn Mheadhonach next to Beinn a'Ghlo and Carn a'Chlamain, Queen Victoria's first Munro. To the north the Cairngorms still hold large snow patches early in June and

I can see the remote Munros, An Sgarsoch and Carn an Fhidhleir, standing at the headwaters of the rivers Feshie, Tarf and Geldie, an isolated corner of Scotland once described by Hamish Brown as; '… wild mistmoor, unlived-in, lonely as a sad heart, the silence more crashing than any sound could be.'

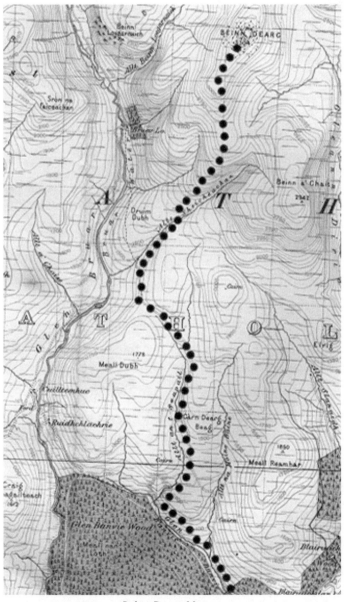

Beinn Dearg Map

BEINN DEARG (1,008m)

Grade	***
Map:	OS Sheet 43
Distance/Ascent:	28km/890m
Starting height:	155m
Time to top:	5h (+cycle from Blair Atholl) +breaks
Public Transport Start:	Blair Atholl railway station.
Car Start/Finish:	Glen Tilt Car Park near Blair Atholl

An 18 mile round trip across featureless moorland to one of the remoter Munros. While there is a path all the way to the foot of Beinn Dearg which is obvious in summer, even a light fall of snow can hide the path in winter.

ROUTE:

1   From Blair Atholl cycle/drive to Old Blair.

2   If driving, park before reaching Old Blair in car park NN87448 66262 (busy at weekends, toilets in Blair Atholl) signposted *Glen Tilt Parking*. (Atholl estates suggest drivers make a £1 donation towards footpath maintenance). At entrance to car park turn left along road (first 3km of route way marked with black arrows).

3   Keep right at driveway to Gardener's Cottage.

4   Where tarmac ends at cross roads NN86800 66700 continue straight ahead following unsurfaced track along NE side of Banvie Burn.

5   At a gate continue straight ahead into forest. Follow track through woods keeping Banvie Burn on your left.

6   Keep left at fork in track (way marked black arrow).

7   Do not cross Rumbling Bridge (moss covered) NN85906 67324. Keep Banvie Burn on left.

8   Follow signpost reading *long route*.

9   Leave way marked route just before gate NN85313 67852 at edge of forest. Go through gate and follow track across moorland (gate sometimes locked but there is a stile).

10 Pass Lady March Cairn NN 85200 69100.

11 Cross Allt na Moine Baine at concrete bridge NN85033 69450.

12 Continue along track on E side of Allt an t-Seapail.

13 Reach Allt Sheicheachan bothy (leave bikes about 0.5km before/south of bothy, track very rough beyond here).

14 Behind bothy cross Allt Sheicheachan and follow track along NW (left) bank of stream.

15 When track reaches ford NN84908 74959 do not cross stream. Continue straight ahead on narrow stony stalkers' path.

16 Follow obvious eroded path N up Meall Dubh nan Dearcag (above about 800m path becomes fainter).

17 Reach scree and a short distance before summit pass a cairn (931m) NN84938 77032.

18 Reach summit of Beinn Dearg (1,008m) NN85302 77777 (shelter and trig point).

19 Return by the same route.

PUBLIC TRANSPORT: train leaves Edinburgh 6.32am (7.06am from Glasgow) arriving Blair Atholl 8.55am (not Sundays). Last train back from Blair Atholl 9.53pm. Bikes carried free but must be booked onto trains in advance. Full public transport details at www.travelinescotland.com or phone 0871 200 22 33.

STALKING: This is deer stalking country so between 12 August and 20 October go to www.outdooraccess-scotland.com and click on Walking and Stalking link or see notice in car park at start of walk (information updated by 8am each day).

CYCLING: A gate about 3km from Old Blair at NN85313 67852 is sometimes padlocked, bikes can be lifted over stile (Atholl Estates Ranger Service telephone 01796 481355). Bikes carried free on trains but must be booked in advance

Somewhere Else: Allt Sheicheachan bothy is conveniently situated at the foot of Beinn Dearg.

CHAPTER TWENTY FIVE

Ben Vrackie

Dead Man Walking

SEEN FROM THE FOOTBRIDGE at Pitlochry railway station Ben Vrackie rises above the trees beyond the slated rooftops of the town. Standing there I thought of Caleb at the dawn of the 20th century sketching the Cairngorm Mountains from the footbridge at Aviemore station 50 miles up the line and understood what inspired him to create a mountain panorama.

Peter Drummond describes Ben Vrackie (841m/2,759ft) as;

> geologically a whirl of black schists, grey micashcists, white quartzite and greenish epiorite, all with characteristic screes, soils and therefore plants to give it 'speckle'.

Ben Vrackie's name reflects the geology of the mountain: it comes from the Gaelic word *breac* meaning dappled or speckled and used to describe hills with patches of scree among the heather. Similarly Allan Breck Stewart one of the central characters in Robert Louis Stevenson's novel *Kidnapped* was so named because his face was pitted with small-pox scars.

Local historian Colin Liddell has a slightly different take on the name; Ben Vrackie is 'the speckled mountain' because white quartz rocks used to be scattered across its slopes and were visible from some distance away. Almost all these rocks were taken away during the 19th century to decorate the houses and gardens of Pitlochry. Today near the summit of Ben Vrackie one or two (well embedded) white quartz rocks can still be seen near the path.

It has been suggested that some of the 50 or so Scottish mountains called Beinn Bhreac or Beinn a'Bhric were named after a mythical creature from Gaelic folklore. Tales are told of an old woman who disguised herself in deerskins and capable of being a true friend or deadly enemy to solitary travellers. She was named the Cailleach Beinn a'Bhric meaning the 'spirit of the speckled mountains'.

Climbing Ben Vrackie

Dark suited commuters on their way to work streamed past me as I sat on a bench outside Edinburgh's Haymarket station at 8.15am on a Tuesday morning. I felt as if I was following in the footsteps of early Scottish mountaineers like Ronnie Burn and AE Robertson. Although rail access to the hills is more restricted than 100 years ago because of the Beeching cuts to the network, Ben Vrackie can easily be reached by public transport from the central belt of Scotland.

The train is a relaxing alternative to driving up the A9, arguably the most dangerous bit of many a 21st century mountaineering expedition in Scotland. Instead of negotiating heavy traffic on the Forth Road Bridge and the M90 I settle back in my seat enjoying the view of Arthur's Seat across the Firth of Forth as the train rattles through Burntisland. The journey from Perth with its vast station, overgrown tracks and derelict buildings, to Pitlochry seems quicker than by car. I catch my first glimpse of Ben Vrackie as the train crosses the River Tay on a girder viaduct with castellated piers I have seen many times from the A9. I leave Edinburgh at 8.37am, arrive in Pitlochry at 10.15am and reach the summit of Ben Vrackie at 12.40pm.

Outside Pitlochry station turn right along the main street and take the first left, Moulin road for about a kilometre until you come to Moulin village on the outskirts of Pitlochry. Behind iron railings beside the pavement the Moulin Burn flows down through the town. The burn rises on the moor above Moulin on the lower slopes of Ben Vrackie and keeps me company for the first part of the climb. In the past the burn provided power for meal, lint, tweed and saw mills along its length.

On the platform at Pitlochry station stands a white painted iron drinking fountain in the shape of a heron. Halfway up Moulin Road on a grassy bank by a pine tree a real heron stands motionless at the side of the Moulin burn. There are dippers and wagtails on the stream too.

Passing the Craigvrack Hotel I remember staying there one icy January and climbing Ben Vrackie, with gums bleeding, drenched in sweat. On a bleak Monday morning a few weeks later I was diagnosed with AIDS and it was 14 months before I climbed another mountain. Eighty years, the time it takes a virus to replicate its way from the Congo to the River Tummel, from the heat of central Africa to the cold of Pitlochry in winter.

I walk past Moulin Church with its cockerel weather vane on the steeple. Behind the churchyard wall two of the oldest gravestones are called the Crusader graves because each has a sword carved on it. In days gone by petty offenders were punished by being fastened by an iron collar to a tree in the graveyard. Propped up against the wall in the porch of the church is a small gravestone known as the Grand Gutcher Stone. *Gutcher* is Scots for grandfather and inscribed on the stone are the words;

> Tis My Lot
> This Day It Is
> Your Lot
> Tomorou

The village of Moulin dates back to Bronze Age times. Around 150AD the Greek geographer Ptolemy published a map of the world based on information from Roman soldiers returning home. Some have claimed that the name of the settlement of Lindum on the north bank of the River Tay on Ptolemy's map is in fact the village of Moulin. Moulin stood at a major crossroads but after 2,000 years as an important settlement was bypassed when the new Great North Road through Pitlochry was built by General Wade in 1728.

Turn left at the Moulin Inn along Baledmund Road and follow road signs for *Ben-y-Vrackie*, a local spelling (see chapter 20). Swallows come back from Africa year after year to nest under the eaves of the Moulin Inn. The Inn first opened its doors in 1695, 50 years before Bonnie Prince Charlie's Jacobite rebellion of 1745. The old stables for the inn today house a microbrewery established in 1995 to make good quality beers.

At the edge of the village a road sign to *Ben-y-Vrackie* points the way. The standing stone in the field to the left of the road is known as the Dane's Stone. Moulin market used to be held in this field each March at the end of the winter. Deals struck at the market were sealed by a clasping of hands at the Dane's Stone. The market was a major event of the year and was notorious for bad weather; 'Moulin market weather' was a local expression. A memorial stone by the A924 east of Pitlochry commemorates a shepherd who died in a blizzard walking the five miles home to Stronhavie from Moulin Market on the evening of Thursday 3 March 1887.

Follow the road into woodland bearing right at the gates to Baledmund House. In spring primroses and daffodils grow along the edge of the road here. Turn right into a small car park, the footpath to Ben Vrackie starts at an information board and waymarker.

Follow the waymarkers uphill through beech, silver birch and pine trees. Brown and yellow boletus mushrooms sprout up through the mossy woodland floor in autumn. Cross a timber footbridge. Broom grows here, its seed pods popping in the warm sunshine of early October. There are wild raspberries too among the bracken and in places rhododendron is invading the woods.

Where the path emerges from the trees on to the open moorland that forms the lower slopes of Ben Vrackie, a tall pine felled by a winter storm lies near the path. Stones and pebbles protrude from the circle of earth uprooted when the tree fell.

Go through a gate in a deer fence where a yellow sign warns walkers to be well prepared for climbing Ben Vrackie. The track cuts a line through the heather and bog myrtle. A black ground beetle scuttles across the sandy path in front of my boots while aeroplanes leave vapour trails in the clear blue sky above the scree covered slopes of Ben Vrackie. In summer many wild flowers grow on the hillside among them tormentil, wild thyme, yarrow, and marsh cinquefoil.

Bay Boletus
Mushroom

Ahead a wisp of cloud touches the top of Ben Vrackie. Looking back, farmland stretches to the edge of the moor. Pitlochry nestles in the wide strath below and the River Tummel glints in the sunshine. A church bell tolls in the town and a few moments later I hear a train sound its horn at Pitlochry station.

WHO OWNS BEN VRACKIE?

Most of Ben Vrackie lies within the boundaries of the Baledmund estate which is owned by Alastair Finlay Fergusson, Pitfourie, Pitlochry, Perthshire, PH16 5QZ.

In June 1881 Robert Louis Stevenson, the Edinburgh born author and poet, came to spend the summer at Kinnaird Cottage below Ben Vrackie. While there Stevenson wrote three short stories; *Thrawn Janet*, *The Body Snatchers* and *The Merry Men*. Of this holiday Stevenson wrote;

We have a lovely spot here: a little green glen with a burn, a wonderful burn, gold and green and snow-white... Behind, great purple moorlands reaching to Ben Vrackie. Hunger lives here, alone with larks and sheep. Sweet spot, sweet spot.

At a fork in the track take the right hand path signposted *Ben Vrackie.* The left hand path leads to the Bealach na Searmoin, the pass of the sermon between the two rounded hills to the north-west. In autumn devil's bit scabious and the last few bluebells brighten the grass between white lichen and moss covered rocks. A buzzard circles high above the moorland. The path clings to the hillside as it skirts some little crags and passes through the gap between Meall na h-Aodainn Moire, the mountain of the big face and Creag Bhreac. An old stone wall stretches out across the moor. The steep scree covered south face of Ben Vrackie comes into sight as the path dips down to Loch a Choire. That January in 1997 the loch was frozen solid. We hurled rocks at the ice but it did not crack.

Follow the path up past the screes below the summit that give the mountain its name. Ben Vrackie is a site of special scientific interest because rare species of plants including alpine milk-vetch grow on inaccessible crags and ledges on the hill. After a steep climb the trig point marking the top of Ben Vrackie (841m/ 2,759ft) is reached. Hamish Brown wrote; 'The view from the summit is tremendous, especially westwards along the Tummel-Rannoch trench to distant Rannoch Moor and its hills. Beinn a'Ghlo looms large, and southwards, there is a good view of the Lowland hills...'

In October the overwhelming impression was of blue sky and brown heather and the scree covered upper slopes of Beinn a'Ghlo beyond Loch Moraig. Blair Castle is a distant white dot from Ben Vrackie and the

Stonechat

industrial site next to the A9 is the limestone quarry at Shierglas. By a little lochan tucked in a fold of hillside below Ben Vrackie, lines of sheep trailed across the heather, their fleeces splodged with red dye. Schiehallion a triangular cone in the distance.

Many boots on the grassy summit of Ben Vrackie have worn a circle of bare earth and rock around the trig point. During the Second World War children and schools were evacuated from other parts of the country to the Pitlochry area and billeted on families or housed in hotels. The direction indicator on the summit of Ben Vrackie is a memorial to the Leys school in Cambridge evacuated to the Atholl Palace Hotel in 1940. The materials for the indicator were carried up the mountain by environmentally friendly donkey. According to the view indicator the Arthurs that can be seen from the summit of Ben Vrackie in clear weather include Ben Chonzie, Ben Vorlich, Ben Lomond, Stob Binnein, Ben More, Ben Lawers, Meall Garbh, Schiehallion, East Lomond, West Lomond, Lochnagar, Beinn a'Ghlo, Beinn Dearg and Arthur's Seat itself.

Return to Pitlochry by the route of ascent, I was back in time to catch a train that got me to Edinburgh at 16.16. The train ticket cost £18.10, less than the price of petrol for the car journey. And I even had time to buy a Compton Mackenzie paperback from the second hand bookshop on Pitlochry station.

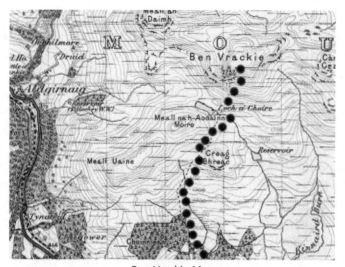

Ben Vrackie Map
(Please note that this route is over two OS map sheets)

BEN VRACKIE (841m)

Grade	**
Map:	OS Sheet 43 and 52
Distance/Ascent:	10km/741m
Starting height:	100m
Time to Top:	2h 30min +breaks
Public Transport Start/Finish:	Pitlochry
Car Start/Finish:	Ben Vrackie car park near Moulin

This popular route up Ben Vrackie has a good path all the way, is easily accessible by public transport and passes the historic Moulin Inn.

ROUTE:

1   Outside station turn left, walk through car park, and then turn right along Atholl Road (the main street).

2   From Atholl Road (the main street) in Pitlochry turn left up Moulin Road following signposts for *Moulin*.

3   Walk/drive along Moulin Road for 1km. Turn left at Moulin Inn along Baledmund Road following road signs for *Ben Vrackie*.

4   Follow road as it bears right at entrance to Baledmund House. Turn right into car park NN94414 59771 (overflow car park a few hundred metres back down road to Moulin). Footpath to Ben Vrackie starts in corner of car park (waymarker).

5   After short distance cross unsurfaced road (red waymarker) and go through wooden gate in deer fence. Follow path through woods.

6   Path joins another unsurfaced road at blue waymarker. After short distance leave road as it turns left and go straight ahead along footpath (red waymarker NN94353 60353).

7   Go through gate in deer fence NN94183 60774 onto moorland.

8   At fork in path NN94254 61395 turn right (signposted *Ben Vrackie*).

9   Go through gate NN94631 61829.

10 Cross stepping stones at SE end Loch a 'Choire NN94858 62534 and follow path steeply uphill to summit Ben Vrackie NN95000 63200.

11 Return by the route of ascent.

PUBLIC TRANSPORT: Trains every two hours from Pitlochry. Full public transport details at www.travelinescotland.com or phone 0871 200 22 33.

DOGS: some sheep on open hillside.

WINTER CONDITIONS: ice axe and crampons needed.

Somewhere Else: The Moulin Inn, Pitlochry.

CHAPTER TWENTY SIX

Beinn a'Ghlo

Red Deer

Now she flies high – now she flies low –
And she lights on the summit of huge Ben-y-gloe.

The Witch of Ben-y-Gloe, MG LEWIS

AS THE *UISGE BEATHA* flowed on the long summer evenings at the shielings tales were told around the fire of a witch who lived on top of Beinn a'Ghlo with the power to wrap a grey cloak of mist around the hill. The witch cast spells to get people to do her bidding; changing the direction of the wind and letting loose storms. Maybe the meaning of the name Beinn a'Ghlo has its roots in the old stories.

The minister for the parish of Blair Atholl in the 1790s had perhaps heard the folk tales for he called the hill *Beinn-glo;* the mountain with the veil of clouds or snow. *Glo* is an old Gaelic word meaning a hood or a veil of mist. The 16th century mapmaker Timothy Pont recorded it as *Bin Gloin* and in 1769, on his tour of Scotland, Thomas Pennant described: '... the great hill of Ben y glo, base is 35 miles in circumference, and whose summit towers far above the others.' Hill of mist is a good explanation of the meaning and the mountain's great height of 1,121m/3,678ft combined with its tendency to be in cloud probably explains its name.

Beinn a'Ghlo is located on the east side of Glen Tilt 63½ miles from Arthur's Seat and 20 degrees west of north. It is a huge, complex mountain with many ridges, summits and corries, covering around 40km². To Adam Watson the mountain ecologist Beinn a'Ghlo is 'one of the most beautiful and mysterious hills of Scotland'. There are three Munro peaks on Beinn a'Ghlo; Carn Liath 975 metres (grey hill), Bràigh Coire Chruinn-bhalgain 1,070 metres (height of the corrie of round blisters) and Carn nan Gabhar 1,121 metres (hill of the goat). Its highest peak is also its remotest; Carn nan Gabhar is 12 kilometres from Blair Atholl as the crow flies. Only the name Beinn a'Ghlo and the height 3,671 feet is given on Caleb's list which corresponds to the height of Carn nan Gabhar and is consistent with how the mountain appeared on the Ordnance Survey one-inch to the mile, 1st edition, maps of the 1890s.

Geologically Beinn a'Ghlo consists mainly of schists and quartz with some limestone which means the mountain is home to several unusual plants. Where Beinn a'Ghlo sweeps down to Glen Tilt, rare lichens grow on the cliffs of Creag Mhor above the River Tilt and yellow oxytropis is found among the limestone scree near Loch Loch.

Several books about the Scottish hills include the story that a rifle shot in any one of Beinn a'Ghlo's many corries cannot be heard in any of the others. There doesn't seem to be any evidence to substantiate this claim, nor would the ridges of Beinn a'Ghlo appear to be much higher than those of other Scottish mountains. So where did this piece of mountaineering folklore come from? One afternoon in the high windowed Scottish Library on George IV Bridge in Edinburgh I was flicking through the pages of a leather bound edition of *Days of Deer Stalking* by William Scrope published in 1839. On page 171 I found the answer; 'Ben-y-gloe is of vast magnitude,' wrote Mr Scrope, the tenant of Bruar Lodge,

> ... stretching its huge limbs far and wide... it contains twenty-four corries; these corries are separated from each other by such high ridges, that a person standing in one of them could not hear a shot fired in the next.

Climbing Beinn a'Ghlo

Driving along Loch Laggan side from Roy Bridge at 8.00am on an October morning, I'm on my way to Blair Atholl to climb Beinn a'Ghlo. Two days of heavy rain but the forecast for today is better. The sky red in the sunrise and the mountains around Fersit capped with broken cloud above 2,000 feet. As Nevis FM fades to static I realise all the rain in Lochaber over the preceding couple of days has fallen as snow above 800 metres. The first snow of the winter on the Scottish mountains.

From Blair Atholl I take the byroad signposted *Monzie* ignoring turnings to Old Blair and Glen Fender. Its eight years since I've been this way but Cuilean remembers the route and there are sounds of doggy excitement from the back of the car as I drive towards the start of the walk at Loch Moraig.

There is space to park where the public road ends at a double gate, cattle grid and a *No Fishing* sign. There are marshes and reeds but Loch

Moraig is hidden by a pine wood. The hill farm of Monzie lies a mile away across dry stone walls and low rolling grassy hills rising to Carn Liath, first of the Munro summits of Beinn a'Ghlo its southern flank scarred by an eroded hillwalkers' path. The Gaels always had an eye for Highland topography, in Gaelic Monzie means 'a hilly place.'

Sheep and cattle graze unfenced here (dogs out of the car... careful). I remember Cuilean being scared of the cows last time we climbed Beinn a'Ghlo. A BMW jeep pulls up and three men in sunglasses get out (the only people I see that Sunday not climbing Beinn a'Ghlo via Carn Liath).

Go through the gate at the end of the public road and over the cattle grid. Walk a short distance along the private road to Monzie Farm then at the corner of the pine wood turn right through a gate with a sign on it, *Shinagag*.

This is deer stalking country, check www.outdooraccess-scotland.com for information to find out whether stalking is taking place on the east side of Beinn a'Ghlo if doing this walk between 12 August and 20 October. I climbed Beinn a'Ghlo during the stalking season but on a Sunday when traditionally no stalking takes place.

Deer Stalking

You can always tell when there's stalking going on. There you are happily walking along a track somewhere in the Highlands looking forward to a quiet day in the hills when you look round and see a procession of green Landrovers towing ATVs on trailers bumping along the track behind you. Men with florid faces beneath tweed caps scowl from the windows of the vehicles. The sight of Cuilean and the Labradoodle straining at the leash raises their blood pressure to dangerous levels.

Management of red deer in Scotland employs about 300 people full time and 450 on a part time seasonal basis. For all the land devoted to it and fuss made about it, far more employment in the Highlands is provided by hillwalking and wildlife tourism than field sports.

Traditionally an estate deer stalker guides and assists a client to locate the deer, first in a vehicle then on foot. The greatest trophy is a royal stag which has 12 points on its antlers like the one in the novel *Second Sight* by Neil Gunn which centres on the hunt for a legendary stag called King Brude. When close to the deer, stalker and client crawl along using bumps and hummocks in the ground, the direction of the wind and the atmospheric conditions (mist or cold dry air affects the animals' sense of smell) to get near enough the deer for a clear and humane shot.

The deer's stomach and intestines are then removed on the hillside, a gruesome process with a blood drenched name, gralloching, before the carcass is tied to a pony or put on the back of an ATV and taken down the hill to one of those windowless wooden sheds you see behind Highland shooting lodges. I remember vegetarian Farida from Droitwich, turning green in Knoydart one summer, at the sight of a motor boat full of dead deer. And my final word on deer stalking; always remember there is no word for poaching in Gaelic.

I tramp along past a square conifer plantation near the track. On a low hill in the distance a row of ragged Scots pines. Another cattle grid, the dogs cross at the right hand side where the gaps between the iron bars have filled with compacted soil. Looking back I can see Loch Moraig with its little tree covered islands.

WHO OWNS BEINN A'GHLO?

Andrew D Gordon and Duncan Gordon 1999 Trust, Lude and Shinagag Estate, Lude, Blair Atholl, Perthshire, PH18 5TR.

A notice on a gate from the euphemistically named West Grampian Deer Management Group gives information about stalking on the Lude Estate; culling maintains the health of the deer stock and prevents damage through over grazing and trampling, I read. Yet there are hundreds and hundreds of red deer in Atholl and Lude and lots of ground trampled by them. Beinn a'Ghlo is a site of special scientific interest and in 2003 Scottish Natural Heritage found red deer densities on the mountain varying from 15–33 animals per square kilometre, far too many to allow tree and shrub regeneration for which a level of less than six animals per square kilometre would be required.

Archaeologists have found evidence of people living around Loch Moraig since early times. Traces of hut circles and the remains of a settlement of half a dozen buildings and fields enclosed by earth banks have been found on the hillside above the west shore of the loch. On a summer's morning in 1689 Bonnie Dundee led his army along the edge of Loch Moraig on his way to the Battle of Killiecrankie.

Running along the side of the track is a turf and stone wall which may be part of an old agricultural boundary. Continue along the track past two old wooden sheds with corrugated iron roofs. Ignore the footpath to Carn Liath that starts here (everyone else will be going that way) and keep heading east on the track. At the sheds Cuilean stops and sniffs the air while looking along the path to Carn Liath, then sniffs the road to Shinagag and looks up at me, wondering which way?

The track crosses a burn at a shallow ford, white flowers of yarrow in the grass here, grazing animals usually avoid its strong smelling, bitter tasting leaves. The track crosses flat moorland, peat and heather and grass, below the grey scree covered slopes of Carn Liath. To the south I can see Ben Vrackie, less steep here than on the Pitlochry side with Farragon Hill and Schiehallion in the distance. The rooftops of the house at Shinagag poke up between square plantations of pine and a few scattered broad leaved trees.

MARY QUEEN OF SCOTS AND THE GREAT TINCHEL

The view from the summit of Beinn a'Ghlo today is one of deserted moorland and empty glens. But these hills were not always quiet. In the August of 1564 thousands of people filled Glen Loch when Mary Queen of Scots visited Perthshire and took part in a deer hunt at the south end of Loch Loch. The Queen and her nobles stood on a rise known ever after as Tom nan Ban Righ, the queen's hillock (not marked on maps) from which she watched the tinchel, a Scots word that means a deer hunt derived, from the Gaelic word *timchioll*, meaning 'a circuit'.

Deer hunting in the 16th century was very far from the silent stalking of today. Deer were driven by dozens, sometimes hundreds of men and dogs towards a narrow gap in the hills called an *elrick*, their antlers appearing over the hill 'making a show like a wood' according to one contemporary description. Meall na h-Eilrig below Carn nan Gabhar is named after the *elrick* where the hunters armed with bow and arrow, spear and club lay in wait to ambush the deer.

In Glen Loch on an August afternoon five centuries ago 2,000 Highlanders form a chain to push the deer towards the waiting huntsmen and dogs. 360 animals are slaughtered that day. As the deer thunder towards the royal party on Tom nan Ban Righ, Mary Queen of Scots thrills to the chase and orders her favourite deerhound be released. The dog panics the massed deer and they stampede back towards the crowds of men acting as

---

beaters. Unable to escape the men throw themselves face down in the heather covering their heads with their arms as the deer run over them. Three Highlanders are trampled to death before the deer are corralled and the hunt resumes.

About 200 metres before the fork in the track to Shinagag look out for several grass covered mounds and stones at the side of the track. They mark the start of a hillwalkers' path not shown on the OS map that bears north-east across the moorland, contouring round the foot of Carn Liath at a height of about 500 metres. This path is easy to miss. I did – result; much tramping through deep heather. There's no cairn marking the path but if you look carefully to the left of the track you can see it cutting a thin line north-east through the heather. After passing some wooden grouse butts the path becomes more distinct as it approaches the lower slopes of Beinn Bheag.

Soon another of Beinn a'Ghlo's peaks comes into sight; Airgiod Bheinn. An old description of Scotland records;

> on Airghead-bheinn, a part of Beinn-glo, there are stones, that shine, as if they had been vitrified, and give it the appearance of a volcano, which probably give the name of Airghead-bheinn, or the silver mountain, to this pinnacle...

The path dips down to cross a burn before skirting Beinn Bheag. By October the heather in the corries below the ridge linking Carn Liath and Bràigh Coire Chruinn-bhalgain had ceased flowering and turned brown. Looking around I see mile upon mile of brown heather covered moorland, these glens seem deserted today but Loch Loch below Beinn a'Ghlo lies in the centre of an area once known as the Seven Shielings, remote and deserted today, but two centuries ago hundreds of people worked there in summer tending livestock and making cheese.

Today hundreds of pairs of climbing boots have exposed the woody stems of the heather and trampled it into the peat at the edges of the path. Dry where it crosses stony bits of ground, for long stretches the surface of the path is slippery black peaty earth. Two red grouse rocket up from the heather, down curved wings whirring, startling the dogs with their throaty alarm call *go-bak, go-bak-bak-bak-bak.*

Great lines of a hundred or more deer file past a huge boulder on the hillside high above, they have caught my scent and are nervous. It is

October and the animals fear the crack of rifle shots and sudden death. As I follow the path down to cross a small stream the dog literally stops in her tracks, ears pricked up listening to a stag at the foot of Airgiod Bheinn roaring across to the stags on Bràigh Coire Chruinn-bhalgain. Facing Beinn a'Ghlo across Glen Loch is Beinn Vuirich, the hill of the roaring of stags... *vuirich*, the word resonates with the primordial sound of autumn in the Scottish hills.

In summer the deer move high up the hills to escape the midges and clegs. As snow and blizzards cover the high ground in winter the deer move lower down the hills. Kellan aged nineteen spends New Year 1982 with his younger sister and a school friend in a caravan near Aviemore. They have a snow ball fight on a section of the 'new' A9 road that is being constructed nearby. Everything freezes; the milk and the washing up liquid inside the caravan, even his sister's hair in the time it takes to walk back from the shower block. Each morning they awake to a thick covering of hoar frost on the blankets and a half inch thick layer of ice on the plywood interior walls of the caravan. Across the Cairngorms at Braemar the deer are so cold that as the temperature plummets to −27.2 on 10 January, the deer move into the streets of the town at night and at around 3am a stag is photographed standing in front of the Butcher's Shop.

Follow the path by the Allt Bealach an Fhiodha up through the corrie to the Bealach an Fhiodha which in clear weather is obvious on the sky-line. At about the 650 metre contour the path, faint in places and hard to follow, crosses to the east bank of the burn. Little side streams flow down the hillside almost invisible in the long grass. Large black patches of peaty earth are exposed on the eroded hillside. The rocks beside the path are covered in the same red lichen I'd seen on Schiehallion. Crimson cushions of sphagnum moss grow among the heather and at one place white feathers are scattered across the path, the site of a kill by a bird of prey. High above the scree two stags stand silhouetted on the ridge of Bràigh Coire Chruinn-bhalgain.

When seen from the upper slopes of Beinn a'Ghlo, Beinn Bheag (little hill) is dwarfed by Carn Liath, the Gaels' unfailing eye for topography again. Higher up heather gives way to grass and the apple-green foliage of blaeberry as the path, high on the east bank of the burn climbs towards the bealach. Blaeberry is more tolerant of snow than heather and is often found growing at high altitudes.

I once climbed Beinn a'Ghlo with my mother. Back then she was a member of the LSCC, the Ladies Scottish Climbing Club founded in 1908 by Jane Inglis Clarke because she was fed up with Mr Inglis Clarke spending all his time on the hills with the Scottish Mountaineering Club. We struggled up Carn Liath in near gale force winds and when we reached the bealach north of Carn Liath, Mum who a year earlier had celebrated her last Munro on Ben Dorain with a reading of Duncan Ban Macintyre's Farewell to the Bens and a party at the Bridge of Orchy Hotel afterwards, decided she would rather pick blaeberries than struggle on along the ridge. In the time it took me to bag Bràigh Coire Chruinn-bhalgain she'd filled half a Tupperware box with little blue-black berries and her fingers were stained purple.

Alpine ladies-mantle and fir club moss grow at the stony Bealach an Fhiodha (847m – not marked on the OS 1:50000 map) which lies at the heart of the Beinn a'Ghlo massif. To the north the Cairngorms were white with the first snow of winter at the beginning of October.

From the Bealach an Fhiodha a gravelly path worn in the wind cropped heath leads east up to the wide shallow col between the scree covered summit of Carn nan Gabhar and Airgiod Bheinn. On the way back down I meet a group of hillwalkers with a black and white border collie. The dogs have a mad charge around in circles instigated by Cuilean (who had looked a bit stiff on the summit of Carn nan Gabhar as she picked her way between the rocks).

From the col below the summit of Carn nan Gabhar bear north-east up a broad stony easy-angled ridge. Freezing level that October day was at 985 metres, and a light dusting of snow covered the mountain's top. It was very cold, sunny but the wind was icy. Too cold to stop for food, I just took photos and entered GPS waypoints.

The almost level summit ridge of Carn nan Gabhar has three cairns, the furthest away one is the highest. From the summit ridge there are views to Airgiod Bheinn and Carn Liath and you look down to Ben Vrackie and little Loch Valigan. The smooth rounded hills of the Grampians, in October green fading to brown, stretch away into the distance. Continue north-east to another little bump about 250 metres away which has a trig point on it.

THE WITCH OF BEINN A'GHLO

William Scrope recorded the old stories, told him by ghillies and stalkers on long days tramping the heather. 'There is great talk of a witch that still haunts Ben-y-gloe' he wrote in 1839;

> ... She is represented as of a very mischievous and malevolent disposition, driving cattle into morasses, where they perish, and riding the forest horses by night, till covered with mire and sweat, they drop down from fatigue and exhaustion. She has the power of taking the shape of an eagle, raven, hind... She destroys bridges, and allures people to the margin of the flood, by exhibiting a semblance of floating treasures, which they lose their lives in grasping at.

According to William Scrope the last sighting of the witch of Beinn a'Ghlo took place in Glen Tarf. Two hunters left Braemar on a winter's day under a leaden grey sky. The old pines in the glen creaked in the icy north wind... or was it the east wind; sometimes it seemed suddenly to change direction. Soon big flakes of snow began to fall and by the time the two men reached Glen Tarf they were lost in a blizzard and forced to seek shelter at a bothy. The door was opened by a wild looking, haggard old woman with long, lank dishevelled hair and deep-set, piercing grey eyes. So scared were the men of her that they could hardly eat the food she prepared for them. When the witch discovered they had brought no venison with them she told them that to make amends they must leave a fat stag at midnight on the first day of every month at Frasers' Cairn in Glen Bruar. Then flying into a terrifying rage the witch told them; 'If ye neglect this my bidding, foul will befall ye... ye shall surely perish on the waste; the raven shall croak your dirge; and your banes shall be pickit by the eagle.' Next morning when the men awoke from a deep sleep it had stopped snowing, the sun was shining and the witch had vanished, never to be seen again...

Thomas Grierson an early summit bagger, credited by Ian Mitchell in *Scotland's Mountains Before the Mountaineers*, with the ascent of 12 Munros climbed Beinn a'Ghlo around 1811. In April 1886 Hugh Munro traversed all the summits of Beinn a'Ghlo in a great stravaig from Spittal of Glenshee to Blair Atholl.

Snow fills the gaps between the rocks on the boulder strewn summit plateau of Carn nan Gabhar. From the trig point 150 metres of rough walking in a north-easterly direction brings me to the third and highest summit of Carn nan Gabhar (1,121m) which has a substantial cairn on it.

Caleb's fascination with the hills visible from Scottish mountains was a characteristic he shared with other early mountaineers; the view from the summit of a hill was still a new and novel phenomenon. Hugh Munro wrote at length in *The Scottish Mountaineering Club Journal* in May 1893 on the view from Beinn a'Ghlo which;

> ... from its great height and commanding position on the frontier of the Lowlands is very extensive... Eighteen miles E.N.E. Lochnagar stands out... Farther off to the right the two Fifeshire Lomonds are conspicuous; while, when there is a strong wind to blow away the smoke, the Pentlands, seventy-five miles away, are plainly seen. Due south... are the billowy Ochils. Close at hand Ben Vrackie, above Killiecrankie... Standing out from the heathery uplands, which rise to the south side of Loch Tay, is Ben Chonzie... Next come Ben Vorlich and Stuc a Chroin, Ben Ledi, forty-seven miles off; Am Binnein, seen over Ben Lawers, Cairn Mairg, and Schiehallion... while across Glen Tilt, Ben Dearg, nine miles W.N.W., completes the circle.

And once you have searched the summit of Beinn a'Ghlo for witches, return by the same route.

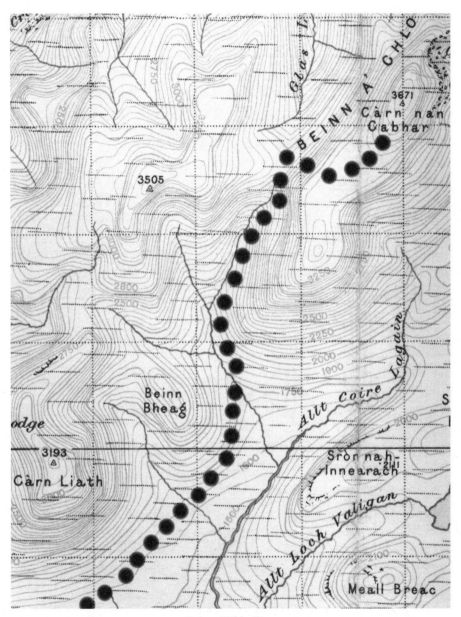

Beinn a'Ghlo Map

BEINN a'GHLO (1,121m)

Grade	***
Map:	OS Sheet 43
Distance/Ascent:	20km/790m (from Loch Moraig)
Starting height:	330m (Loch Moraig)
Time to top:	4h (+cycle from Blair Atholl) +breaks
Public transport start/Finish:	Blair Atholl railway station
Car Start/Finish:	Loch Moraig near Blair Atholl

A long heathery tramp to the remotest summit of Beinn a'Ghlo.
Something of a challenge by public transport. Navigation needed.

ROUTE:

1   From Blair Atholl drive/cycle along quiet single track road signposted *Monzie*. Ignore left turns to Old Blair and Glen Fender.

2   Park where public road ends at Loch Moraig NN90561 67088 (double gate/cattle grid/*No Fishing* sign).

3   Go through the gate (right hand side of cattle grid easiest for dogs) and continue about 50m along private road to Monzie.

4   At corner of plantation of pine trees turn right through gate with signs on it *Shinagag* and *No Cars*.

5   Continue along the track past two old sheds at the foot of Carn Liath. Ignore path that branches left up Carn Liath.

6   Keep east on the track which crosses shallow ford over stream.

7   Go through gate on track.

8   NN93801 68273 about 200m before fork in track to Shinagag look out for grass covered mounds and rocks at side of track and bear left along indistinct hillwalkers' path that cuts a faint line north-east through the heather as it contours below Carn Liath at height of about 500m (path is easy to miss).

9   Path climbs up a little grass topped hummock and past some wooden grouse butts. Path faint as it crosses a patch of short cropped green turf – look out for a solitary wooden fencepost to left of path at this point.

10 If can't find path pick it up at NN94375 68807

11 Path becomes more distinct as it dips down to cross a burn NN94793 69558 before beginning to skirt Beinn Bheag.

12 Follow path up by Allt Bealach an Fhiodha NN95178 71196. At about 650m the path (faint in places and hard to follow) crosses to east bank of stream NN95479 71869.

13 Reach Bealach an Fhiodha 847m NN95860 72661 (not marked on OS 1:50000 map).

14 From Bealach an Fhiodha follow gravelly path east up to wide shallow col between Carn nan Gabhar and Airgiod Bheinn. Ignore left fork in path NN96050 72544 at 930m.

15 When col below summit of Carn nan Gabhar is reached at 1,010m NN96462 72629 bear north-east up the broad easy-angled ridge.

16 Pass a cairn on mound of scree and rocks.

17 Continue 250m north-east across boulders to trig point.

18 From trig point walk 150m north-east to highest point of Carn nan Gabhar (1,121m) NN97117 73301.

19 Return by the same route.

PUBLIC TRANSPORT: train leaves Edinburgh 6.32/7.06am from Glasgow arriving Blair Atholl 8.55am (not Sundays). Bikes carried free but must be booked onto trains in advance. Last train back from Blair Atholl 9.53pm. Full public transport details at www.travelinescotland.com or phone 0871 200 22 33.

DOGS: sheep and cattle on first part of walk along track. Also three cattle grids (fairly easy to cross). Higher up big herds of deer.

STALKING: This is deer stalking country so between 12 August and 20 October go to www.outdooraccess-scotland.com and click on Walking and Stalking link.

WINTER CONDITIONS: some experience of winter mountaineering needed before tackling this route in winter.

CHAPTER TWENTY SEVEN

The Magic Stones

The magic stones are filthy, coated in soot and grime. The stones cured illness they said. The mill stands by a narrow stone bridge where the road bends to cross the River Dochart. He had come to see the magic stones, braving the vicious snarling collies outside in the yard. The magic stones are kept in a soot filled recess in the wall of the mill near the chimney. Caleb cleans the largest stone with a linen handkerchief and now it seems to resemble a grotesque human face with sunken eyes.

BROWSING THE SHELVES of musty books in the Royal Scottish Geographical Society's library at Strathclyde University, searching for Caleb's world, I recalled the scene in Carlos Ruiz Zafon's *The Shadow of The Wind* when Daniel and his father visit the Cemetery of Forgotten Books;

> Every book, every volume you see here, has a soul. The soul of the person who wrote it and of those who read it and lived and dreamed with it. Every time a book changes hands, every time someone runs his eyes down its pages, its spirit grows and strengthens... In this place, books no longer remembered by anyone, books that are lost in time, live forever, waiting for the day when they will reach a new reader's hands.

No one had looked at CG Cash's books for a very long time. On a remote shelf near the end of a forgotten row I found *Stone Circles*, a slim volume with a red cover containing two articles on archaeology published in *The Proceedings of the Society of Antiquaries of Scotland* and subsequently privately printed by Caleb, something he often did. As I turned the last page I saw there was an envelope pasted to the inside of the back cover. I lifted the flap of the envelope almost with a shiver and pulled out half a dozen brown and white faded photographs of the hill fort on Tor Beag at the foot of Ben Ghuilbnich in Strathspey that Caleb had spent the summer of 1909 exploring. A square of paper was folded around the photos. The dehumidification of the university library's air conditioning system had kept the paper and its 'Imperial Note' watermark almost as white as the day 100 years before when, in neat handwriting I immediately recognised, Caleb had written on it *with compliments CG Cash.*

Archaeology developed out of antiquarianism at the end of the 19th century. The volumes of *The Proceedings of the Society of Antiquaries of Scotland* are bound in a thick brown flaky sort of leather with faint gold writing on the covers and sit today on the bottom shelf of the general periodicals section on the fifth floor of the Andersonian Library. On Monday 13 January 1908 Caleb was elected a Corresponding Member of the Society of Antiquaries of Scotland. The first *Law* of the Society defines its purpose as; '... the study of the antiquities and history of Scotland, more especially by means of archaeological research.' CGC was delighted to be elected. More letters to put after his name; Corr. Mem. Scot. Soc. Ant. to go after FRSGS.

The Magic Stones.
St Fillan's healing stones photographed for Caleb's 'Archaeological Gleanings From Killin'.

Argyll in the 1970s; Kellan and his little sister stand at the top of Beregonium the little hill fort below Beinn Lora, above the beach at Ardmucknish Bay looking at bumps in the turf, wondering if they mark the remains of walls and trying to puzzle out what on earth a vitrified fort is. On bike rides along the little byroads between Loch Etive and

Loch Creran they pass chambered cairns in the fields; piles of stones half covered with turf and surrounded by a few trees. Kellan thinks... an instant in deep time the 10,000 years people have lived in Scotland.

Caleb and Alice spent several summers in the Scottish Highlands looking for chambered cairns, exploring hill forts, making observations of stone circles and seeing a great many cup marked stones. That Alice accompanied Caleb on his archaeological expeditions shows it was a shared interest, something they could enjoy together, unlike mountaineering.

Caleb was often guided to hill forts or chambered cairns by local farmers or shepherds who told him of the existence of sites of archaeological interest. In 1909 Caleb explored chambered cairns around the village of Aviemore with Robert Anderson editor of *The Aberdeen Daily Journal* and a past president of the Cairngorm Club. The two men stayed in the cottage of the county roadman. Early mountaineers often paid to stay in private houses (today's bed and breakfast). Alex Sinclair, the road man, had a non-archaeological interest in chambered cairns, he used the stones from them to repair the main road, forerunner of the A9.

Autumn and winter evenings back in Edinburgh were spent writing up his observations which Caleb then submitted as papers to the Society of Antiquaries of Scotland. Politely described by Jeffrey Stone as; 'substantial', Caleb's writings for *The Proceedings of the Society* consist of page after page of detailed descriptions of stone circles illustrated with neatly drawn diagrams and drawings all initialled CGC. Today *The Proceedings of the Society of Antiquaries of Scotland* provide a rich source for websites devoted to standing stones and menhirs.

Caleb's excavation techniques consisted of a shovel and help from the local farmer's son, a world away from the painstakingly careful methods familiar to us today from TV programmes about archaeology. Caleb did seek advice from his mentor Sir Arthur Mitchell Vice President of the Society of Antiquaries as to how to proceed with the excavation of a chambered cairn at Avielochan near Aviemore. In 1873 Mitchell had made some of the first notes and observations of local archaeological remains while on holiday in Strathspey and advised; 'the inner enclosure and passage should be entirely cleared out.'

Characteristically Caleb enjoyed the exercise and physicality involved in archaeology, later writing; 'I did some labourer's work in excavation.' When all the digging and shovelling became too much for him Caleb roped in the son of the farmer on whose land the cairn stood to help him dig it out. (What the farmer's son thought of archaeological digging in addition to his other work on the farm CGC does not record). Caleb wrote they found nothing apart from a small piece of a jet bracelet and some fragments of bone. Caleb showed the pieces of bone to an acquaintance who was a doctor but the fragments proved too small to identify as human or animal.

Never one to pass up an opportunity, during the Easter holidays of 1909 Caleb was able to get a close look at another chambered cairn near Aviemore when the surfacemen of the Highland railway were removing the smaller stones covering the cairn to use as ballast on the railway line and in doing so exposed the inner structure of the cairn.

Though his methods seem amateurish by 21st century standards Caleb approached the new science of archaeology with great energy and enthusiasm. In cyberspace CG Cash's discoveries are recorded on the pages of the RCAHMS (Royal Commission on the Ancient and Historical Monuments of Scotland) website. Were it not for Edwardian antiquarians like Cash and their painstaking documenting of sites of archaeological interest many chambered cairns and hill forts and standing stones would have been lost. Caleb's excavations and archaeological observations were carried out at a time when there was little protection for sites and antiquities and their preservation was not regarded as important. As with nature conservation Caleb and his fellow members of the Society of Antiquaries had ideas in advance of their time.

A story recounted by Caleb illustrates the different attitudes towards archaeology in the opening decade of the 20th century; in 1908 Alex Sinclair the road man was helping a local farmer demolish a chambered cairn in one of his fields. Under a stone at the site of the chambered cairn they found a bronze pin. Realising it was not gold the roadman gave it to the farmer's young son Alec. But when Caleb heard about this, the following summer, he arranged to take the pin, which probably dated from Viking times to the Museum of Antiquities in Edinburgh.

Caleb's sketch of the bronze pin found in a chambered cairn near Aviemore in 1908.

Caleb always carried a large sheath knife with him. He used it to hack back the heather from paths and it came in handy for cutting branches of juniper to use as beaters when Rothiemurchus forest caught fire. Working as a schoolteacher in Edinburgh for most of the year, during those six weeks spent in the Highlands each summer (I like to think) there was a hint of Indiana Jones about Caleb: scaling crags in search of rare alpines and eagles' nests, sending secret messages, fighting forest fires, and seeking out magic stones. The locals clearly thought so too;

> When excavating at Avielochan I was several times asked, half jocularly, perhaps, whether I was searching for treasure; and on each occasion I took good care to explain that treasure in the sense of money or valuables was not to be expected in such places, but that their structure and arrangement gave interesting information, and that articles of archaeological interest might be found, and should always be reported to competent authorities.

Over the years Caleb published further articles with titles like 'Archaeological Gleanings from Aberfeldy' describing sites of archaeological interest visited during holidays spent with Alice. They looked at stone circles near Tegarmuchd and sketched cup marked stones at Urlar.

I turn off the A827 east of Aberfeldy and drive along the track towards Lundin Farm. I get out of the car. Behind me on the wooded slopes of the Perthshire hills the leaves of the birch trees are turning orange. I walk a short distance along the track. A solitary oak tree stands on a grassy mound with five moss and white lichen covered standing stones in a rough circle. I think of Caleb and Alice riding their bicycles along here as I turn and walk back to the car.

During September 1911 CGC spent some time in Killin. Armed with the Society of Antiquaries *Reports on the Perthshire Stone Circles* Caleb set out to visit the sites and duly reported 'our additional gleanings' to the Society. Near Duncroisk Caleb found a boulder with 18 cup marks on it and 'in pouring rain crouched over it to make a hasty sketch.' Caleb went from standing stone to cup marked boulder along Loch Tay on his bicycle. In 1912 Caleb spent some of his holiday time at Yarrow in the Scottish Borders (this time staying in the comparative luxury of the Gordon Arms) where he explored Peel towers, cup marks, standing stones, stone circles and a cist.

CGC submitted his paper 'Notes on Some Yarrow Antiquities' to the

Society in 1913. It would be his last. Caleb's world was coming to an end. It would be swept away by the First World War. Even as he sketched the standing stones of Perthshire and spent those 'delightful days' with Alice making notes, measurements and drawings of cup marked boulders during the summer of 1911, the grey hull of the German gunboat *Panther* was nosing its way into the harbour at Agadir in Morocco beginning the sequence of events that would culminate in the outbreak of the First World War in September 1914. Soon CG Cash – mountaineer, teacher, archaeologist and geographer – and the Edwardian world in which he lived would vanish and be as forgotten as the people who built the chambered cairns and hill forts that so fascinated Caleb.

The Victorian world and its Edwardian encore perished in the trenches. A whole generation of climbers was lost in the First World War. The gentleman mountaineers of Edwardian Scotland were no more. It was the 1930s before climbing recovered and when it did it was led by men like Jock Nimlin and Tom Weir. Sometimes unemployed they had to earn a living, and formed new clubs like the Craig Dhu and the Ptarmigan.

Ironically the war that ended Caleb's world helped save the osprey as the gamekeepers and Edwardian shooting parties who had massacred birds of prey were themselves gunned down in the mud and barbed wire of no man's land. Two world wars led to reduced game keeping pressure and probably helped osprey numbers begin to recover.

The bound volumes for the years 1914–19 of *The Scottish Geographical Magazine* and *The Proceedings of the Society of Antiquaries of Scotland* shrink in size and occupy less shelf space in the Andersonian library as fewer articles were submitted for publication as contributors were killed and war time restrictions made geographical and archaeological field trips impossible.

Caleb perhaps realised his world was disappearing. In 1917 he referred wistfully to 'those peaceful pre-war days'. Sufficient time remained though for Caleb to complete his greatest labour.

CHAPTER TWENTY EIGHT

West Lomond

Blowing up John Knox

Now the ice lays its smooth claws on the sill
Scotland's Winter; EDWIN MUIR, 1956

WEST LOMOND IS A BEACON HILL. A hill I see every day from the top of Lilyhill Terrace in Edinburgh. Taking the dogs out one winter afternoon there was great clarity of light; West Lomond snow covered, white against an icy blue sky. Back in the house I look out of the window and see the snow has started to fall again. Plans to climb West Lomond from Glen Vale postponed for the byroads are snow covered. I read on the BBC website this winter has been the coldest in Scotland for 100 years. Reluctant to leave the warmth of kitchen and Rayburn I go back to the computer and start typing again.

That day in 1898 when Caleb stood at the summit of Arthur's Seat, with his list of mountains the twin peaks of East and West Lomond were among the closest and most prominent hills he could see from Edinburgh. West Lomond is visible from Arthur's Seat over the entrance to Leith docks 15 degrees west of north.

Most people see West Lomond through a car window. From the motorway between Edinburgh and Perth the Lomond hills seem higher than they actually are. The early Scottish mountaineers travelled to the Lomonds by train. The station at Mawcarse near Kinross on the direct railway line from Edinburgh to Perth was conveniently situated for climbing West Lomond Hill. The line closed in the 1960s and soon after the M90 was built on top of it.

Given their closeness to Edinburgh when seen from Arthur's Seat, the Lomond Hills are relatively inaccessible by public transport today in comparison to the journey described by two Victorian hillwalkers; 'Leaving Edinburgh (Waverley) at 1.40 p.m., one can be at Mawcarse at 3 o'clock, and at the top of West Lomond (1,712ft) an hour and a half later...'

Rising to 522 metres West Lomond Hill is a prominent landmark like its namesake Ben Lomond. In 1915 W.J. Watson became Professor of Celtic at Edinburgh University. His book, *The History of the Celtic Place-Names of Scotland,* has been called the 'Old Testament' of Scottish place names and in it Watson suggests the name *lomond* comes from Cumbric, an ancient language once spoken in the Scottish Lowlands. In Cumbric the word *llumon* means a blaze or light. Fires lit on beacon hills were an ancient means of communication in time of war.

The Fife Lomonds are visible from Edinburgh to Dundee. Ben Lomond can be seen from many parts of Glasgow. From Stirling Castle rock both Ben Lomond and the Lomond Hills of Fife can be seen. Long ago these hills formed a chain of communication. In *The Lord of the Rings* by JRR Tolkien fires are lit on the beacon hills of Gondor as the enemy approaches and war looms.

Climbing West Lomond

As I set off from the car park on the byroad between Glenlomond and Strathmiglo one icy morning towards the end of February a tractor was ploughing a nearby field. The weathering of the rock that makes up the Lomond Hills gives rise to a fertile soil rich in natural phosphates, iron and calcium – good farmland. Dozens of rooks sat on the crests of the ploughed furrows and each time the tractor approached they flew up and flapped a little further down the field.

After a short distance, the byroad crosses a mossy old stone bridge over the Glen Burn and enters a wood. Turn left through a green metal gate, signposted *Footpath to Glenvale.*

A freezing February day, bright blue sky. It read minus six on the car thermometer when I turned the key in the ignition setting off from Edinburgh that morning. The path passes under the bare branches of wintry trees. Last autumn's leaves, white with frost, cover the ground. Soon I leave the wood behind emerging into open ground, scattered silver birches among the dead bracken.

A tall Scots pine stands next to the path. Ahead, West Lomond and Bishop Hill, streaked with patches of snow. Glen Vale lies in the dip between the hills. This path to Harperleas follows the old county boundary of Fife and Kinross. On a winter morning the flattened dead bracken thickly coated in white frost resembles a lacy tablecloth laid on the ground.

Half a dozen rough stone steps lead down to a wooden footbridge across the Glen Burn. Streams, puddles and boggy pools all frozen solid, the ice too hard to break with a climbing boot. By afternoon the dogs are thirsty. Though very cold, the air is dry. Cuilean presses her nose to the ice, smelling water but unable to drink.

The path climbs up more stone steps to reach moor land. Grass, heather, bracken all dusted with frost. Two grouse whirr up. The path runs high above the burn (covered in sheets of ice, water bubbling beneath). A wintry shower the previous day has left a dusting of snow on north and east facing slopes and among the dead bracken at the foot of Bishop Hill.

From the moor land I look back across the yellow and brown fields of Fife; houses, little squares of woodland, distant traffic on the motorway. Ten miles away the Ochils and beyond them the snow covered mountains of the southern and central Highlands.

At a metal gate keep close to the burn, ignoring a faint path that climbs higher up the hillside. In winter when the vegetation dies back the outline of an old building or animal enclosure can be made out beneath the flattened dead bracken and undergrowth.

Where Glen Vale begins to narrow, a rock outcrop called John Knox's pulpit stands on the hillside, a few metres above the path. Initials and names are carved into the stone. Several years ago part of the 'pulpit' was demolished in a controlled explosion after it became unsafe. When I walked through Glen Vale John Knox's pulpit was occupied by sheep. Crows circled around the rocky crag but there was no sign of the angel with drawn sword who appeared to protect the minister while he preached to the Covenanters during 'the killing time'.

Blowing up John Knox's pulpit.
[CP12/123 British Geological Survey © NERC. All rights reserved.]

John Knox would be called a religious extremist today; a revolutionary Protestant whose *First Blast of the Trumpet against the Monstrous Regiment of Women* published in 1558 declared that women were 'weak, frail, impatient feeble and foolish creatures' unfit to rule men. Yet in August 1561 a young Catholic woman, Mary Stuart, returned from France to become Queen of Scotland. Knox lived in Edinburgh's High Street and in the words of Antonia Fraser acted 'as a demoniac chorus' for all the young Queen's actions. There is no evidence that John Knox ever preached in Glen Vale. But in the 17th Century, during the period of religious persecution known as 'the killing time', the Covenanters held secret Protestant services in the Lomond Hills, meeting at the strange rocky outcrop marked on today's OS maps as John Knox's Pulpit.

Beyond John Knox's Pulpit Glen Vale becomes a narrow cleft between West Lomond and Bishop Hill and the burn flows through a gorge. A waterfall has partially frozen and dripping icicles hang from the rocky walls.

Curlew

Moor land with a few lonely scattered trees stretches across to Bishop Hill. A flock of sheep huddles by a dry stone wall. I head north across rough heather aiming for the rocky bank named on the map as the Devil's Burdens. Legend tells that while the devil was building West Lomond he quarrelled with a witch called Carlin Maggie. The devil laid down his burdens here before turning the witch to stone on nearby Bishop Hill.

WHO OWNS WEST LOMOND?

East and West Lomond are part of the Lomond Hills Regional Park which covers roughly 65 km² of West Central Fife. Fife Council own 500 hectares of land and Scottish Water own 620 hectares but most of the land within the Regional Park, 5,355 hectares, is in private ownership.

There are many sheep tracks in the heather on this part of West Lomond but no clear footpath so navigation will be needed in bad weather. Climb up through the Devil's Burdens picking a route between the crags and boulders or avoid them completely by going a short distance to right or left. The hillside to the east of the Devil's Burdens is strangely eroded; rocks and islands of heather stand on the exposed ochre soil. Over the years this eroding hillside has yielded many archaeological finds telling a little of the people who once lived and hunted on West Lomond. Small blades and barbs made of stone. They would have been used as cutting tools. Arrowheads too. In 1994 heavy rain washed away stones and soil, revealing a Bronze Age battle axe carved from hard volcanic rock.

Past the Devil's Burdens East Lomond comes into sight and Ballo reservoir, ice covered but for a patch of dark water in the middle. To the south the Firth of Forth and its islands, Arthur's Seat with the Pentland Hills as backdrop, the Bass Rock and North Berwick Law. To the west the Cleish hills and the Ochils spiked with wind turbines.

Something moves in the heather a few feet away; a stoat running along the path. Wary of the dogs it quickly disappears towards a cavity among the nearby rocks. These hills were once the royal hunting grounds for nearby Falkland Palace. Mary Queen of Scots ran her deerhounds and flew hawks on the Lomond Hills. The two roe deer I see in a ploughed field on the by road from Strathmiglo, descendants of the deer Mary Stuart hunted. For Mary a prisoner on Castle Island it was bleak those ten months in 1567, gazing across the grey waters of Loch Leven to the slopes of West Lomond.

The colours of the Lomond Hills in February all burnt umber and ochre with a dusting of white frost. Above the Devil's Burdens easier walking on shorter heather and cropped grass. At about 400 metres cross a fence and climb steep grassy slopes towards the top of West Lomond. Just below the summit I kick steps in a long strip of spring snow scattering frozen crystals in the sunshine.

The stones heaped on the summit of West Lomond are the ruins of a Bronze Age burial cairn. From the hill top there are wide views to East Lomond and Largo Law and across the brown and yellow fields of the Howe of Fife to the tower blocks of Dundee. Further away stand Ben Ledi, Ben Vorlich, Stuc a'Chroin, Ben Lawers, Meall Garbh, Schiehallion and Lochnagar. A sharp eye can make out Maiden Castle with its defensive ditch. To the east a stone tower rises above the trees on Black Hill, a memorial to the man who built Falkland House and planted thousands of trees, the splendiferously named Onesiphorus Tyndall Bruce. From the top of West Lomond descend north-west to reach the flat ground below the summit. Paths here are many, indistinct and potentially confusing. Aim to hit the path marked on the map near Hoglayers where it descends a cleft in the steep escarpment and leads back down to the road. Make sure to find the path as there are crags and very steep ground in places on this side of West Lomond.

The name Hoglayers reflects the importance of sheep farming in the history of the Lomond Hills. A hog is a yearling sheep and hoglayers refers to the *lairs* or hollows on the hillside where the sheep shelter in bad weather in winter. Hill sheep are tough creatures. Last night the temperature in the city dropped to −6°C.

Once on the path follow it steeply down through the cleft in the escarpment. Lower down it descends more gently along a grassy terrace between large boulders to a fence with a smile and waymarker. Fungi grow among the grass below the overgrown remains of an old stone wall set into the hillside. This wall marks the boundary between the yellow-brown grass of the open hillside and the farm fields below. Follow the grassy path across the hillside down towards the Bonnet Stone.

From the Bonnet Stone field head north towards the road, through a gap in a dry stone wall. Sheep and a few black and white cattle graze among the clumps of gorse. Green shoots poke up from the ploughed fields. A kestrel hovers in the air. In the distance the leaves of a copse of trees round a stone farmhouse are turning to autumn colours

---

THE BUNNET STANE

The mushroom shaped 'bonnet' and the strange holes in the rock are probably the result of erosion by sand, wind, water and ice. The cave in the Bunnet Stane is known as 'The Maiden Bower'. Information boards at the Bunnet Stane tell how a local girl fell in love with the son of a rival family. The Bunnet Stane was the couple's meeting place. One evening the girl waited as usual. As her lover drew near to The Bunnet Stane a band of her father's men lying in wait suddenly appeared and slew him. The girl refused to leave the Bunnet Stane and pined away the rest of her life alone in the cave. It is said if you are pure in heart any wish you make whilst in the cave will come true within a year.

More prosaically the name 'Maiden Bower' appeared on the first Ordnance Survey map in 1855 as 'Maiden Bore'. The term *maiden* meaning *first* or *initial* and *bore* as in mining. The cave was probably constructed by a local landowner in the early 1800's for exploratory geological work or as a folly.

Walk along a track by the edge of the fields, past a stone gate post in the long grass. Behind you the Lomond Hills rise up like a wall. When the track joins the very quiet byroad from Strathmiglo to Glenlomond, turn left and walk about two kilometres back to the car park. There are pheasants in the fields. Rooks nest in the trees by the road and at Lappiemoss a smell of wood smoke from the chimney of a whitewashed cottage.

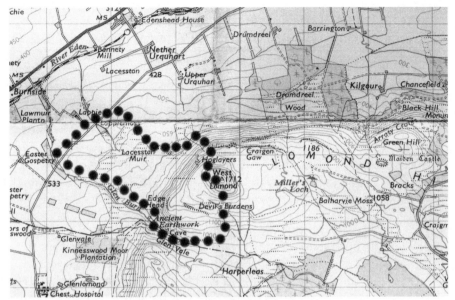

West Lomond Map

WEST LOMOND (522m)

Grade   **

Map: OS Sheet 58

Distance/Ascent: 8km/372m

Starting height: 150m

Time to top: 2h (3h30min for whole circuit) +breaks

Car Start/Finish: Car park on byroad between Glenlomond and Strathmiglo

A circular route starting and finishing on farmland, crossing moor land, involving easy navigation at the summit of the hill and with some interesting geology.

ROUTE:

Ascent

1   Start from car park NO17270 06969 on byroad from Glenlomond to Strathmiglo about 2km north of Glenlomond.

2   Walk out of car park and turn left along road.

3   After short distance turn left through green metal gate, signposted *Footpath to Glenvale.*

4   Go through trees and cross wooden footbridge NO17515 06619 over Glen Burn (stile/gate). Path stays on north bank of burn for rest of walk.

5   Go through metal gate NO18546 06144. Keep to main/lower path here which stays near burn, ignoring faint path that climbs higher up hillside.

6   Pass John Knox's pulpit, Glen Vale narrows here.

7   Keep on path until you reach vehicle track near gate in wall NO19375 05629 at height of about 280m.

8   Climb north up Devil's Burdens picking route between crags and boulders or avoid them completely by going to right or left. No clear footpath.

9   At about 400m cross fence NO19570 06434 and climb steep grassy slopes aiming for top of West Lomond (522m) NO19725 06620 (cairns and trig point).

Descent

10 From trig point descend NW to reach flat ground below summit of West Lomond. Aim to hit path marked on the map near Hoglayers NO19410 06920 where it descends cleft in steep escarpment and leads back down to the road. Make sure you find the path as there are crags and very steep ground on west side of West Lomond.

11 Once on path follow it steeply down through little cleft in escarpment. Lower down, follow path along a grassy terrace between large boulders.

12 Reach fence with stile and waymarker. Follow path across the hillside. Towards the Bonnet Stone beside fence along top of field.

13 Follow path steeply downhill short distance to top corner of Bonnet Stone field (small wooden waymarker with white arrow).

14 From Bonnet Stone field head north towards road through gap in wall.

15 Follow faint path beside wall to gate and stile then join well defined track along edge of fields.

16 Go through a gate NO18481 08159 and turn left along the road.

17 Walk back along very quiet road for 2km to return to car park /start of walk.

NAVIGATION: compass bearings may be needed to find the summit of West Lomond from head of Glen Vale and to find the safe descent route near Hoglayers in bad weather.

DOGS: lots of sheep on West Lomond and cows near Bonnet Stone.

Somewhere Else: Pillars of Hercules Organic Farm Shop and Café on A912 just west of Falkland.

CHAPTER TWENTY NINE

East Lomond

The Fortress of Fife

EAST LOMOND, A BEACON HILL to signal from with an Iron Age fort on its summit. A hill visible from the streets of Edinburgh. Taking the dogs out this morning I see a rise in temperature during the night has left the snow cover on East Lomond less pristine, white and gleaming than it was yesterday.

When Caleb compiled his list of the Scottish mountains visible from Arthur's Seat he used a tower from a more recent war as the guide line for East Lomond. Built in 1809 to defend the entrance to Leith Harbour during the Napoleonic wars and now half-buried in the East Break-water, the Leith Martello Tower is today land-locked. A key to the tower remains in the possession of Forth Ports plc.

Standing as it did on offshore rocks, to Caleb at the summit of Arthur's Seat in 1898, the Martello tower would have been a prominent feature in the sea off Leith. Today East Lomond (434m/1,423ft) can be seen from Arthur's Seat seven degrees west of north in line with Easter Road football stadium.

'Fifeshire is admittedly weak in hills, but it can boast of at least two which are well worth a visit...' wrote an early stalwart of the Scottish Mountaineering Club in 1894 and he went on;

> These are the Lomonds, East and West, so familiar to everyone who has stood on the Mound in Edinburgh, on a bright clear day, and looked northwards across the vista of chimney-cans and roofs which lies spread out beneath. To the Edinburgh man upon whom the Pentlands are beginning to pall, I cannot recommend a more agreeable variety for a Saturday afternoon than a walk across these hills...

Climbing East Lomond

The guided tour of Falkland Palace moves on to the King's Chamber but I pause at a leaded window on the spiral staircase watching the mist drift across the top of East Lomond. When I catch up the guide is explaining how architecturally the building is dominated by the twin towered gate-house completed in 1541 by the same master mason who designed the north-west tower of the Palace of Holyroodhouse, at the foot of Arthur's Seat. Falkland Palace, the guide continues, has a distinctly French look but with characteristically Scottish crow steps.

THE ROYAL KENNELS

Mary Queen of Scots loved dogs, she adored the small dogs at court (two loaves of bread a day were set aside for them) as well as the great Scottish Deerhounds used for hunting. At the royal palaces of Scotland, a hierarchy of servants cared for the Queen's hunting dogs which were kept outside in kennels. Page boys slept in the kennels, to look after the dogs and keep them from fighting. The warm doghouse often more comfortable than the servants' sleeping quarters indoors. Those 19 years a prisoner in England did Mary's mind sometimes escape from her prison cell back to her dogs running free on the moor beneath Beinn a'Ghlo?

In an age long before newspapers and TV, a 16th century monarch had to show himself to his people as their ruler. The Scottish kings were con-stantly on the move between royal residences, often staying only a few nights and rarely more than a month. The most common route was Edinburgh, Linlithgow, Stirling, Perth, Falkland and St Andrews. The royal household and the court travelled with the King along with dozens of mule hauled carts carrying tapestries, coffers, tableware, clothing and even furniture. The royal accounts record that in May 1539 three carts were needed to take 'the king's great green bed' from Falkland to St Andrews.

Despite being on the northern edge of the continent the Scottish court was known across 16th century Europe for its nurturing of the arts and sciences. A Renaissance masterpiece at the cutting edge of con-temporary architecture at the time it was built, Falkland Palace provided a fitting backdrop for the court of King James v who surrounded himself with poets, playwrights, scholars, composers and musicians. Sir David Lindsay, author of the play *Ayne Satyre of the Thrie Estates* rose to prominence in James v's court. In *Complaint of the Papingo* Lindsay wrote;

Fare weill Faulkland, the fortress of Fyfe
Thy polite park under the Lowmound law

To climb East Lomond begins at the stone fountain with its red painted heraldic lions in the High Street of Falkland. The lions hold shields displaying the town coat of arms, a stag lying beneath an oak. Walk past the old white washed stone houses of Falkland with their red tiled roofs and crow stepped gables, some have historic inscriptions carved into their walls. The Lomond Inn looks inviting but I keep straight on along Cross Wynd towards trees, fields and low hillside at the edge of the town.

Continue past a large factory built in 1931 to manufacture linoleum (today it makes paper bags.) The small town is dominated by the factory on the south and the palace on the north. Just beyond the factory car park where the street ends keep straight ahead along a track signposted *Footpath to East Lomond*. Climb up through the woods and before long the spires and towers of Falkland appear below.

Splendid old beech trees line the path forming an avenue and in autumn red-orange leaves cover the ground. Higher up the beeches give way to the conifers of the Douk Plantation. Ferns grow by the side of the path-pine needles and pine cones replacing beech leaves underfoot.

The path emerges from dense woodland onto open hillside. Far below the houses of Falkland lie tucked into the flank of East Lomond and beyond the Fife countryside; green fields, ploughed fields and yellow stubble. A clear path climbs the hillside taking a direct line towards the top of East Lomond through grass, moss and blaeberry.

Cross an overgrown dry stone wall topped with heather and when you reach a fence cross it at the stile. Once across the fence climb steeply to the top of East Lomond (434m). Unusually on East Lomond the trig point is not on the top of the hill but on a shelf of level ground ten metres below the summit.

It's a 'sair pech' but before long you will be standing on the top with its mountain indicator, Arthur's Seat, the Ochils and Lochnagar among the hills listed, a mountain panorama in steel. Today Jonathan de Ferranti's computer generated mountain panoramas show dozens of peaks it is possible to see from East Lomond; Ben Ledi, Ben Vorlich, Ben More, Ben Chonzie, Ben Lawers, Meall Garbh, Schiehallion, Meall Dearg, Ben Vrackie, Beinn Dearg and Beinn a'Ghlo among them.

From the hill top, Falkland looks like a toy town surrounded by miniature fields and copses of trees. Below, the larches in the Douk plantation are turning yellow and the beech trees orange. As on West Lomond a mole has been at work turning up hills of dark brown loam.

Descend quite steeply west from the summit down a path a little eroded in places. Aerial photos show the outline of ancient ramparts and ditches encircling the hillside here, long hidden beneath moss, grass and heather. An Iron Age hill fort occupied the entire summit of East Lomond Hill. A piece of yellow sandstone with a Pictish symbol, a bull, carved on it was excavated from the site of one of the walls of the fort in 1920. The symbol stones of the Picts are still not fully understood; the bull may be a clan emblem, or a fertility symbol. It dates from between 500 and 800AD but who carved it and what does it represent? In JRR Tolkien's saga of Middle Earth *The Lord of the Rings*, Legolas the elf recalls another long forgotten people who once lived in the land of Hollin;

> ... the trees and the grass do not now remember them. Only I hear the stones lament them; *deep they delved us, fair they wrought us, high they builded us; but they are gone. They are gone.*

Reach the flatter ground below the summit of East Lomond, the path leads on towards Craigmead and West Lomond. I looked across the Fife country-side; a solitary tree leafless in October sheltered by a low stone wall. In autumn some fields brown and ploughed, some green and grassy, others yellow stubble. What I remember about that October week in Fife were the geese. Arriving in long noisy skeins every still day it seemed. I heard the sound of geese in the distance as I stood near the old lime kiln below East Lomond. A large skein flew overhead; a leading v shaped formation followed by a second v formation, black lines against a grey autumnal sky.

CRAIGMEAD MEADOWS

The fields around the lime kiln on the western flank of East Lomond are known as Craigmead Meadows and are a site of special scientific interest. The excavation of limestone here in the past coupled with lime dust from the kiln blowing around has resulted in a fertile soil. The many wildflowers that grow in Craigmead Meadows have evocative names; marsh cinquefoil, northern marsh orchid, mountain everlasting, alpine bistort, adder's tongue fern, moonwort, mare's tail, ladies mantle, wood horsetail and marsh lousewort. Butterflies and other insects depend on the summer flowers that grow in the meadows. Industry has left its mark on the Scottish hills visible from Arthur's Seat – slate quarries on Ben Venue, hydro-electricity generation on Ben Lawers, wind turbines on the Ochils and the lime kiln here on East Lomond where the special wildlife value of Craigmead Meadows is a product of its industrial history.

The rocks of the Lomond Hills began to form hundreds of millions of years ago when this part of Fife was a shallow tropical sea near the equator. Warm sea currents washed sand into deep layers. Eventually these became pale, honey coloured sandstone. Limestone too was formed in the sea bed from the shells of the many creatures that lived there. A period of intense volcanic activity followed. The peaks of East and West Lomond are the eroded remains of volcanoes and the area between them consists mainly of volcanic rock.

Millions of years later people made use of these different kinds of rock. The Picts carved the yellow sandstone with a symbol of a bull. King James v's master mason remodelled Falkland Palace into a renaissance masterpiece using stone quarried on the Lomond hills and carried downhill on sledges and horse drawn carts. And in the 19th century a lime kiln was constructed at the foot of East Lomond to turn stone into fertiliser.

LIME KILN

During the Industrial Revolution people moved from rural areas into the towns and this led to a need for increased food production in the surrounding countryside. The soil could not produce extra food without enrichment so this created a demand for lime, an agricultural fertiliser which boosts yields of some crops.

Limestone was quarried near the kiln and broken into pebble sized bits for burning. Two men, the 'breakers' worked on top of the kiln smashing up the limestone and shovelling it into the kiln. The breakers had a hard life; working from 4am to 5pm, surrounded by clouds of acrid smoke, they usually broke up two tons of stone a day.

A lime kiln is just a huge furnace. The breakers shovelled in a constant supply of limestone and coal from above. Within the stone walls of the lime kiln was a thick layer of sand and clay which encased and insulated the brick lined kiln. The archways in the walls were opened or closed to control the speed of burning in the kiln depending on the strength of the wind and its direction. The archways also allowed the burned lime to be collected as a powder and loaded on to customers' waiting carts to be transported to the nearby industrial areas of Fife. As the finished product was a powder which needed to be sheltered from the wind and rain, this is why the archways face in different directions.

A line of Scots pines in the distance… West Lomond on the skyline. On the hillside above the path a kestrel is hunting, scanning the slopes of East Lomond for prey.

I follow the track down to a conifer plantation at Craigmead beside the byroad that crosses the Lomond hills from Leslie to Falkland. At this point the walk can be lengthened (allow at least two hours extra) to include West Lomond by following the route on page 271.

When the path leaves the woodland north of Craigmead cross to the east bank of the stream at Yad waterfall and return to Falkland through the little wooded gorge called Maspie Den: ferns sprout from the rocky sides of the gorge and beech leaves cover the path. Fungi grow on the moss covered roots of old pine trees. Shiny green rhododendron leaves and the bare branches of silver birches in early winter. Water flows clear over smooth flat sandstone on the stream bed.

Maspie Den is criss crossed by a network of footpaths, estate roads and footbridges, but just keep the stream in sight or sound until you get to the ivy covered walls and elaborately carved chimneys at the back of Falkland House. Once it was the home of Onesiphorus Tyndall Bruce (1790–1855), today it is a school. When an estate road is reached near the house turn right along it.

Kestrel

ONESIPHORUS TYNDALL BRUCE

The wealthy Bruce family made their money from the British East India Company and bought Falkland estate in the 19th century. In 1839 Onesiphorus Tyndall Bruce, commissioned William Burn, a famous Victorian architect, to build a mansion, the House of Falkland. With wide open views across lawns and parkland to the Howe of Fife, the house is one of the best surviving Jacobean style country houses and is a grade A listed building. Inside are enormous rooms elaborately decorated in styles influenced by Byzantine architecture, religion and symbolism.

Onesiphorus was a great 'improver' planting thousands of trees on the estate and creating a network of pleasure walks which provided a picturesque experience for the gentry. In Maspie Den footpaths and bridges were constructed up to the strangely undercut Yad waterfall. After Onesiphorus's death a stone obelisk was built on Black Hill as a monument to him.

Walk along the road through mature woodland keeping straight on, ignoring left and right turns. Rusty iron railings line the side of the road as it passes through parkland with views of East Lomond through the trees. The roofless shell of Crichton-Stuart Memorial Chapel stands in the fields. Begun in 1912 the building was never completed. Go past the old stables with courtyard and octagonal wooden clock tower to arrive back at the car park and the start of the walk.

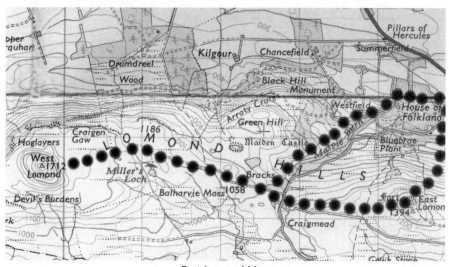

East Lomond Map

EAST LOMOND (434m)

Grade   *

Map: OS Sheet 58&59

Distance/Ascent: 6km/359m

Starting height: 75m

Time to top: 1h30min (2h 30min for whole circuit) +breaks. Add 2h if
                 climbing West Lomond too.

Start/Finish: Falkland

*A circular walk with an interesting descent through Maspie Den. Good
walk for older children.*

ROUTE:

1   Find your way to ornate fountain in centre of Falkland. Drive past
fountain and along High Street. Where road turns left continue straight
ahead along West Port (signposted *Cricket Club*).

2   Pass street sign reading *The Hidden Place* and go past Falkland estate
lodge house. Car park NO 24724 07466 just past lodge house on right.

3   From car park walk back into Falkland to fountain.

4   Take a right turn opposite fountain and walk up Cross Wynd. Keep
straight ahead at crossroads where it becomes East Loan.

5   Pass factory on left. At factory car park where street ends keep straight
ahead along track signposted *Footpath to East Lomond* then follow
signposted path uphill through woods.

6   Path emerges onto open hillside (275m) NO24973 06468 and takes
direct line to top of East Lomond.

7   Cross fence at stile and climb steeply to summit East Lomond (434m)
NO24408 06195.

8   Descend west from summit quite steeply down path to flatter ground
below summit of East Lomond.

9   Go through gate and follow track down to byroad from Leslie to
Falkland.

10   Turn right and walk short distance down road, go past entrance to
Craigmead car park (toilets) then turn left along track signposted *West
Lomond*. After short distance leave track, turning right on to path (not
marked on OS maps) into woodland (opposite a gate).

(At this point the walk can be lengthened (extra 6km) to include West Lomond by continuing along the track which runs between two stone walls. Reach a metal gate then follow track gently downhill for short distance before final climb up to summit of West Lomond NO 19725 06620 (cairns and trig point). Add at least two hours if climbing West Lomond too).

11 Once out of trees ignore right turn (it leads back to Falkland to Leslie Road).

12 The path reaches two bridges located close together at NO23018 06687. Cross left hand bridge and go through wooden gate NO 23409 06879.

Maspie Den is criss crossed by a network of footpaths, estate roads and footbridges but just keep the stream in sight or sound until you get near Falkland House and you will find your way back to the walk's starting point. Having said that it's worth trying to follow the directions below which give the most interesting descent.

13 Ignore the first right turn NO 23473 06894 after wooden gate but take the second right turn about 10m further down path (the one that leads to the Yad waterfall).

14 Follow this path which crosses to east side of gorge and follows stream down through Maspie Den. Near foot of gorge path crosses back to west side of stream.

15 Keep following path by stream until you come to Falkland House then turn right onto an estate road.

16 Keep straight ahead, ignoring left and right turns onto other estate roads.

17 Go past the old stables with clock tower to arrive back at car park and start of walk.

DOGS: may be sheep on open hillside on East Lomond. I did not see any but there were lots on nearby West Lomond and notices saying to keep dogs under control.

Somewhere Else: Pillars of Hercules Organic Farm Shop and Café on A912 just west of Falkland.

CHAPTER THIRTY

The Age of Lists

Bibliography: from the Greek βιβλιογραφία, (*bibliographia*, book writing); a systematic list of books on any subject.

Topography: from the Greek τόπος (topos, place) and γραφία (graphia, writing); the detailed description of particular places.

The New Elizabethan Reference Dictionary

Caleb stands in the front room of the top flat in Comely Bank Road, a coal fire burns in the grate, sleet beating at the windows, the floor is strewn with Sir Arthur's slips of paper. He runs his hand through his beard. He picks a slip of paper off the floor randomly and reads...

Smith, WA   Benderloch, or notes from the West Highlands. Map.80, *Paisley, 1883.*

Then another...

Rutherford, J Beregonium; with remarks by Dr Garnett in his tour through Scotland [Tour in 1800]. MS.fol. no. 89, in Lib. Perth Lit. and Antiq. Soc.

Thinks. What had possessed him to take on this monumental task?

'THE HARDEST THING to write is a great poem or great reference book' wrote Candia McWilliam. 'To last and succeed the reference book should have something of the great poem to it.' Caleb's last book, his final epic topographical swansong, had its genesis in 1901 when the eminent Scottish doctor and historian Sir Arthur Mitchell KCB, MD then in his seventies contacted Caleb for information about Timothy Pont for a list of historical tours of Scotland he was compiling. Like Caleb, Mitchell was deeply interested in the topography and landscape of Scotland and the two men became friends. To begin with Caleb enjoyed helping out, the afternoons spent at Mitchell's home, 'when we chatted about everything under the sun and moon'. As he sat drinking china tea with Sir

Arthur, did Caleb's mind sometimes drift to Ladywood Lane and his father the brass finisher from the backstreets of Birmingham?

Mitchell, a doctor who specialised in mental health and at one time held the splendidly named post of Commissioner in Lunacy for Scotland, had literally made it the habit of a long lifetime (1826–1909) to note down all the books he came across which contained topographical information about Scotland. Mitchell wrote down these details on strips of notepaper torn from the unused portions of letters and then stored them in cardboard boxes. Mitchell showed Caleb this 'chaotic multitude' of scraps of paper in cardboard boxes and asked for his help in sorting them with a view to publishing them as a reference book or bibliography.

Caleb wrote that he accepted after some hesitation; 'I think I should not have done so if I had foreseen how big the task was to be, and how little of it Sir Arthur himself would be able to do.' From 1904 onwards Caleb set to work in his spare time, bringing order to Mitchell's vast accumulation of bibliographical notes. He took cardboard boxes filled with thousands of the strips of paper home to sort them into what he called the List. Caleb wrote the work was '… necessarily slow, because I could devote to it only part of my scanty leisure.'

After Mitchell's death at the age of 83 in October 1909 Caleb continued with work on the List rewriting all the slips of paper in a standardised format, a task which took him a year and a half. Around this time work on the bibliography seems to have taken over his life. When published it ran to 700 pages but even then Caleb felt it could 'make no pretensions to completeness or finality' feeling that a team of researchers could compile a final, ultimate, comprehensive and complete list. In the preface to the bibliography Caleb makes a rare mention of his brother Albert who helped with the work, enabling CGC to include maps of Scotland kept in the British Museum in London. Jeffrey Stone saw that; 'the labour of preparing this monumental reference source must have far exceeded Cash's earlier work on the Pont manuscript map collection in the Advocates' Library'.

As the British, French and German armies became bogged down in the trenches of northern France Caleb's own war of attrition with Mitchell's scraps of paper was nearing an end. When the List was finally complete it was published with Caleb's own additions and modestly titled *A Contribution to the Bibliography of Scottish Topography* with volume I appearing in March 1917 and volume II in May.

In June 1917 Caleb gave a signed copy of *A Contribution to the*

Bibliography of Scottish Topography to the library of the Royal Scottish Geographical Society. For all Caleb's labours only 400 copies of the bibliography were printed in 1917 and when my copy purchased on the internet arrives through the post I have to fetch a sharp knife from the kitchen so many of the pages are still uncut. Alas, Caleb, nobody has opened this book in nearly one hundred years.

And Sir Arthur's scraps of paper had worn Caleb out. Twelve long years spent working on the List had taken an invisible toll of his health and in the summer of 1917 as the Battle of Passchendaele dragged on the *Edinburgh Academy Chronicle* reported 'with great regret that Mr. Cash is unable to take his work for the term owing to ill health... we hope a term's rest will enable him to return with renewed vigour in October.'

The bibliography was well received by reviewers, one likened it to a labour saving device like the Singer sewing machine. It was an interesting comparison. Caleb lived on the cusp of the modern age and flicking through the pages of *A Contribution to the Bibliography of Scottish Topography* I am struck by how like they are to the pages on Google.

Caleb referred to the bibliography as the List. One of Caleb's earliest published pieces of work, the Scottish mountains visible from Arthur's Seat, like his last book, took the form of a list. In the 21st century lists are everywhere. Playlists, shopping lists, wedding lists, tick lists, gift lists, wish lists, mailing lists, electoral lists, black lists, short lists, task lists, threatened species lists, lists of favourites.

In the National Library of Scotland in Edinburgh which in the 1930s replaced the Advocates Library where Caleb worked on Pont's maps, a well-thumbed copy of *A Contribution to the Bibliography of Scottish Topography* sits on a shelf of reference volumes behind the counter where books are issued. There's another in the reading room. The kind of book you'd think the internet would have replaced, but no the librarian tells me, they use it all the time to find sources of Scottish history when responding to inquiries from members of the public. So Caleb did not labour in vain after all. The library staff sitting in front of their computer screens are able at the click of a mouse to bring up lists on Google of a length undreamed of one hundred years ago as Caleb toiled to compile *A Contribution to the Bibliography of Scottish Topography*.

During the latter half of the 20th century Scottish mountaineering too would come to be dominated by lists. Lists of Munros, lists of Corbetts, lists of Grahams. The age of lists had begun.

Epilogue

At 9.45pm on the sultry evening of 21 August 1917 Caleb dies. He is 60 years old. His obituary will appear in the same edition of The Cairngorm Club Journal *as the review of* A Contribution to the Bibliography of Scottish Topography. *Alice sits at his bedside. Next day she will register the death at the Registrar's Office in Davidson's Mains. In the sandstone house near Cramond William Muir the doctor notes the time of death then slides his fob watch back into his waistcoat pocket and turns to gaze out the window across the trees. Caleb's last synapses flicker. A million silver sparks flow over the cliffs of the Sticil. The osprey circles above the loch rising higher and higher into the vertical distance then vanishes.*

CHAPTER THIRTY ONE

Lochnagar

5 degrees West of North

FROM THE 1550S TO THE 1850S Scotland saw extremes of weather; storms, heavy rainfall, summer droughts and many severe snowy winters, a period of climate deterioration known as the Little Ice Age. At this time the tops of Scotland's highest mountains were snow covered all year round. Today the ghosts of these perpetual snows linger in An Garbh Choire of Braeriach and below the east facing cliffs of Aonach Mor in Lochaber. Thomas Pennant toured Scotland during the summer of 1769 and wrote; 'I saw the great mountain Laghin y Gair, which is always covered with snow.'

The perpetual snows had melted by 1898 when Caleb put Lochnagar (1,156m/3,793ft) as the most easterly of the Scottish mountains on his list, located south of the River Dee to the east of Braemar, five degrees west of north and 68 miles from Arthur's Seat. Caleb used the east end of the recently opened Imperial dock at Leith as a guide line for Lochnagar. The Imperial Dock is still in use today and is easily identified by the large concrete grain silo on the quayside. If Ben Lomond is Glasgow's mountain then Aberdeen has Lochnagar and an old rhyme from the North East goes;

> *Fecht for Britain? Hoot awa!*
> *For Bonnie Scotland? Imph, man na!*
> *For Lochnagar? Wi crook and claw!*

Open the page entitled Aberdonia & Banfia in Blaeu's 1654 *Theatrum Orbis Terrarum*; the mountain's name is given as Bin Chichues with at its foot L. Garr. (I see Caleb lift the white vellum bound volume down from the shelf in the front room of the top flat in Comely Bank Road. Rain beating on the cobbles in the street outside).

'On this hill we can observe the strange sight of a loch "running uphill"…' wrote Peter Drummond in *Scottish Hill Names* – the old Gaelic name for Lochnagar was Beinn nan Cìochan, mountain of the breasts after the granite tors on its corrie rim known today by their Scots' names, Meikle Pap and Little Pap, the big and the little breast.

On the map William Roy made of Scotland around 1750 the mountain was named Loch-na-Garr and Lochnagar, the lochan of noise or laughter from the Gaelic word *gàire* still lay in the corrie a thousand feet below the summit. As the years passed the name of the noisy loch below began to be used for the peak above it with 18th century writers referring to The Hill of Lochan-y-Gar. Writing in the 1790s Charles McHardy, minister of Crathie and Braemar called the mountain Loch-na-garaidh and reckoned that some of the hills in his parish were; '... probably the highest in Scotland.' The change of name was completed with Byron's 19th century poem *Lachin y Gair*;

> *Oh for the crags that are wild and majestic!*
> *The steep frowning glories of dark Loch na Garr!*

Climbing Lochnagar

Deeside. Permeated by the presence of the British monarchy. Lochnagar, sometimes called the royal mountain, stands entirely within the boundaries of the Balmoral Estate with its castle, shooting lodges, Marie Antoinette garden cottage and pyramid shaped memorial cairns. The long running soap opera that is the British royal family continues to this day and still has episodes set at Balmoral. All part of what Ian Mitchell writing in 2000 dubbed *Balmorality*; 'what is on Deeside may be a never-never land, but it is a real never-never land'.

Leave the grey granite streets of Ballater where the butcher's, the green grocer's and the huntin', shootin', fishin' shop each have an ornate 'By Appointment' royal crest hung above the door. Drive the 12 kilometres down Glen Muick (pronounced Mick) to the car park at the end of the road. Walk across a wooden bridge over the River Muick towards the Balmoral Estate Visitor Centre.

In a field beside the track lies the long abandoned township of Spittal of Glenmuick. In the 15th century the Bishop of Aberdeen set up a refuge for travellers here. The word *spittal* in a name signifies the site of a hospice, a medieval kind of inn. Old estate documents refer to 'the sheallings called hospital haugh'. Two hundred years ago Spittal of Glenmuick was a thriving community where several families struggled in a harsh climate to eke a living from farming. Little can be seen of the township today, only the low remains of walls, grass covered bumps in a field. Among the buildings that once stood here; a corn drying kiln, a barn, longhouses (people lived at one end of the house, animals at the other) and, this is Scotland remember, a whisky still.

Today Spittal of Glenmuick seems remote, the end of the road, but in the past hill paths linked the township to other parts of what today is the Cairngorm National Park, much more directly than the 21st century road network. The cattle of Aberdeenshire were driven south through Glen Muick to the markets at Crieff and Falkirk. An old path to Glen Clova in Angus, the Capel Mounth passes through Spittal of Glenmuick and was an important north-south route for over 500 years, the A9 of its day.

Retreating Jacobite soldiers passed through Spittal in 1746 after defeat at Culloden. In 1771 James Robertson visited the township while in the Cairngorm area on behalf of the Annexed or Forfeit Estates Commission set up by the British government to seize the land of clan chiefs who had supported Bonnie Prince Charlie. As Iain R Thomson succinctly put it in his book *The Long Horizon*, the Commission was; 'archetype of a form of administration still familiar in the Highlands, the 'Quango.'

The Annexed or Forfeit Estates Commission's work included topographical and mineralogical surveys of the Highlands which foreshadowed the discovery of North Sea Oil 200 years later. 'On the hill called Lochnagan [*sic*] a variety of crystal is found,' wrote Robertson, 'this is the highest mountain here and it is the only one on which for some time, I have observed the rocks formed into inaccessible precipices.' While travelling through the Highlands James Robertson made first ascents of several Scottish mountains including Ben Nevis but did not record for posterity whether he climbed to the summit of Lochnagar or merely viewed the lochan and cliffs from the corrie.

Walk past the wooden Balmoral estate visitor centre. At a metal barrier turn right along a track signposted *Lochnagar Path* past a belt of tall pine trees planted to shelter the farm buildings. The track curves its way across the grassy river flats with the cliffs of Lochnagar on the skyline. Cross a wooden bridge over the River Muick where the yellow flowers of bog asphodel grow in the marshy ground near the riverbank.

Tall pine trees surround the buildings at Allt-na-Guibhsaich and the driveway to the house is dark and shaded by dense rhododendron bushes which have spread far beyond the garden wall. A gloomy air of mourning still hangs about the substantial house Queen Victoria called her 'bothy' while playing Marie Antoinette.

WHO OWNS LOCHNAGAR?

Trustees under Deeds of Nomination and appointment by HM Queen Elizabeth, Balmoral Estates Office, Ballater, Aberdeenshire, AB35 5TB.

Turn onto a stony track towards a boarded up building, the old carriage house and stables for the lodge at Allt-na-Guibhsaich, its doors and windows are painted the same Farrow and Ball grey green as all wood-work on the Balmoral Estate; a sign points the way, *Lochnagar Path*.

A rough track crosses an open area of ground before heading into a plantation of tall pines. The mossy remains of dry stone walls stand among the trees, blaeberry bushes cover the ground and roots poke up through the sandy pine needle covered path. Beyond the trees, as it skirts around the base of Conachcraig, the track wide and clear cuts a deep line in the heather moorland exposing sand deposited when the glaciers melted. Cross the Allt-na-Guibhsaich (the burn of the pine tree) at a ford, there is no bridge and the stream might be difficult to cross in very wet weather. There are the remains of shielings near here, low circles of stones in the heather, built by a people long gone from Glen Muick.

North of the stream the path begins to climb uphill by the side of a deep trench where bog myrtle and yellow tormentil grow among the grass. On the wetter areas of hillside vivid green sphagnum moss grows in great cushions. The Little Pap, the Meikle Pap and the cliffs of Lochnagar draw the eye west.

At a small cairn beside the track near the head of Glen Gelder take a footpath that leads west across heather moorland strewn with rocks towards the col between Lochnagar and Meikle Pap. Shooting butts (and a stone carved with a B) marked as *Ptarmigan Butts* on the 1:25000 map stand alongside the well maintained path. Clumps of blaeberry grow among the heather and rocks. Line after line, the rounded Grampian Mountains stretch to the horizon. Long strips of muirburn give the hill-side a dappled look. A few yards to the left of the path at a height of 850 metres lies the Fox Cairn Well. Alpine ladies mantle grows here among the stones by the spring. The sun is hot and Cuilean drinks the cold water from the well.

THE FIRST ASCENT OF LOCHNAGAR

Reverend, Dr George Skene Keith made the first recorded ascent of Lochnagar on 14 July 1810 to measure its height. Using a barometer he calculated the mountain to be almost exactly 3,800 feet. The Reverend Keith and his companions stayed on the top for three hours, eating, drinking and admiring the view until a sudden change in the weather blanketed the mountain in thick mist. The drink taken at the summit seems to have kicked in on the way down the hill; 'our descent was accompanied by a number of awkward tumbles and one of the gentlemen was rolled nearly 100 feet: but no accident happened to any of us, except the loss of my spirit level. After 12 hours absence we returned... completely drenched with rain.'

Nearby stands a memorial; Bill Stewart was a 21-year-old from the Kaimhill area of Aberdeen. Most weekends in the early 1950s he would take the bus to Ballater on a Friday night to go rock climbing on the cliffs of Lochnagar. In the summer of 1953 Bill was climbing Parallel B gully with James 'Chesty' Bruce and two female friends when he slipped. His initial fall was short but the rope severed where he had looped it behind a spike of rock as a running belay and he fell to the corrie floor sustaining fatal injuries. Like many households in the Aberdeen of the 1950s, Bill Stewart's family did not have a telephone. It was only when they saw James Bruce returning alone along the street in Kaimhill that the awful realisation dawned there had been an accident.

The path bears south to reach the foot of the steep hillside known as the Ladder. Walk a short distance west from the path to view the cliffs and scree that rise above the loch from which Lochnagar takes its name. Martin Moran, first man to climb all the Munros in one expedition in winter, was avalanched here in January 1980 as he approached the foot of Parallel B Gully; 'Then a crack, and everything was moving – me, the slope and the mountain.' Buried in the snow on the corrie floor and unable to breathe Moran was lucky... he was quickly rescued by his climbing partner.

The path climbs up through the jumble of green lichen spattered boulders heaped on the steep slope of the Ladder and soon reaches the flat plateau of Lochnagar above the cliffs near Cuidhe Crom. The name means the crooked snow wreath and here on the mountain's shaded north-east facing slopes snow often remains into summer. Ben More in

Perthshire has a Cuidhe Chrom too but while the Alps have Mont Blanc and the Weisshorn, mountain features named after long lying snow patches are very rare in the Scottish hills.

Cairns mark the top of The Ladder; from here the path follows the rim of the corrie round to Cac Carn Mor and just below the 1,100 metre contour joins a well maintained path that comes up from Glas-allt-Shiel at the head of Loch Muick. The top of Lochnagar is flat and plateau like but you are always conscious of the edge, the cliffs that fall away down to the corrie.

In summer the path round the rim of the corrie is an obvious scar, wide and eroded as it climbs gently up to Cac Carn Mor the little granite tor that stands above boulder studded heath on the mountain top. A lost crampon, a relic of winter is wedged among the stones in the cairn. Deer graze high up on the flat summit of the White Mount to the south, as a glider flew overhead with a quiet swishing sound.

Keech and *paps*. Good earthy Scots words. Too earthy for the Victorians and it led them to promote Lochnagar as the name for the whole mountain massif. Not only did the old Gaelic hill of the breasts have two paps, its highest points are named Cac Carn Beag and Cac Carn Mor; the Gaelic word *cac* is related to the Scots word *keech* known in English as faeces. Hardly the sort of name that would have amused Queen Victoria when pointing at a mountain and asking what it was called.

Alpine ladies mantle grows up here sheltering among the granite boulders that litter the summit plateau. The rocks of Lochnagar formed 415 million years ago, the result of a massive collision of continents that forced molten granite up towards the earth's surface, like bubbles rising to the surface of water. North of Cac Carn Mor the path crosses the head of the Black Spout (*Sit!* Dogs on leads quick) near a vertigo inducing drop down to the loch.

PROFESSOR MACGILLIVRAY AND THE BLACK SPOUT

William Macgillivray, Professor of natural history at the University of Aberdeen in the 1840s climbed many Scottish mountains in search of rare plants and wild animals At the age of 11 he walked to Aberdeen from Harris in the Outer Hebrides to begin his education and as a student he walked to London from Aberdeen to visit the British Museum. He often slept outdoors while exploring the Cairngorms, wrapping his coat around him and making a bed from heather and grass. Macgillivray climbed Lochnagar many times. In 1850, he scrambled down the gully today known as the Black Spout; 'Of the fissures or rents by which the great precipice is scarred,' he wrote, 'one of the largest of all, commencing not far from the eastern summit, may be descended to the base of the rocks.'

A gentle rise leads up to Cac Carn Beag (1,155m – the highest point of Lochnagar) a granite tor shaped like a Henry Moore sculpture. The tors on Lochnagar are the result of weathering during warm sub tropical periods in the earth's history tens of millions of years ago. Many of the tors in the western Cairngorms were ground down by glaciers during the ice age but Cac Carn Beag and Cac Carn Mor survived... on the summit of Lochnagar you are looking at a pre ice age landscape.

In 1848 on her very first visit to Balmoral Queen Victoria set off to climb Lochnagar for the first of what were to be several ascents. Victoria and husband Prince Albert drove in a carriage to the Old Brig o' Dee in the Ballochbuie forest. They climbed up the shoulder of the Stuic where in mist they crossed the plateau to the top of Lochnagar. The Queen made good time on her first ascent of Lochnagar though 'Albert was tired, and remounted his pony' for the last part of the climb and she was in for a disappointment at the summit; '... Alas! Nothing whatever to be seen; and it was cold, and wet, and cheerless. At about 20 minutes after two we set off on our way downwards, the wind blowing a hurricane and the mist being like rain...' Lochnagar was Victoria's second Munro, her first was Carn a'Chlamain in Glen Tilt in 1844.

From the summit of Cac Carn Beag retrace your steps south over Cac Carn Mor to the fork in the path (passed on the way up the hill) that leads down to Glen Muick by the Glas Allt burn. This is an impressive piece of engineering that recalls the construction of the network of stalkers' paths across the Scottish hills in the 19th century. You'll appreciate it as you walk along it. Fit for royalty.

The Glas Allt foams white down through the heather in little water-falls and waterslides and clear pools. Above the burn, on the stone and heather hillside a hind stands motionless, watching me and the dogs. Lochnagar is home to golden eagles, I watch two large (unidentified) birds tumbling and chasing in the air high above the rim of the corrie.

MUNRO BAGGING MUNROS

Hugh Munro climbed Lochnagar as part of a three day round of hills in the Eastern Grampians in January 1890. On New Year's Day he walked from Milton of Clova over Broad Cairn onto Lochnagar, through Glen Callater and down to Braemar: 40 kilometres with 1,280 metres of ascent. The next day, 2 January, he walked through Glen Ey, climbing Ben Iutharn Mhor and Glas Tulaichean to Glenshee: 34 kilometres with 1,370 metres ascent. On 3 January he walked home to Lindertis near Kirriemuir, a distance of 35 kilometres on roads in ten centimetres of new snow. As Martin Moran points out, living in a generation that considers a 24 kilometre hillwalk in snowy conditions exceptional, how many 21st century mountaineers would care to emulate Munro's January 1890 round today?

The path drops down to follow the east side of the Glas Allt as far as a wooden bridge where it crosses to the west bank. Cottongrass, tormentil and blaeberry grow by the burn. South, across the deep trench of Loch Muick, lies the Munro Broad Cairn.

Follow the path and take care as it climbs down by a spectacular, Alpine like waterfall to the pines that shelter the house of Glas-allt-Shiel hidden among the trees on the shores of Loch Muick. Wild thyme and common butterwort grow among the lichen and moss covered rocks by the path. A lone rowan sprouts from a crack in a huge boulder and birch trees straggle up the hillside above the sandy beach at the head of the loch.

Near the pine plantation that surrounds the house the path runs close to a deer fence along the heather and blaeberry covered banks of the Glas Allt burn. The path enters the trees at an iron fence post. Cross the foot bridge over the burn and follow the pine needle covered path down through the wood to an old wall where it joins the estate road along the shore of Loch Muick. In its name Glas-allt-Shiel, the shieling of the grey burn, recalls a way of life before the people were cleared from the Balmoral estate to make way for deer forest in the 1830s by landowner Sir Robert Gordon.

The house at Glas-allt-Shiel is known as the Widow's House, built after Albert's death for Victoria who could not bear to go to her 'bothy' at Allt-na-Guibhsaich. On 1 October 1868 it opened with Highland dancing and John Brown plying Victoria with whisky-toddies. In the words of Ian Mitchell, for Victoria Glas-allt-Shiel was; 'another, even more substantial and comfortable residence to play the bereaved Marie-Antoinette in.'

Follow the road for two kilometres or so along the side of Loch Muick below steep hillside topped with crags. Downy birch, eared willow, aspen and rowan grow by the shore. Several areas of birch woodland, an important lochside wildlife habitat, have been fenced off to allow regrowth of seedlings and saplings safe from grazing red deer. Some of the mature birch trees by the lochside are 150 years old and are growing at one of the highest altitudes in Scotland. Bog asphodel, bog myrtle and heather overhang the old stone embankment at the side of the road. On the far side of the loch the track leading to Broad Cairn snakes up the hillside.

At the north-east end of Loch Muick stands a stone boat house. Just before you reach the building turn right on to a footpath and walk along the shore to join a track that runs east beside Loch Muick. In summer there are sandpipers on the narrow strip of stony beach. The bleached white stumps of Scots pines still grip the edge of the shingle. Cross the bridge over the River Muick at its outflow from the loch. Walk back along the estate road beside the river as it curves its way along the floor of the glen. Keep straight on where the track signposted *Public Footpath to Glen Clova by Capel Mounth* joins the road and in another half kilometre arrive back at the old farm buildings at Spittal of Glenmuick.

In 1924 the Cairngorm Club gathered on Cac Carn Beag for the 'opening' of the mountain indicator. Among the members of the Cairngorm Club who erected the indicator and attended its unveiling ceremony were people who'd climbed with Caleb. Alexander Inkson McConnochie reading the report about the ceremony in *The Cairngorm Club Journal* some weeks later thinks perhaps of his old friend's unwearying step, ceased these seven years. Like Caleb's list of Scottish mountains visible from Arthur's Seat the indicator gives the heights and distance in miles of the hills visible from Lochnagar. There are 12 Arthurs on the indicator: East Lomond, West Lomond, Ben Cleuch, Ben Chonzie, Ben Vorlich, Ben Lomond, Stob Binnein, Ben More, Ben Lawers, Schiehallion, Beinn a'Ghlo and Beinn Dearg. A list of mountains on a ceramic disk set in stones and cement on the summit of Lochnagar: *This indicator shows the direction of the most important hills that can be seen in clear weather from the summit of Lochnagar.* Caleb's list of the Scottish mountains visible from Arthur's Seat, on a page of *The Cairngorm Club Journal* in a red cloth bound volume with titles in gilt on the spine, lies on a remote library book shelf... forgotten for now.

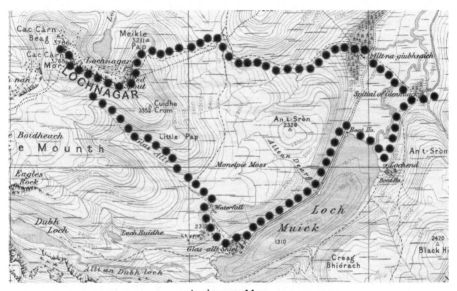

Lochnagar Map

LOCHNAGAR (1,156m)

Grade   **

Map: OS Sheet 44

Distance/Ascent: 18km/800m

Starting height: 410m

Time to top: 3h 30min (7h for whole circuit) +breaks

Start/Finish: Spittal of Glenmuick

A long but fairly straightforward route on good paths passing a spectacular waterfall and a royal playground. Some navigation needed.

ROUTE:

Ascent

1   In centre of Ballater from the main street (A93) turn into Bridge Street, cross River Dee and turn right along B976 following signposts

to *Braemar*. After 1km where road bears right to cross stone bridge continue straight ahead on to byroad signposted *Glen Muick*. Drive about 12km to end of road NO31000 85100. Park in pay and display car park (£3). Toilets.

2 From car park walk down estate road and across bridge over River Muick. Go past Balmoral Estate Visitor Centre.

3 Just after metal barrier turn right along track signposted *Lochnagar Path*.

4 Follow estate road over bridge across River Muick. Turn left onto stony track to board up building where sign points the way, *Lochnagar Path*.

5 Follow rough path into plantation of pine trees. Ignore left turn and head towards wooden bridge/small stone shed at edge of plantation NO29500 85950.

6 Follow track across heather moorland as it skirts around base of Conachcraig. Cross Allt na Guibhsaich burn at ford (no bridge – might be difficult to cross in spate).

7 At 670m reach small cairn beside track NO27390 86100. Fork left here on to obvious footpath that initially goes downhill and leads w towards col between Lochnagar and Meikle Pap.

8 At col below Meikle Pap follow path as it bears south to foot of boulder slope (The Ladder) NO26050 85765. Path becomes slightly harder to follow here. After short climb path reaches flat plateau (1,050m) and cairns near Cuidhe Crom.

9 From here follow eroded path round rim of corrie to Cac Carn Mor. (At NO25075 85235 path joins well constructed path from Glas-allt-Shiel. Take note of this path as it is descent route).

10 From Cac Carn Mor (cairn on small granite tor) NO24450 85670 follow path N for 400m past head of Black spout to Cac Carn Beag (1,156m) NO24400 86135. (Trig point and indicator on large granite tor reached by very easy scramble).

Descent

11 From Cac Carn Beag retrace your steps south over Cac Carn Mor (1,150m) then south-east 800m along path to NO25075 85235.

12 At NO25075 85235 take right fork in path and follow well engineered path SE to E bank of Glas Allt burn.

13 At bridge path crosses to W bank of stream. Take care as path descends beside waterfall to pine plantation at Glas-allt-Shiel house on shores of Loch Muick.

14 Path enters pine plantation at iron fencepost NO27400 82500. Cross footbridge over burn and follow path down through trees to estate road. Turn left and follow the road 2.5km along the shore of Loch Muick.

15 At NE end of Loch Muick reach boat house. About 50m before the building turn right on to footpath and walk along shore in front of boathouse to join track running E beside shore of Loch Muick.

16 Cross bridge over River Muick at its outflow from loch. After short distance track joins estate road. Turn left along road.

17 Ignore track signposted *Public Footpath to Glen Clova by Capel Mounth* and after 500m arrive back at metal barrier, Balmoral Estate Visitor Centre and car park.

NAVIGATION: the plateau of Lochnagar is featureless in mist and compass bearings will be needed in bad weather. **Be careful to stay on the path.**

STALKING: mid-August–20 October go to www.outdooraccess-scotland.com and click on Walking and Stalking link.

WINTER: winter mountaineering experience needed to tackle Lochnagar in snow and ice.

Somewhere Else: The Hungry Highlander chippie in Braemar.

The City on the Hill

He sleeps fitfully on the old brass bed beneath the plaster cornice with its pattern of wheat sheaves. Over the decades the upholsterers' twine binding the clumps of horsehair in the mattress together has stretched creating corries and ridges. He woke in the night a film of sweat between his skin and the sheets... dreams he's walking down a grassy hillside in mist. Suddenly the mist clears and below, beyond a wall where the grassy hillside ends he sees closely packed rows of stone houses and streets sloping down towards the sea.

CHAPTER THIRTY TWO

Arthur's Seat

I will be your 'steady guide' to Arthur's Seat, and if I prove weari-some, you have only to close your book and so dismiss me.

CG CASH, 1894

EDINBURGH. THE CITY ON THE HILL. Called the Athens of the North because of its fine architecture, Scotland's capital is a town built on the stubs of ancient volcanoes. The largest of these volcanoes, Arthur's Seat, a sleeping lion guarding the city since time immemorial first erupted into a tropical landscape 350 million years ago when Scotland lay near the equator. Originally the volcano rose to about 425 metres. In the 18th century James Hutton examined the rocks of Arthur's Seat to further his understanding of how the Earth works. Hutton was one of the great figures of the Scottish Enlightenment and is known as the 'father' of modern geology. Today Arthur's Seat is 251 metres (823 feet) high and is one of the most studied ancient volcanoes in the world.

Five hundred years earlier Geoffrey of Monmouth wrote his imagi-native *Historia Regum Britanniae* (history of the kings of Britain). The book contained all the core elements of the legend of King Arthur; his father Uther Pendragon, Arthur's wife Guinevere, the wizard Merlin and the sword Excalibur. The story of the legendary monarch entranced 12th century Britain and several places in Scotland were named after King Arthur. There is an Arthur's Seat on Hart Fell in the Borders and (a possible connection) with Benarty in Fife. The earliest reference to the name Arthur's Seat is in the 12th century when the clergyman and chronicler of his times Giraldus Cambrensis referred to the hill in Latin as *Cathedra Arturii* (Arthur's Throne). And in 1508 in his poem *The Flyting*, Walter Kennedy, Scots Maker at the court of King James IV, wrote the line 'On Arthuris Sete or on ane hyar hyll'. According to *Scottish Hill Names* Seat is a Scots word expressing; 'the idea of a high throne for the powerful in the land'. Seat is a relatively common Scottish hill name. Hills called King's Seat are found in the Ochils in Clackmannanshire and the Sidlaws near Dundee. The name has its roots in the Old English word *soeti* and the hill word *side* found in the names of hills in the Scottish borders such as Faw Side.

People first came to Arthur's Seat around 9,000 years ago using the hill first for hunting and later for farming. And they climbed to its summit. Centuries later Robert Burns often walked alone to the top of Arthur's Seat to watch the sun rise out of the sea. Robert Louis Stevenson liked to stand on Arthur's Seat on a frosty winter's evening and watch the stars and the lights of Edinburgh. As the tide of war began to turn at Stalingrad and El Alamein the poet and mountaineer Brenda G Macrow climbed Arthur's Seat writing of a future beyond 1942; *And men who climb the hills in after years, They, too, when the leaf falls And summer flickers to a close, shall know the light fading across the dim heights.*

Climbing Arthur's Seat

The Palace of Holyroodhouse at the foot of Arthur's Seat stands silent witness to some of the most turbulent and bloody episodes in Scottish history. In 1745 Prince Charles Edward Stuart held court at the palace holding meetings and dances in the Picture Gallery under the watchful gaze of a hundred portraits of Scottish monarchs. While Mary Queen of Scots was pregnant at Holyrood Palace in 1566 her Italian secretary David Rizzio, was murdered in front of her by a group of jealous nobles. As he was stabbed repeatedly Rizzio clung to the Queen's skirts before being dragged away screaming 'Justizia, justizia! Sauvez ma vie, madame, sauvez ma vie!'

From near Holyrood Palace take the stony track that climbs uphill below the cliffs of Salisbury Crags. The name Salisbury Crags may be derived from the ancient language Cumbric once spoken in lowland Scotland. In Cumbric the words *salis bre* mean willow hill, a name which applied to the entire hill not just the crags. Likewise, the name Willowbrae is linked to the Arthur's Seat area to this day.

Before 1820 only a rough track skirted the foot of Salisbury Crags, 'that wild path' as Sir Walter Scott called it in *The Heart of Midlothian.* In 1820 a committee running a scheme for relief of the unemployed brought across a group of politically radical weavers from the west of Scotland to work on widening the path and when completed it was named... The Radical Road.

Above the track loom the cliffs of Salisbury Crags while below steep slopes of grass, scree and dense gorse drop away to Queen's Drive. From the Radical Road there is an aerial view of the Scottish Parliament commissioned by Donald Dewar and designed by Enric Miralles (the white dome next door is Dynamic Earth). The design was inspired by upturned boats on a beach and the black shapes around the windows on the external walls of the parliament represent the people of Edinburgh peering out from behind their curtains to keep an eye on the politicians.

The landscaping around the parliament blends seamlessly into Holyrood Park. In his original design concept Miralles wrote; 'The building should originate from the sloping base of Arthur's Seat and arrive into the city almost out of the rock'. Following the dark pattern of Scottish history both architect and politician died suddenly before the building was completed in 2004.

Kellan feels the tide of independence rising eight years on... things have come a long way since Mr Leslie the social education teacher, all sideburns and wide ties strummed his guitar and sang *Flower of Scotland* at school camp on the shore of Loch Tay in 1976.

Moss covered blocks of stone lie among the grass in the long abandoned North Quarry on Salisbury Crags. Quarrying took place here for hundreds of years making the outline of the crags much sharper than nature planned. In 1666 'considerable quantities of stone from the quarries...' went south to pave the streets of London; '... its great hardness rendering it excellent for that purpose' as Thomas Pennant reported in 1769. By the beginning of the 19th century quarrying had begun to cut deep indentations into the crags as more and more stone was removed to pave Regent Road and Waterloo Place in the city below. There was an outcry as the crags, Edinburgh's spectacular backdrop, began to disappear under pick axe and gunpowder. In 1831 a decade long legal battle finally resulted in a court order banning the removal of rock from the crags and the abandoned blocks of stone in the North Quarry have lain there in the grass ever since.

WHO OWNS ARTHUR'S SEAT?

Holyrood Park and Arthur's Seat are managed by Historic Scotland on behalf of the landowner HM Queen Elizabeth.

Follow the Radical Road as it climbs higher. Far below in the grassy strip between the foot of the crags and the road is the Rock Trap, a wide trench about 400 metres long excavated in 1984 to prevent falling rocks hitting cars on Queen's Drive. The 1970s tower blocks of Dumbiedykes stand behind the high stone boundary wall of the Queen's Park. Dumbiedykes because, in a house here in 1746, Thomas Braidwood founded the first school in the English speaking world for deaf and dumb children. Dumbiedykes Road was named after the deaf and dumb pupils of Braidwood's Academy who used it to reach the school from the Canongate (the dyke was the boundary wall of Holyrood Park that runs beside the road). Around 1540 James v enclosed the park which Scottish Kings had used as a hunting ground since the 12th century and in 1598 it was described as full of 'hares, conies and deare'.

In 1803 Samuel Taylor Coleridge walked this route at dusk;

> I climbed last night to the Crags just below Arthur's Seat, itself a rude triangle-shaped bare Cliff, & then looked down on the whole city & Firth, the Sun was setting behind the magnificent rock, crested by the Castle – the Firth was full of Ships, & I counted 54 heads of mountains, of which at least 44 were cones or pyramids...

On Salisbury Crags look out for fulmars, these ocean going sea birds related to the albatross began to nest on the crags about 30 years ago. Back in 1878 the fulmar's only British nest site was on St Kilda in the Outer Hebrides, where the inhabitants hunted the bird for its flesh and oil. As hunting declined the fulmar began to spread around the British coast, reaching the Firth of Forth in 1920. As sea cliffs became crowded, the birds moved to inland crags to find nesting spaces.

At the highest point of the Radical Road the Pentland hills to the south of Edinburgh come into view with Blackford Hill and the Braid Hills in the foreground.

Near here is the break in the crags known as Cat Nick. Caleb climbed Arthur's Seat for the first of many times around 1886 writing in *The Cairngorm Club Journal*;

> An interesting walk may be had along the Radical Road, round the foot of the Salisbury Crag... At its most westerly point the 'Cat Nick' offers an easy gully whereby to ascend to the top of the cliff.

The Ladies Scottish Climbing Club
on Salisbury crags in 1900 when long skirts and sun hats were *de rigueur* for women rock climbers.

[*LSCC ARCHIVE*]

Beyond Cat Nick the Radical Road passes the site of Long Quarry and then South Quarry as they are named on old maps. At the edge of the road on the left stands Hutton's Rock. In one of the earliest examples of geological conservation 18th century scientist James Hutton persuaded the quarry men to leave the rock intact because it contained a good example of a vein of iron ore. Standing there I see CGC on one of his geographical excursions to Arthur's Seat gather the boys of Class III.A around Hutton's Rock one July morning in 1897.

Past Hutton's Rock keep close to the crags bearing left onto a rough footpath along the base of the cliffs and leaving the Radical Road which continues downhill to join Queen's Drive. Common rockrose with its yellow flowers grows alongside purple milk-vetch and wild thyme. Towards the end of the Crags the path passes a small rock face known as Hutton's Section NT27201 72838.

Follow the footpath through the gap known as The Hause (Scots for throat or narrow entry) between the end of Salisbury Crags and Arthur's

Seat. The bend in Queen's Drive near here is called Powderhouse Corner after a (long gone) building where gunpowder used for quarrying the crags was stored.

Page 378 of *The Old Statistical Account* (*Parish of Duddingston*) records;

> On the 13th September, 1744, a water-spout broke upon the top of Arthur's Seat, and dividing its force, discharged one part upon the western side, and tore up a channel or chasm, which still remains a monument of its violence...

The 'water-spout' a violent thunderstorm, unleashed hail and deluging heavy rain on Edinburgh from 10 in the morning until three in the afternoon. The rain created a new storm channel on the west face of Arthur's Seat and washed a large amount of loose stones and gravel to the base of the hill. When the rain stopped and the mist cleared from Arthur's Seat the people of Edinburgh saw in the landslide debris the shape of a fish and gave the storm channel the Scots name the Guttit Haddie.

At the foot of the Guttit Haddie the path forks at a boulder embedded in the ground. Take the right hand path. Paved with stones it zig zags steeply up the hillside. The left hand path derives its name from 'The Affair of the Wild Macraas' in 1778 when soldiers of the Seaforth Highlanders at Edinburgh Castle mutinied after hearing rumours the regiment was to be shipped from Leith to India. In protest the soldiers marched to the old hill fort on Arthur's Seat and camped there for several days. To keep the mutineers' spirits up a piper playing the bagpipes walked up and down the path below the summit of Arthur's Seat to this day marked on some maps as Piper's Walk.

Follow the well-engineered Guttit Haddie path up the hillside with views across to the backslope of Salisbury Crags. The path climbs past an outcrop marked on old maps as Raven's Rock after the large black birds that were once welcome scavengers as they cleaned the streets of Edinburgh. Numbers dwindled and the last pair nested on Arthur's Seat in 1837. After an absence of 150 years ravens are again sometimes to be seen in Holyrood Park.

Writing in 1894 Caleb mentions Hunter's Bog, the upland valley 'almost like a fragment of a Highland glen' that lies between the back slope of Salisbury Crags and Arthur's Seat. It was used as a rifle range by soldiers from Edinburgh Castle in the 1830s and later by the Home

Guard during the Second World War. One Sunday afternoon after a weekend of heavy rain... Scott comes through the front door, back from the dog walk clutching a rusty bullet found on Whinny Hill. Put that in your book, he says.

Near the top of the Guttit Haddie ignore a footpath to the left that turns into a scramble, keep to the main path as it traverses along the hillside high above Edinburgh University's Pollock Halls of Residence and the Prestonfield House Hotel before reaching the top of Nether Hill.

Until the 1990s, where the buildings thin out giving way to fields and woods to the south-east of Arthur's Seat, the Queen's Park was still joined to the open countryside of Midlothian. Then houses were built on a last strip of greenbelt and Holyrood Park was encircled by the city for the first time in its history.

FLORA AND FAUNA OF ARTHUR'S SEAT

Arthur's Seat is unique among urban areas as its grassland has been left largely unchanged since the 16th century and over 40 different species of grass have been recorded including wavy hair-grass, crested hair-grass and Yorkshire fog. In the past sheep were the most visible mammals on Arthur's Seat and first grazed the hill as early as 1541. The mammal most likely to be seen today is the rabbit. There are also a handful of brown hares but I have seen them only twice in eight years, both times on very misty days. Mole hills are a common sight on Arthur's Seat and other small mammals present include voles, shrews, stoats and weasels. After dark I often see foxes and bats on Whinny Hill and sometimes a hedgehog.

Walk across the grassy top of Nether Hill through heath bedstraw and yarrow towards the summit of Arthur's Seat gazing across to Edinburgh Castle and the Old Town, seen by Walter Scott in Marmion as; '... piled deep and massy, close and high, mine ain romantic toun.' Nether Hill's other name is the Lion's Haunch with the summit of Arthur's Seat being the Lion's Head. Nether Hill in the sense of the lower or more westerly top of Arthur's Seat is the older name. Lion's Haunch first appeared on the 1852 Ordnance Survey map, an indication the Victorians began to see the hill's shape as a crouching lion around the time Prince Albert was busy landscaping the Queen's Park.

Follow one of the eroded paths or scramble easily up the rocks to the summit of Arthur's Seat (251m) with its trig point and mountain indicator less comprehensive than Caleb's List but testament to the enduring appeal of the mountain panorama. The last few metres to the trig point where Caleb once stood are across slippery rock worn smooth by generations of people climbing to the summit of Arthur's Seat.

During the First World War there was a gun emplacement on Arthur's Seat, the concrete base and rusty securing rings can still be seen. The summit is too eroded for much plant life but wild thyme with its little purple flowers still clings tenaciously on. In August, flying ant day Kellan calls it, winged ants gather on the summit of Arthur's Seat and use the hill as a launch point for their mating flight.

Climb the concrete spiral staircase to level 4 of the Museum of Scotland in Chambers Street, Edinburgh. Among the objects on display in dimly illuminated glass cases in the section *Daith Comes In* are 17 hand carved miniature coffins found hidden in a crack in a rock by children playing near the summit of Arthur's Seat in June 1836. No one knows why they were there or who buried them. Theories range from witch-craft to a mock burial for the 17 victims of the murderers Burke and Hare. These objects are among the most mysterious and sinister in the museum's collection. Seen on a webpage the coffins make my flesh creep. I click the mouse and send them back into cyberspace.

Sometimes the rocks at the top of Arthur's Seat are covered by a granular grey substance like fine cat litter. Crematorium ash. The dogs find it irresistible. Something worth bearing in mind if thinking about scattering a loved one's ashes up here; the dearly departed will end up sprinkled on Arthur's Seat but it will be via a dog's lower intestine.

From the trig point head east down smooth, worn and slippery rocks then pick up a paved path and follow it to the head of the Dry Dam, the narrow valley between the Lang Rig and Whinny Hill. *Dam* is a Scots word for a pent up head of water and only in the wettest weather have I seen a little stream drain the hillside here. Grassy slopes sweep gently down to Dunsapie Loch described by Caleb as; 'nestling at the foot of its crag with not a little of the beauty of a Highland loch...' The easiest route up Arthur's Seat starts from here or as Caleb puts it;

> The Queen's ascent is made by following the Queen's Drive to Dunsappie [*sic*] Loch, and then walking up the last slope to the summit of the hill, which is in full view.

The Lang Rig (Scots for *long ridge* marked on some maps as Long Row), edged with low cliffs on its western side, is thought be the first lava flow from the Arthur's Seat volcano. Kestrels can be seen hunting here and the yellow flower heads of Lady's bedstraw grow among the grass. Follow the clear path down to the ruined 15th century St Anthony's Chapel.

The chapel's dedication to St Anthony suggests the monks who lived there cared for people suffering from skin diseases. Old stories tell the chapel was built to guard the nearby holy well of St Anthony and at night a light illuminated the tower as a guide to ships in the Firth of Forth.

From the chapel follow a stepped path below the cliff face down to St Margaret's loch past silver birches and Scots pines. The loch was created in 1856 from a marshy area by Prince Albert, Queen Victoria's consort, as part of the landscaping of Holyrood Park. At that time the land behind the palace was described as both marshy and smelly. The sewers from Edinburgh's Old Town emptied onto the land at the foot of Salisbury Crags and a guidebook to the Palace of Holyroodhouse published in 1838 described this area as 'most odiferous'.

When the stepped path reaches the water's edge turn sharp left and follow it around St Margaret's Loch then across the grass back towards Holyrood Palace (on the left a boulder on the hillside near Haggies Knowe seals St Anthony's Well). The swans and greylag geese on the loch are sometimes joined by mallard, tufted duck, and black headed and common gulls and occasionally in winter the rare Iceland gull.

ARTHUR'S SEAT (251m)

Grade   *
Map: See map at start of book and OS 1:25000 Sheet 350
Distance/Ascent: 2.5km/255m
Starting height: 35m
Time to top: 1h (2h including breaks for whole circuit)
Start/Finish: Holyrood Palace

A circular walk taking in some of the most impressive features of Holyrood Park-the most dramatic route up Arthur's Seat.

ROUTE:

1 Start from car park near Holyrood Palace Broad Pavement NT27044 73708 in Queen's Drive (£1 per hour charge Mon-Fri 0830-1730). Cross Queen's Drive and take the Radical Road (stony track) uphill below Salisbury Crags (marked by falling rocks warning sign).

2 Follow Radical Road along base of cliffs. Towards SE end Salisbury Crags pass Hutton's Rock then where Radical Road goes downhill bear left onto rough footpath, keeping close to cliffs and pass Hutton's Section (information board) NT27201 72838.

3 Follow footpath through gap (The Hause) between end of Salisbury Crags and Arthur's Seat

4 At foot of Guttit Haddie take right hand fork in path at boulder embedded in ground NT27434 72735. Follow paved path as it zig zags up hillside.

5 Near top of Guttit Haddie ignore left turn and keep on maintained path which traverses SE *away from summit* of Arthur's Seat, along hillside above golf course for short distance and tops out on Nether Hill (237m).

6 Walk across Nether Hill straight towards summit of Arthur's Seat. Follow eroded paths or scramble easily up (slippery) rocks to Arthur's Seat (251m) NT 27534 72942 (trig point).

7 From near trig point head E in direction of Dunsapie Loch aiming for chain fence. Pick up paved path and follow for short distance to end of fence at head of Dry Dam (valley between Lang Rig and Whinny Hill).

8 From here take obvious path NT27680 73018 down Lang Rig (starts with a few stone steps) heading for (ruined) St Anthony's Chapel.

9 After 50m ignore left hand fork in path, keep heading for ruined chapel. Near chapel bear right onto footpath through gorse bushes that leads to ruined chapel.

10 From chapel follow stepped path below cliff face down to St Margaret's loch

11 At lochside turn sharp left and follow path around the loch then across grass back to Holyrood Palace/car park.

PUBLIC TRANSPORT: Lothian Buses no.35 from South Bridge/no.36 from Waverley Bridge every 15/20 min (www.lothianbuses.com or phone 0131 555 6363) or 20 mins walk from city centre.

TOILETS: in Holyrood Park Education Centre (small modern building at northern edge of large expanse of grass to east of Holyrood Palace).

Somewhere Else: The Sheep's Heid Inn, The Causeway, Duddingston Village.

CHAPTER THIRTY THREE

The Mountain in the City

Many a Highland Ben of ten times its bulk has less of the real mountain about it than has Arthur's Seat.

HAROLD RAEBURN, 1897

THE THEME MUSIC from *The Archers* fades. The rain's beating at the kitchen window and the trees in the garden outside thrash back and forth in the gale force wind. The smell of coal smoke from the Rayburn blown back down the chimney seeps into the kitchen through the tightly shut vent on the firedoor.

Cuilean performs a perfect dog stretch as I lace up my boots. Time for the dog walk.

Up the steeply sloping street the Labradoodle pulls at the lead. Around half ten at night I often see a vixen here running through the back gardens that now cover her ancestral hunting grounds on the lower slopes of Whinny Hill. 'Tight packed suburbia' Nikolaus Pevsner called it in *The Buildings of Edinburgh*, just beginning to be built when Caleb stood on the summit of Arthur's Seat compiling his list. The city encroached on the vixen's territory. This urban fox a hill fox once.

The wind has stripped the last leaves off the trees at Lilyhill Gate. The first throw of the tennis ball on Whinny Hill is hurled back towards me by the strong wind. I think I see the kestrel, a flash of a red brown back rolling in the wind above the gorse where it nested last summer. Hungry, using the absence of people and dogs to hunt.

Hail mixed in the rain stings the dogs' muzzles. Cuilean's first hail storm was on Druim Coire nan Eirecheanach high up on the South Cluanie ridge in Kintail. She's hated hail ever since. She puts her head down, one eye closed and runs towards the gorse bush.

Icy white hail on the slippery grass. I slip and sit down with a spine jarring slide. New boots needed these ones only good for the allotment now. And I'm getting cold – thin summer weight trousers soaked through. A few streetlamps and car headlights are on in the city down below though it's only just past three in the afternoon. Rain blowing horizontally across the hillside. The dogs driven mad by the gale race round and round in huge circles, chasing each other through the orange brown clumps of bell heather on Whinny Hill.

An old *Scottish Mountaineering Club District Guide to the Southern Uplands* declares; 'Edinburgh's citizens are fortunate to have this marvellous little mountain in their neighbourhood.'

But is Arthur's Seat a mountain? Or just a hill?

Caleb had no doubts on the subject writing in 1894 that Arthur's Seat; '... though only 822.9 feet in height, may well be called a mountain from its geologic structure, and the fine abruptness of some of its crags.'

The potential for danger... another characteristic Arthur's Seat shares with its higher cousins. Someone dies on Arthur's Seat most years.

A hill can become a mountain in winter. On the 5 December 2010 with up to two metres of snow lying in hollows on the hillside the City of Edinburgh Council issued an avalanche warning for Arthur's Seat.

'When the North Sea "haar" hides the city and the green slopes below, and exaggerates and distorts the rugged basaltic ribs and buttresses,' wrote Harold Raeburn in 1897, 'one feels as far above the world as on some splintered crag in a wild north-eastern corrie 2,000 or 3,000 feet above sea-level...'

Another early Scottish mountaineer William Inglis Clark thrashed up Cat Nick in the winter of 1897 over icy rocks buried deep in powder snow;

> Far below were the snow-covered houses... The children were sliding their toboggans on St Leonard's Hill, and the hum of the city rose to our ears. Yet here we were, almost as completely shut off from human help as if we had been in the heart of the Highlands.

A grade III winter climb scales 150 metres of crumbling rock, scree and gorse bushes on the north-west face of Arthur's Seat. The Scottish Mountaineering Club's climbing guide *Lowland Outcrops* records that 'Excalibur' was first ascended in 1996 at night using head torches to 'avoid alarming the locals' and is possibly the longest urban winter climb in Britain.

Climb Arthur's Seat in a storm in November or in icy frozen winter conditions. Then decide. Mountain or hill?

The morning of 6 January. With Arthur's Seat covered in foot deep snow I walked alone, leaving the dogs at home for once, over Whinny Hill in bright sun, blue sky, and deep snow. Strapping crampons on at the foot of the final rise to Arthur's Seat I climb a miniature gully on the north side of the hill. Steel spikes scrape on volcanic rock in a crack full of deep powder snow crystals. On the summit the crampons claw into boiler plate ice. I feel I've had a taste of the longest urban ice climb in Britain. Now I truly believe Arthur's Seat to be the mountain in the city.

November. At the top it's hard to walk it's so windy. Today the Pentlands are clear but Edinburgh Castle is disappearing into a grey murk. There's a rainbow going straight up from Lochend Park. No one else on the hill despite the city being so close. The sound of sirens blown on the gale. I'm as alone here as on the top of any Munro. A ferocious gust of wind and then the rain starts.

May. At first the helicopter is just a black dot bright light over the grey estuary. A minute then its whirring thumping blades are overhead before it curves round and hovers level with the summit of Arthur's Seat before beginning a slow drop down to the green lawn of Prestonfield House and the waiting satellite TV vans. Seen from the top of Nether Hill the trees around the white painted mansion form the shape of an ace of clubs, planted by an 18th century gambler after he won the house in a game of cards. Now in the 21st century as the helicopter's landing skids touch the carefully tended grass in front of Prestonfield House, a political game where Scotland is the stake plays out in the shadow of Arthur's Seat.

June. Swifts fly low circles over Whinny Hill. The Italian boys in their garish red kilts purchased from The Scotland Shop on the corner of South Bridge and the High Street are having their photo taken at the trig point. On Nether Hill three American students are writing their names with stones from the scree at the base of Arthur's Seat. A puff of blue smoke from the one o' clock gun drifts across Edinburgh Castle. The sun shines from an azure sky. At the mountain indicator two Spanish women are feeding Cuilean crisps and pieces of ham sandwich.

The crows are tumbling, somersaulting in the strong breeze at the summit of Arthur's Seat. I stand at the trig point where Caleb stood with his list of mountains that day in 1898, gazing north and west across the rooftops of Edinburgh beyond the Firth of Forth, straining my eyes to see... *Ben Lomond... Ben Venue... Ben Ledi... Benvane... Dumyat... Stob Binnein... Ben More... Ben Vorlich... Ben Cleuch... Ben Lawers... Meall Garbh... Ben Chonzie... Schiehallion... Meall Dearg... Beinn Dearg... Ben Vrackie... Beinn a'Ghlo... West Lomond... East Lomond... Lochnagar.* A line of a Norman MacCaig poem in my head, '... a frieze and a litany', this line of hills, the Scottish mountains visible from Arthur's Seat.

How to Use this Book

When planning to do one of the walks in this book first read the **Route Summary** in the grey box for your chosen walk, make a note of the grid references and directions given, then compile a short route card to take on the hill with you.

The mountain chapters also contain information and additional grid references for points of interest passed on the walks.

A NOTE ON THE MAPS

The maps are taken from the author's collection of pre-1962 Ordnance Survey maps (heights are marked in feet) because it proved too expensive to use modern mapping and are reproduced by kind permission of the Ordnance Survey.

GRADING OF WALKS

* Mainly on good paths. Map reading needed.

** Some steep, rough ground. Some experience of summer hillwalking and basic ability to navigate with map and compass needed.

*** Ability to navigate in featureless terrain on remote high ground over long distances in mist needed. Use of hands on rock may be required for short distances.

Gradings apply to summer conditions only.

ROUTES

The choice of routes on CG Cash's 20 Scottish mountains visible from Arthur's Seat is subjective rather than comprehensive. I've included routes I enjoyed. Since there are only 20 Arthurs each hill is treated separately though some (like Ben More and Stob Binnein) can and often are climbed together. Heights are in brackets throughout the text. All routes have been walked by the author, Cuilean and the Labradoodle.

NAVIGATION

Modern technology such as GPS should be used as a complement to basic map and compass.
Alfie Ingram, Tayside Mountain Rescue Team Leader, 2007.

Many of the Scottish hills visible from Arthur's Seat are Munros or Corbetts – Scotland's highest mountains so if you want to tackle the ** and *** routes in this book you will need to know how to read a map and use a compass. Do not use a mobile phone for mountain navigation. Going on a course is the best way to learn how to navigate.

WARNING!

Remember; always be prepared to turn back on a hillwalk if weather conditions deteriorate. The Scottish mountains will still be there next week or next year. Mobile phone coverage on the Arthurs is patchy so leave someone a note of your route and stick to it.

WHAT EQUIPMENT TO TAKE ON THE * RATED WALKS IN THIS BOOK

... we enlivened our diet by consuming between us one pint of 'Mummery's blood.' This mountain elixir consists of equal parts of navy rum and Bovril served boiling hot... it lowers angles, shortens distances, and improves weather.
WH Murray, 1947

Walking boots
Waterproof jacket
Waterproof over-trousers
Spare fleece
Hat
Gloves
OS Map (wrapped in clear plastic bag)
Torch
Whistle
A small supply of food and a bottle of water
Wrist watch
Mobile phone – fully charged and switched off
Basic first aid kit

FOR THE ** AND *** RATED WALKS YOU'LL ALSO NEED

Silva compass (and know how to use it)
Survival bag
GPS (optional)

AND IN WINTER...

Ice axe
Crampons (and know how to use them)

THE ARTHURS IN WINTER CONDITIONS

Anyone intending to do one of the ** and *** routes in this book between November and March should carry an ice axe and crampons and be familiar with basic winter mountaineering techniques like ice-axe arrest. The best way to learn about winter mountaineering is to go on one of the courses run by Scotland's National Outdoor Training Centre based at Glenmore Lodge at the foot of the Cairngorms.

PUBLIC TRANSPORT

Ian McEwan wrote we live; '... in the last decades of the petroleum age, when a 19th century device is brought to final perfection in the early years of the twenty-first...' The device he refers to is of course the car. Because of the effects of climate change on the Scottish mountains, where it is reasonably straightforward to reach the start of a route by public transport, I have given basic information. Roughly half the 20 Scottish Mountains visible from Arthur's Seat can be accessed by public transport from Edinburgh or Glasgow for a day walk. I have climbed several of the Arthurs by public transport accompanied by the Labradoodle. In the route summaries, the section headed *Somewhere Else* suggests somewhere else to go for a beer, a cup of tea or something to eat after a walk. I haven't included one for every hill, just chosen places I like.

Who Owns the Arthurs

Who possesses this landscape?
The man who bought it or
I who am possessed by it?

A Man in Assynt, Norman MacCaig.

In so far as it is possible to I have endeavoured to find out who owns the Scottish mountains visible from Arthur's Seat. Land ownership changes over time so some landowner details may be out of date.

In many European countries the agricultural land on the lower slopes of the mountains is in private hands but the mountain peaks themselves – an important national asset – are owned by the government. Yet in Scotland, a country defined by its iconic bens and glens, it is still possible for a wealthy individual to buy a Scottish mountain and many hills remain in private hands.

Land ownership in Scotland remains controversial today despite the changes brought in when the Scottish Parliament passed the Land Reform Act in 2003 and Alasdair Morrison, MSP for the Western Isles, rose to his feet and silenced the chamber with the words: Tha latha an uachdarain seachad. Tha e criochnaiche. *The landowners' day is over. It is done.*

Bibliography

A Contribution to the Bibliography of the Scottish Mountains Visible from Arthur's Seat

BEN LOMOND

ANDERSON, G. & P. *Guide to the Highlands and Islands of Scotland*, John Murray, London, 1834.

BAKER, E.A. *On Foot in the Highlands*, Alexander Maclehose & Co, London, 1933.

BARRINGTON, J. *Loch Lomond and the Trossachs*, Luath Press, Edinburgh, 2006.

DRUMMOND, *Scottish Hill Names*, Scottish Mountaineering Trust, 1991.

DUNBAR, J.G (ed.) *Sir William Burrell's Northern Tour*, 1758, Tuckwell Press, East Linton, 1997.

McOWAN, R. *Loch Lomond and the Trossachs*, The Pevensey Press, Newton Abbot, Devon, 2000.

MITCHELL, I. *Scotland's Mountains before the Mountaineers*, Luath Press, Edinburgh, 1998.

MITCHELL, J. *Loch Lomondside*, Collins, London, 2001.

RACKWITZ, M. *Travels to Terra Incognita*, Waxmann, Munster, 2007.

SIMMONS, Andrew. *A Tour in Scotland* by Thomas Pennant 1772, Canongate Venture, Edinburgh, 1998.

THOMSON, I.D.S. *May the Fire Always Be Lit*, The Ernest Press, 1995.

TURNBULL, *Walking Loch Lomond and the Trossachs*, Cicerone, Milnthorpe, 2009.

WOOD, E. *The Hydro Boys*, Luath Press, Edinburgh, 2002.

www.snh.gov.uk

BEN VENUE

DENNIS, R. *A Life of Ospreys*, Whittles Publishing, Dunbeath, 2008.

HOLDER, G. *The Guide to Mysterious Perthshire*, Tempus Publishing, Stroud, Gloucestershire, 2006.

MOUNTAINEERING Council of Scotland and the Scottish Landowners' Federation. Heading for the Scottish Hills, Scottish Mountaineering Trust, 1988.

RODGER, D. et al. *Heritage Trees of Scotland*. Tree Council, London. 2006.

STORER, R. *100 Best Routes on Scottish Mountains*. Warner Books, London. 1987.

SCOTT, W. *The Lady of the Lake*. John Ballantyne & Co., Edinburgh. 1810.

STOTT, L. *Aberfoyle Slate Quarries*. Stirling Council, Stirling. 2007.

VERNE, J. *The Underground City*. Luath Press, Edinburgh. 1877.

WORDSWORTH, D. *Recollections of a Tour Made in Scotland*. Yale University Press. 1997.

www.roydennis.org

BEN LEDI

CRUMLEY, J. *Among Mountains*. Mainstream, Edinburgh. 1993.

McOWAN, R. *Walks in the Trossachs & Rob Roy Country*. Saint Andrew Press. 1983.

NOCK, O.S. *The Caledonian Railway*. Ian Allan Limited, Shepperton, Surrey. 1963.

WELSH, M. & ISHERWOOD, and C. *Walking the Trossachs Loch Lomondside and the Campsie Fells*. Clan Books, Doune, Perthshire. 2005.

WOOLISCROFT, D. & HOFFMANN, B. *The Romans in Perthshire*, Perth and Kinross Heritage Trust, 2005.
www.incallander.co.uk

BENVANE
BROSTER, D.K. *The Dark Mile*, Heinemann, 1929.
BROWN, H.M. *Climbing the Corbetts*, Victor Gollancz Ltd, London, 1988.
DEVINE, T.M. *Clearance and Improvement*, John Donald. Edinburgh, 2006.
LISTER-KAYE, J. *Song of the Rolling Earth*, Time Warner, London, 2003.
McKIRDY, A., GORDON, J., CROFTS, R. *Land of Mountain and Flood*, Birlinn, Edinburgh, 2007.
TAYLOR, K. *Glen Finglas*, Woodland Trust, Auchterarder, 2004.
www.whoownsscotland.org.uk

DUMYAT
BAKER, P. *The Ochils, Campsie Fells and Lomond Hills*, Cicerone, Milnthorpe, 2006.
BROWN, C. *Robert the Bruce*, 2004.
CORBETT, L., ROY, E.K. & SNADDON, R.C. *The Ochil Hills*, Forth Naturalist & Historian, 1994
KELSALL, R.A. *Blairlogie Boyhood*, Robin Kelsall, 1999.
MACDONALD, D. & BARRETT P. *Mammals Field Guide*, HarperCollins, 1993.
PEVSNER, N. (ed.) *The Buildings of Scotland, Stirling and Central Scotland*, Yale University Press, London, 2002.
RCAHMS, *Well Sheltered & Watered*, RCAHMS, Edinburgh, 2001.
SMITH, R. (ed.) *Call of the Wild*, Rucksack Readers, Dunblane, 2005.
SWAN, A. *Clackmannan and the Ochils*, The Rutland Press, Edinburgh, 2001.
WATSON, A. *The Ochils*, Perth and Kinross District Libraries, 1995.

STOB BINNIEN
CLIFF, P. *Mountain Navigation*, Edinburgh, 1978.
MURRAY, W.H. *Rob Roy MacGregor*, Canongate Press, Edinburgh, 1982.
POUCHER, W.A. *The Scottish Peaks*, Constable, London, 1965.
McNEISH, C. *The Munros*, Lomond Books, Edinburgh, 1996.

BEN MORE
BURT, E. *Letters from a Gentleman in the North of Scotland*, Volume Two, 1754.
GREIG, A. *At the Lochan of The Green Corrie*, Quercus, London, 2010.
J.M.M. *The Ben More Group, The Scottish Mountaineering Club Journal*, Volume 1, Number 6, September 1891.
MOUNTAIN, *Moor and Loch*, Sir Joseph Causton and Sons, London, 1895.
STORER, R. *The Ultimate Guide to the Munros*, Luath Press, Edinburgh, 2008.
THOMAS, J. *The West Highland Railway*, Pan Books Ltd., London. 1965.
gdl.cdlr.strath.ac.uk

BEN VORLICH
ALLAN, E. *Burn on the Hill*, Bidean Books, Beauly, Inverness-shire, 1995.
BENNET, D.J. *The Southern Highlands*, Scottish Mountaineering Trust, 1991.
COVENTRY, M. *Castles of the Clans*, Goblinshead, Musselburgh. 2008
GORDON, S. *Highways and Byways in the Central Highlands*, Macmillan, London, 1949.

BEN CLEUCH

WATSON, A. *The Ochils, Placenames, History, Tradition*, Perth and Kinross District Libraries, Perth, 1995.

WATT, H.B. *May-Day on the Ochils*, Cairngorm Club Journal, Vol 1, 1893–96, no.2, January 1894, pp.73–76.

SINCLAIR, Sir John (ed.) *The Statistical Account of Scotland*, 1791.

New Statistical Account of Scotland, William Blackwood & Sons, Edinburgh, 1834.

www.friendsoftheochils.org.uk

BEN LAWERS

GILLIES, W.A. *In Famed Breadalbane*, The Munro Press, Perth, 1938.

MARDON, D. *Ben Lawers*, The National Trust for Scotland, Edinburgh, 1993.

SIMPSON, M. *Skisters, the Story of Scottish Skiing* Landmark Press, Carrbridge, 1982.

www.killinmrt.org.uk

MEALL GARBH

BROWN, H.M. *Hamish's Mountain Walk*, Victor Gollancz Ltd, London, 1978.

KEMPE, N. & WRIGHTHAM, M. (eds.) *Hostile Habitats*, Scottish Mountaineering Trust, 2006.

MURRAY, W.H. *Scotland's Mountains*, Scottish Mountaineering Trust, 1987

BEN CHONZIE

BUTLER, K. *Wild Flowers of the North Highlands of Scotland*, Birlinn, Edinburgh, 2009.

BUTTERFIELD, Irvine. *The Famous Highland Drove Walk*, Grey Stone Books, Lancashire, 1996.

DARTON, M.A *Dictionary of Scottish Place Names*. Lochar Publishing, Moffat, 1990.

HULL, R. *Scottish Mammals*, Birlinn, Edinburgh, 2007.

MACFARLANE, R. *The Wild Places*, Granta Books, London, 2007.

MAXWELL, G. A. *Gathering of Eagles*, Birlinn, Edinburgh, 1998.

MILLER, J. *The Dam Builders*, Birlinn, Edinburgh. 2002.

NETHERSOLE-THOMPSON, D. and WATSON, A. *The Cairngorms*, Scottish Mountaineering Trust, 1981.

W.D. *Ben Chonzie. The Scottish Mountaineering Club Journal*, Volume 4, Number 3, September 1896.

CAMPBELL, C. *The Rise and Progress of Mountaineering in Scotland, The Scottish Mountaineering Club Journal*, Volume 3, Number 4, January 1895.

SCHIEHALLION

BROWN, H. (ed.). *Poems of the Scottish Hills,* Aberdeen University Press, 1982.

BROWN, H. *The Last Hundred*, Mainstream, Edinburgh. 1994.

DANSON, E. *Weighing The World*, Oxford University Press, New York, 2006.

GRAY, M. *The First Fifty,* Mainstream. 1991.

GREIG, A. *In Another Light,* Weidenfeld and Nicolson, London, 2004.

MORGAN, E. *Collected Poems*, Carcanet, 1990.

THE Scots Magazine, Scotland, September 1774.

MEALL DEARG

DEMPSTER, A. *The Grahams*, Mainstream Publishing, Edinburgh, 1997.

DUFFY, C. *The '45*. Cassell, London, 2003.

WIGHTMAN, A. *The Poor Had No Lawyers*, Birlinn, Edinburgh, 2011.
www.ordnancesurvey.co.uk

BEINN DEARG
ANDERSON, J. *Atholl Estates: A Brief History*, Perth and Kinross Heritage Trust.
BURNS, R. *The Humble Petition of Bruar Water*, 1787.
HOSIE, R.S (ed.) *Book of British Birds*, Reader's Digest, London, 1969.
SCROPE, W. *Days of Deer Stalking*, John Murray, London. 1838.
STORER, *Exploring Scottish Hill Tracks*. David&Charles, Newton Abbot, Devon, 1994.
www.mountainbothies.org.uk

BEN VRACKIE
FFORDE, C.A. *Summer in Lochaber*, House of Lochar, Colonsay, 2002.
LIDDELL, C. *Pitlochry A History*. 2008 Watermill Books, Aberfeldy, 2008.
MADDERS, M. *Where to Watch Birds Scotland*, A & C Black, London. 2002.
McLYNN, F. *Robert Louis Stevenson*. Pimlico, London. 1994.
WELSH, M. *Walks in Perthshire*. Clan Books, Doune. 1992.

BEINN A'GHLO
SCOTT, M. *Scottish Wild Flowers*, HarperCollins, Glasgow, 1995.
KERR, J. *Life in the Atholl Glens*, Perth and Kinross Libraries, 1993.
MURRAY, W.H. *The Scottish Highlands*. Scottish Mountaineering Trust, 1976.
www.mcofs.org

LOMOND HILLS
BROWN, H. *25 Walks Fife*, Mercat, 1995.
BROWN, M., McKIRDY, A. & McADAM, D. *Fife & Tayside: A Landscape Fashioned By Geology*, Scottish Natural Heritage, Edinburgh. 2001.
BROWN, W. *The Fife Lomonds, The Scottish Mountaineering Club Journal*, Volume 3, Number 1, January 1894.
FRASER, A. *Mary Queen of Scots*, Wiedenfeld & Nicolson, London, 1969.
HORROCKS, H. *Falkland Palace and Garden*, The National Trust for Scotland, Edinburgh, 2009.
LINDSAY, D. *Complaint of the Papingo*, 1530.
TOLKEIN, J.R.R. *The Lord of the Rings*, George Allen & Unwin, 1954.
www.rcahms.gov.uk

LOCHNAGAR
GREIG, A. *The Return of John MacNab*, Headline Book Publishing, London, 1996.
MITCHELL, I.R. *On the Trail of Queen Victoria in the Highlands*. Luath Press, Edinburgh. 2000.
MILES, H. & JACKMAN, B. *The Great Wood of Caledon*, Colin Baxter Photography Ltd., Lanark, 1991.
MORAN, M. *Scotland's Winter Mountains*, David & Charles, Newton Abbot, Devon, 1988.
ROWE, R. *Wildlife Traveller Scottish Mainland*, Pocket Mountains Ltd., Bo'ness, West Lothian, 2006.
STRANGE, G. *The Cairngorms, 100 Years of Mountaineering*, Scottish Mountaineering Trust. 2010.

THOMSON, I.R. *The Long Horizon*, Strathglass Books, Inverness, 1999.
TURNBULL, R. *Walking in theCairngorms*, Cicerone, Milnthorpe. 2005.

ARTHUR'S SEAT

ANDREW, K.M. *The Southern Uplands*, Scottish Mountaineering Trust, 1992.
HARRIS, S. *The Place Names of Edinburgh*, Steve Savage Publishers Ltd., London. 2002.
MacCAIG, N. *Collected Poems*, Chatto and Windus: The Hogarth Press, London 1985.
MACROW, B.G. *Unto The Hills*, Oliver and Boyd, Edinburgh.
PEVSNER, N. (ed.) *The Buildings of Scotland Edinburgh*, Penguin Books, Middlesex. 1984.
TURNBULL, M. *The Edinburgh Book of Quotations*, B+W Publishing, Edinburgh, 1991.
McADAM, D. *Edinburgh and West Lothian*, Scottish Natural Heritage, Perth, 2003.
PRENTICE, T. (ed.) *Lowland Outcrops*, Scottish Mountaineering Trust, 2004.
WICKHAM-JONES, C.R. *Arthur's Seat and Holyrood Park*, HMSO, London. 1996.
WRIGHT, G., ADAMS, I. & SCOTT, M.A *Guide to Holyrood Park and Arthur's Seat*, Gordon Wright Publishing, Edinburgh, 1987.
maps.nls.uk.

CALEB

ALLEN, J. *Cairngorm John*, Sandstone Press, Dingwall. 2009.
BARTLAM, N. *Ladywood*, Sutton Publishing, Stroud, Gloucestershire. 1999.
BENNETT, D. & ANDERSON, R. (eds.) *The Munros*, Scottish Mountaineering Trust, 1985.
BLAEU, J. *Theatrum Orbis Terrarum*, J. Blaeu, Amsterdam, 1654.
BROOKER, W.D. *A Century of Scottish Mountaineering*, Scottish Mountaineering Trust, 1993.
BROWN, H. (ed.). *Seton Gordon's Cairngorms*, Whittles Publishing, Dunbeath, Caithness, 2009.
CASH, C.G. (1894) *Arthur's Seat, The Cairngorm Club Journal*, Vol 1, no.3, July 1894, pp.145–151.
CASH, C.G. (1895) *Cairn Toul in August*, The Cairngorm Club Journal, Vol 1, no.5, July 1895, pp.336–7.
CASH, C.G. (1896) *Mist On The Sgoran Dubh, The Cairngorm Club Journal*, Vol III, 1899–1902, no.18, July 1896, pp.122–23.
CASH, C.G. (1897) *The Mountains of Scotland Over 2,000 Feet, The Cairngorm Club Journal*, Vol II, no.8, 1886–1899, January 1897.
CASH, C.G. (1897) *Braeriach In April, The Cairngorm Club Journal*, Vol II, 1896–99, no.8, January 1897, pp.184–86.
CASH, C.G. (1897) *Luminous Phenomena Observed on Mountains*, Nature 56, 13 May 1897, p.31.
CASH, C.G. (1899) *Mountains Visible from Arthur's Seat, The Cairngorm Club Journal*, Vol III, 1899–1902, no.13, July 1899, p.21.
CASH, C.G. (1900) *The Rothiemurchus Forest Fire, The Cairngorm Club Journal*, Vol III, 1899–1902, no.14, January 1900, pp.96–104
CASH, C.G. (1900) *The Ordnance Survey And The Cairngorms, The Cairngorm Club Journal*, Vol III, 1899–1902, no.14, pp.85–88.
CASH, C.G. (1900) *The Ordnance Survey of Scotland, The Scotsman*, Tuesday 18 September 1900, p.7.

CASH, C.G. (1901) *Recent Progress of the Ordnance Survey of Scotland, The Scotsman,* Tuesday 17 September 1901, p.7.

CASH, C.G. (1901) *The First Topographical Survey of Scotland, Scottish Geographical Magazine,* Volume XVII, 1901, p.399–414.

CASH, C.G. (1902) *Nights and Days On The Cairngorms, The Cairngorm Club Journal,* Vol III, 1899–1902, no.18, January 1902, pp.317–26.

CASH, C.G. (1904) *Storm on the Garbh Coire Crags, The Cairngorm Club Journal,* Vol IV, 1902–05, no.22, January 1904, pp.194–204.

CASH, C.G. (1904) *At Creag Na H'Iolaire, The Cairngorm Club Journal,* Vol IV, 1902–05, no.22, January 1904, pp.205–211.

CASH, C.G. (1904) *How To Make A Panorama. The Geographical Teacher,* Vol II, 1902–04, pp.174–175.

CASH, C.G. (1904) *Timber Floating at Rothiemurchus, The Cairngorm Club Journal,* Volume IV, 1902–05, no.23, July 1904, pp.301–05.

CASH, C.G. (1905) *Three Visits To The Garbh Coire, The Cairngorm Club Journal,* Vol IV, 1902–05, no.24, January 1905, pp.337–49.

CASH, C.G. (1905) *The Capercailzie in Rothiemurchus, The Cairngorm Club Journal,* Vol V, no 25, July 1905, pp.52–55.

CASH, C.G. (1907) *Notes on the View From Arthur's Seat, The Edinburgh Academy Chronicle,* Vol XIV, 1906–07, May 1907, p.108.

CASH, C.G. (1910) *Archaeological Notes from Aviemore,* Proceedings of The Society of Antiquaries of Scotland, Vol XLIV, 1910, pp.189–203.

CASH, C.G. (1912) *Archaeological Gleanings from Killin,* Proceedings of the Society of Antiquaries of Scotland, Vol XLVI, 11 March 1912, pp.264–285.

CASH, C.G. *History of the Loch an Eilein Ospreys,* Privately Printed, Aberdeen, 1907.

CASH, C.G. (ed.). *The Story of the North-West Passage,* Thomas Nelson and Sons, Edinburgh, 1899.

CASH, C.G. (ed.). *Cook's Voyages,* Blackie & Son, Glasgow, c.1902.

CASH, C.G. (ed.). *Anson's Voyage Around the World,* 1740–44, Alston Rivers Ltd., London, 1909.

CAMPBELL, R.N. *The Munroist's Companion,* Scottish Mountaineering Trust, 1999.

COGHILL, H. *Lost Edinburgh,* Birlinn, Edinburgh, 2005.

COOPER, P.A. *Round About Glas Tulaichean and Glas Maol, The Cairngorm Club Journal,* Vol VII, no.38, 1912, pp.110–118.

CUNNINGHAM, I.C. *The Nation Survey'd,* Tuckwell Press, East Linton, 2001.

DEMPSTER, A. *The Munro Phenomenon,* Mainstream Publishing, Edinburgh, 1995.

GLEN, A. *Old Grantown to Aviemore Upper Strathspey,* Stenlake Publishing, Ayrshire, 2009.

LAMBERT, R.A., *Contested Mountains,* The White Horse Press, Cambridge, 2001.

MACFARLANE, R. *Mountains of the Mind,* Granta Books, London, 2003.

MACNEISH, C. & Else, R. *The Edge,* BBC Books, London, 1994.

MAGNUSSON, M. *The Clacken and the Slate,* Collins, London, 1974.

MILNE, R. & Brown, H.M. (Eds.) *The Corbetts and Other Scottish Hills,* Scottish Mountaineering Trust. 1990.

MINTO, C.F. *Scotland Yesterday,* BT Batsford, London, 1990.

MITCHELL, A. & CASH, C.G. *A Contribution to the Bibliography of Scottish Topography,* Edinburgh University Press, 1917.

MITCHELL, I. *The First Munroist,* The Ernest Press, 1993.

MORRIS, R.J. *Scotland 1907*, Birlinn, Edinburgh, 2007.

MUIR, E. *Scottish Journey*, William Heinemann Ltd., London, 1935

MURRAY, W.H. *Mountaineering in Scotland*, J.M. Dent and Sons Ltd., London, 1947.

MURRAY, W.H. *The Evidence of Things Not Seen*, Baton Wicks, London, 2002.

NOCK, O.S. *The Highland Railway*, Ian Allan, London, 1965.

Proceedings Of the Society of Antiquaries of Scotland, 1909–1910, Vol.VIII, 13 January 1908, p.63.

Scottish Geographical Magazine, Volume XXXIII, 1917, p.465.

SHEPHERD, N. *The Living Mountain*, Aberdeen University Press, 1977.

SIMPSON, J. *Touching The Void*, Jonathan Cape, London, 1988.

SPARK, M. *The Prime of Miss Jean Brodie*, Penguin Books, Harmondsworth, and Middlesex, 1961.

The Cairngorm Club Rules, The Cairngorm Club Journal, Vol I, 1893–96, no.5, July 1895, pp.339–40.

THOMSON, I.D.S. *The Black Cloud*, The Ernest Press. 1993.

WALLACE, S. *John Stuart Blackie*, Edinburgh University Press, 2006.

WATSON, D.A. *Simple Introduction to the Stone Circles and Standing Stones of Perthshire*, Photoprint, Scotland, 2007.

WOOD, M. *The Mountain Panorama and Its Significance in the Scottish Context*, Cartographica, Vol 38, Nos.1&2, 2001, pp.103–118.

ZAFON, C.R. *The Shadow of the Wind*, Wiedenfeld & Nicolson, London, 2004.

MOUNTAINS VISIBLE FROM ARTHUR'S SEAT 2012

NAME	Height	POSITION	Distance In Miles	DIRECTION	Degrees West of North	GUIDE LINE	Tick
Ben Lomond[1]	974m/ 3,195ft	E. side of Loch Lomond	59	W. by N.	73	Towers of Church of Scotland General Assembly Building.	1.
Ben Venue[2]	729m/ 2,391ft	S. side of Loch Katrine	53½	W. N. W.	68	Between green dome of West Register House and Tron Church.	2.
Ben Ledi	879m/ 2,883ft	N.W. of Callander	48½	W. N. W.	63	Left of Fettes College, over north approach viaduct of Forth Rail Bridge.	3.
Benvane	821m/ 2,693ft	W. of Loch Lubnaig	52	W. N. W.	62½	Over Dumyat.	4.
Dumyat	419m/ 1,374ft	S.W. extremity of Ochils	31	W. N. W.	62	Over Fettes College.	5.
Stob Binnein	1,165m/ 3,822ft	Braes of Balquhidder	60	N.W. by W.	61	Just to right of Fettes College.	6.
Ben More	1,174m/ 3,852ft	Braes of Balquhidder	60¼	N.W. by W.	60	Just to right of Stob Binnein.	7.
Ben Vorlich	985m/ 3,232ft	S. side of Loch Earn	48½	N.W. by W.	57	Left-hand end of Cramond Isle.	8.
Ben Cleuch	721m/ 2,365ft	Highest point of Ochils	28½	N.W. by W.	55	Right-hand end of Cramond Isle.	9.
Ben Lawers	1,214m/ 3,983ft	N. side of Loch Tay	57¾	N.W.	44	Left-hand end of Inchcolm.	10.
Meall Garbh	1,118m/ 3,668ft	E. peak of Ben Lawers	58	N.W.	43½	Left-hand end of Inchmickery.	11.
Ben Chonzie	931m/ 3,054ft	N. of Comrie	47	N.W.	43	Right-hand part of Inchcolm.	12.
Schiehallion	1,083m/ 3,553ft	S. of River Tummel, between Lochs Rannoch and Tummel	60½	N.W. by N.	35	E. pier at Granton.	13.
Meall Dearg	690m 2,263ft	N. side of Strathbraan	48	N.W. by N.	31	Holyrood Palace.	14.
Beinn Dearg	1,008m/ 3,307ft	W. side of Glen Tilt	69	N.N.W.	22	To the left of the steep scarp of the Lomond Hills.	15.
Ben Vrackie	841m/ 2,759ft	E. of Pitlochry	58	N.N.W.	21		16.
Beinn a'Ghlo	1,121m/ 3,678ft	E. side of Glen Tilt	63½	N.N.W.	20		17.
W. Lomond Hill	522m/ 1,712ft	Between Falkland	21	N. by W.	15	Over entrance to Leith harbour.	18.
E. Lomond Hill	434m/ 1,423ft	and Loch Leven	20¼	N. by W.	7	Easter Road football stadium.	19.
Lochnagar	1,156m/ 3,793ft	S. of River Dee, E. of Braemar	68	N.	5	E. end of Leith docks over concrete grain silo.	20.

1   Today it's easier to see Ben Lomond between the green dome of West Register House and the chimney of Longannet power station.
2   Today Ben Venue can be seen in line over the south tower of the Forth Road Bridge.

Luath Press Limited
committed to publishing well written books worth reading

LUATH PRESS takes its name from Robert Burns, whose little collie Luath (*Gael.,* swift or nimble) tripped up Jean Armour at a wedding and gave him the chance to speak to the woman who was to be his wife and the abiding love of his life. Burns called one of 'The Twa Dogs' Luath after Cuchullin's hunting dog in Ossian's *Fingal*. Luath Press was established in 1981 in the heart of Burns country, and is now based a few steps up the road from Burns' first lodgings on Edinburgh's Royal Mile.
Luath offers you distinctive writing with a hint of unexpected pleasures.

Most bookshops in the UK, the US, Canada, Australia, New Zealand and parts of Europe either carry our books in stock or can order them for you. To order direct from us, please send a £sterling cheque, postal order, international money order or your credit card details (number, address of cardholder and expiry date) to us at the address below. Please add post and packing as follows: UK – £1.00 per delivery address; overseas surface mail – £2.50 per delivery address; overseas air-mail – £3.50 for the first book to each delivery address, plus £1.00 for each additional book by airmail to the same address. If your order is a gift, we will happily enclose your card or message at no extra charge.

Luath Press Limited
543/2 Castlehill
The Royal Mile
Edinburgh EH1 2ND
Scotland
Telephone: 0131 225 4326 (24 hours)
Fax: 0131 225 4324
email: sales@luath.co.uk
Website: www.luath.co.uk

Meall
Garbh

Ben
Lawers

Ben
Chonzie

Schiehallion

Meall
Dearg

Bei
Dea

Inchcolm Island

Inchmickery

Firth of Forth

Granton Harbour

Scottish
Parliament

Holyrood
Palace

N

44 Degrees West of North.....to 31 Degrees West of North